ONCE UPON A TIME AT BARRANDOV

OTA DVORSKÝ

HILLSHIRE
—MEDIA—

Table of Contents

Special Note

I would like to take a moment to share a bit about my father, Ota Hofman, who played a significant role in shaping this story and, in many ways, the direction of my own life. As a screenwriter and dramaturge, Ota worked on some of Czechoslovakia's most beloved children's films and TV series, such as Pan Tau and Three Nuts for Cinderella. His films may have been rooted in the world of children's fantasy, but they always reflected his deep understanding of the real world, especially the challenges faced by those growing up in times of political pressure. He had a way of telling stories that felt both magical and real, capturing the spirit of childhood and the complex world around it.

Ota was a man of strong principles. Even during a time when the country was under strict control, he stayed true to his creative vision. He found ways to bring imagination and wonder into his work, but he also used his stories to show children how to face difficult situations with strength. He believed that imagination could give us the power to overcome any limits, a belief that shapes the themes in this book. His stories often dealt with the struggles of finding freedom in a world that tried to hold you back, a struggle that my characters face in different ways.

His influence is clear in this story, not only through the characters but in the way the book explores themes of freedom, creativity, and standing up for what's right. My father's work was about making space for creativity even when times were tough, and this book reflects that same idea. Ota's values, both as a father and a creator, have guided me throughout my life. This book is my way of honoring his legacy and the lessons he taught me.

Without Ota's spirit and his dedication to his work, this story would not exist. His films showed me the power of storytelling, not just to entertain but to make people think and inspire change. I feel lucky to have been raised in an environment where storytelling was so valued. It is his influence that has shaped everything I write, and I am proud to continue that legacy.

— Ota Dvorsky

Introduction

The greatest truth is hidden in stories that really happened. The book OUTB invites into the world of real heroes who are not really heroes at all. Let's get to know the creative personalities of the children's and youth drama group at the Barrandov film studio, who through no fault of their own found themselves caught up in the turmoil of the turbulent, revolutionary year of 1968. Year when socialist Czechoslovakia was undergoing social and economic changes. In Paris, students are demanding their rights at burning barricades. Western television companies are looking for ways to establish high-quality and economically advantageous cooperation with artists from Eastern Europe. In communist Prague, efforts to find a path to freedom, without hypocrisy or censorship, are reaching their peak. Hope and faith in a better future were growing, because people on both sides of the imaginary barricade wanted to live freely, without fear of persecution and exile. However, fate was not on their side, and brutal force shattered their hopes when the Soviet occupation army entered Czechoslovakia in August 1968. This event interrupted the process of democratization and returned the country to its starting point of brutal oppression, uncertainty, doubt, and mutual distrust.

Each of the characters from both the Eastern and Western world in the book OUTB comes to terms with the new reality in their own way, but none of them give up hope for a better future. Similarly, they are unable to compromise on their artistic and professional standards. Although their work is intended for children, and mostly fairy tales in particular, the circumstances of the time and, to a large extent, minor coincidences influence their fates and trigger a chain of events that they try to resolve with insight and, at times, their own brand of black humor. It is almost unbelievable that in the turmoil of those cruel times, they managed, knowing the enormous risks and consequences of their decisions not only for themselves but also for their loved ones, children, and wives, to create works that were not supposed to exist at all, but which today, more than fifty years later, are considered absolute gems, cinematic pearls that audiences and film historians alike rank among the golden treasures of cinema.

All the very diffferent characters in our story cordially invite you to a time not so long ago – in the spirit of the saying, "We must know well what we do not want to happen again."

Foreword

In November 1931, on the outskirts of Prague, high on a cliff above the Vltava River, construction began on the famous Barrandov Studios. Project financed by Miloš Havel, uncle of Czech President Václav Havel. The Barrandov Studios were a technological marvel of their time and were built incredibly quickly.

Today, the Barrandov film studios are among the largest in Europe and are sought after by filmmakers from all over the world, including famous Hollywood. However, none of this would have happened had it not been for Václav's trip to the US. "After World War I, I was the president of the Czechoslovak Student Union and, at my own expense, I went on a study trip to universities in the United States. While visiting the University of California, Berkeley, I found myself in a beautiful neighborhood of wealthy Californians. And there, in 1924, I had the idea for Barrandov," said Václav Havel, father of Czech President Václav Havel, in an interview.

This grand plan also caught the attention of Václav's brother Miloš, who was already a successful film producer at the time and owned the film company Lucernafilm. Miloš Havel saw a future in sound film, so he did not hesitate to put the whole family into debt and embark on the construction of the Barrandov Studios. The entire area was designed by Max

Urban, who was not only an architect and urban planner, but also a film director.

Although the final design of the individual private villas of the local wealthy was entirely up to them, Václav Havel insisted on a clause in the land sale agreement stating that he had the right to inspect the plans and consult with Urban.

When the first sod was turned at the end of November 1931, few expected that the first film would be shot here 14 months later. "The first day of filming was January 25, 1933, when director Innemann began shooting his film *Murder at Ostrovní Street* in the brand-new studios."

The Havel brothers, in collaboration with Max Urban, managed to build the most modern film studios in Europe. Although they were paying off large debts for the construction and equipment of the studios, they became patrons of Czech film, and throughout the 1930s, their studios produced a number of films that are now considered classics of Czech cinema.

Unfortunately, the glory of the Barrandov Studios did not last long. The sad year of 1939 was fateful not only for Czechoslovakia, but also for the Barrandov Studios. After Czechoslovakia became the Protectorate of Bohemia and Moravia, the Germans began to make extensive use of the first-class studios. Under the baton of German Minister of Propaganda Joseph Goebbels, Nazi propaganda films of the worst kind were produced here. The entire company was confiscated from the Havel brothers and taken over by the Germans. During the war, the Germans managed to shoot 82 films here.

Even after World War II, better times did not come for the studios. Left-wing filmmakers called on the then president, Beneš, to nationalize the studios. This happened, and Miloš Havel, who had first had the studios taken away by the Nazis, lost his "baby" again. This time, the studios fell into the hands of the working people. Havel therefore decided to emigrate. He never returned to Czechoslovakia.

Once upon a time. Want to know how it really was?

The films *Three Nuts for Cinderella*, *I'm Jumping Over Puddles Again*, and *Boys Will Be Boys* Have Something in Common - apart from the fact that they have been finding enthusiastic audiences in new generations for more than fifty years, they also have in common that their creators, the screenwriters, were banned from writing. And yet these films were made. Thanks to brave people who lent their names as authors and signed these screenplays. The early 1970s were quite a tense time. Accept an invitation to the Barrandov Film Studios. This time, however, it will be a little different from what you know from the works of film historians. I invite you to join the Creative Dramaturgical Group for Children's Films during the turbulent period from 1968 to 1973. Film historians do not devote often much of their research time to children's works and their authors. Yet there are films and fairy tales that have remained on the playlists of public and private television stations for decades and without which we cannot imagine the true beauty and generosity of the Christmas holidays.

Characters

Main

Ota Hofman (40–45 years old)

Ota Hofman is often seen with a lit cigarette. He tends to be introverted, rarely allowing others to speak at home, but he chooses his words carefully in public. He doesn't seek attention and has a genuine fondness for children. Ota enjoys engaging with strangers and speaks quickly and naturally, though a slight speech impediment affects his "r" pronunciation, resulting in a flat sound rather than a lisp. His laughter shines through his eyes. An altruist at heart, he helps others without expecting anything in return. He is organized and hails from a family of merchants. Always well-dressed in a suit and tie, he carries natural authority. Ota married young and has two children, a son named Otto and a daughter named Irena. He and his wife have shared their lives together.

Jan Procházka (39–42 years old)

A tragic figure – the Czech Danton. A sturdy man with gray hair who appeared at least a decade older than his years. A committed communist, he embodied the armchair variety. An accomplished screenwriter and articulate speaker, his views struggle to resonate in today's world. During this time, he faced assaults and appeared somber in all photographs. His health issues were evident in his deteriorating physical condition, ultimately leading to hospitalization. He left his

9

position at Barrandov, placing all his hopes on Alexander Dubček, the political leader of Prague Spring 1968. He is married and has three daughters, whom he managed to take to Paris during the events of August. Being considered as traitor of the communists' ideas, he met a tragic end after facing pressure from the StB—State secrete Safety and, seemingly, the KGB.

František Pavlíček (45–49 years old)

He beams with confidence in every photo and video, his bright smile and direct gaze making a lasting impression. This athletic man, known for his way with women, was a motor mouth who rarely paused for breath. His Czech was flavored with Moravian expressions, words like "tož" and "ogaři" that revealed his regional roots. He wove a tapestry of words, embellishing his stories with colorful descriptions that made them feel alive. With a voice that resonated deep in the chest, he held court over a glass of slivovitz or wine, regaling his audience with tales. But behind the easy smile, he had a temper, and wouldn't back down if challenged. Despite this rough edge, he was a devout man, guided by a strong moral compass. When women were around, he was in his element, lavishing them with attention and illustrating his points with a raised left index finger, as if to drive home his words.

Gert Münterfering (33–37 years old)

Gert presents as a typical Bavarian, despite his Austrian roots. He consistently dresses well, often in a shirt, and wears gold-rimmed glasses, though time has taken its toll on his hair. He is notably direct and an effective communicator, addressing issues head-on without shying away from conflict.

Gert has a good sense of humor and holds distinctly center-left views. He is a long-time reader of the Frankfurter Allgemeine Zeitung, a prominent liberal publication among German intellectuals. Ambitious, realistic, organized, and methodical, Gert is self-made, having started working at the age of fourteen. His father fought at Stalingrad and returned from the front seven years after the war ended, passing away shortly thereafter. Gert is married and has a daughter and a son.

Klára Wagnerová (23–28 years old)

A recent college graduate. The type of girl from a good family. Her father is the head of the sales department at Kohinoor. She is a good student and dresses nicely—chic and elegant. She likes France, where she spent her vacation in 1968.

She likes to be liked and knows the rules of the game. She is tougher than she thinks she is. She can take care of herself and is no pushover. She loves her father, and when the secret police come after her, she starts cooperating with them.

However, her goal is to disappear as soon as she has helped her father.

Significant roles:

Kamil Pixa (45–50 years old)

A slim, tall man, energetic, dominant with a strong voice. Emotionally extremely unstable. Since the summer of 1969, he has been missing the last joints of his fingers due to an unexpected adventure in Paris, which he does not like to talk about. He attends all important meetings and is a highly respected figure in Czechoslovak cinema. He is the head of Short Film and also oversees the studios in Gottwaldov. He likes to play. He often thinks he lives in a cowboy movie. He dresses up as a woman, but for him it is more a part of the game. When he speaks, he dictates. He is able to formulate his thoughts and plays for a single team – himself.

Václav Vorlíček (38–43 years old)

A black-haired, tall man with a receding hairline and prescription glasses. He speaks calmly and loudly. He has a speech impediment – he says "v" instead of "r." Compared to his close partner, Miloš Macourek, he has a calm nature, but he is not completely easygoing either. He is very convincing and confident. He pauses before answering and thinks briefly. He weighs his words. He is elegant, speaks standard Czech, and is also fluent in German. He courts women and gets along well with them. He respects his comrades, but at the same time does not mind taking advantage of their favor. He likes British and black humor. He was a communist, not out of conviction, but a classic left-wing opportunist. He speaks rather quietly and deliberately.

Ludvík Toman (48–53 years old

Man of contradictions, where a fondness for vodka and a booming laugh coexisted with a darker, more sinister nature. He was the life of the party, always confident and charismatic, but beneath the charm, he harbored a mean streak. He reveled in making women uncomfortable, often calling himself a boor in their presence, but it was more than just a joke - it was a power play. His communist credentials were murky, but one thing was clear: he was a master strategist, likely KGB-connected, who wielded significant influence from behind the scenes. Moscow had handpicked him to lead Barrandov, and he ruled with an iron fist, shrouding himself in secrecy and avoiding the camera lens. Those who crossed him soon discovered his cruel and vindictive nature, as he played games with people's lives like a master chess player.

001 France, Paris, May 11, 1968

The May afternoon sun struggled in vain to break through the dark clouds that seemed to hang over the Eiffel Tower in Paris. Klára Wagnerová, a young student of international relations, an attractive intellectual girl with a delicate face and an eternal smile framed by light brown hair, had been wandering the streets of Paris all day. She was cursing herself again. You're so stupid. My entire foreign currency allowance is now gone. She remembered the hassle of getting currency allowance in Prague. She'd need to collect stamps on forms and charm officials to get her foreign exchange approved. The strict economy only allowed her to buy a few francs at the official rate from non-convertible currency. Nevertheless, she feared the black market, where getting caught meant confiscation. So, she had to budget carefully now, counting every franc. She glanced at the square box in the paper bag swinging in her hand. In this case, it was impossible to resist...

What am I going to do now? My stomach is growling, my feet hurt, and I don't have anything for dinner. But I'm not going to that awful student dorm! It's my first time in Paris, and who knows when I'll be back. I'm stupid. The voices in Klára's head were fighting a fierce battle, and now the second one had won. No, I'm not stupid. Those shoes are beautiful, and they really stood out in the shop window, and they fit my feet so well! God, so much money... Oh well. I'll walk around a bit more. I still have a few francs left in my pocket. But I don't have anything for Dad. I have to bring him something. So come on, girl, enjoy Paris while you can. Klára resolutely quickened her pace. The agonizing feeling in her stomach was suddenly replaced by the intoxicating aroma wafting from the open door of a small bakery. Klára's feet stopped of their own accord, and she gazed longingly at the window display overflowing with all kinds of baked goods.

The baker in a white apron stood in front of the shop, enjoying her cigarette. Klára Wagnerová, as befits a well-mannered girl, greeted her: "Bon jour." (Good morning.)

The baker looked at her with interest: "Salut. Avez-vous un souhait?" (Good morning. Would you like anything?)

"C'est difficile de choisir, tout est si beau. Je voudrais tout goûter." (It's hard to choose, everything looks so delicious. I'd like to try everything.)

The baker, who had come to see Klára, said, "Si vous aimez les sucreries, je vous conseille les macrons frais." (If you like sweets, I recommend the fresh macarons.)

Klára found the courage to try to put together a more complex sentence. "Merci beaucoup. Ils ont l'air incroyable. D'où je viens, les boulangeries sont un endroit triste, nous n'en avons toujours qu'une seule. Il ressemble à du caoutchouc et n'a pas beaucoup de goût." (Thank you. They look amazing. Where I come from, bakeries are sad places, we only ever have one kind. It looks like rubber and doesn't have much taste.)

The baker smiled when he noticed the foreigner's accent. Where is she from, he wondered. "Vous êtes à Paris ici. Nous misons sur la diversité. Et dans quel pays vivez-vous, s'il vous plaît?" (You're in Paris. We pride ourselves on diversity. And what country do you live in, please?)

Klára replied, "En Tchécoslovaquie." (In Czechoslovakia.)

The baker nodded understandingly: "Ah, alors..." (Oh, I see...)

Klára Wagnerová, aware that her foreign currency allowance was utterly exhausted, forced herself to retreat.

The baker realized that she probably wouldn't buy anything, so he just said, "Attendez un instant." (Wait a moment.) And he went inside. Klára waited, and when the baker returned, he was clutching a bag in his hand.

"Donc, au moins le goût," (Well, at least try it), he urged her and handed her the bag. Klára took it and thanked him: "Merci beaucoup." (Thank you very much.) And she resolutely set off down the sidewalk.

The baker turned to the baker's wife: "C'est une idée terrible. Prenez votre petit-déjeuner tous les matins et n'avez pas le choix. Ce doit être l'enfer sur terre." (That's a terrible idea. Having breakfast every morning and not being able to choose. It must be hell on earth.)

002 France, Paris, May 11, 1968

The corner café Spree Kafe, with a garden, is located on the corner of Rue Vieuville and Rue des Martyrs, near Montmartre, and was bathed in the timid evening rays of the sun. A few tables under blossoming trees lined the adjacent street. The guests were in no hurry, sitting, reading newspapers, or just chatting. Coffee and glasses of wine were served on glass and metal tables. It was peaceful. The calm was palpable. Irena Hofmanová, a kind, smiling middle-aged lady with dark brown hair pulled back with a headband, turned to her husband: "What a great idea to sit down for a while. I've had enough for today. The Eiffel Tower, Montmartre, Sacré-Cœur, Moulin Rouge, that was quite a sight."

Ota Hofman, a slightly graying, elegant man with his hair combed back and wearing a sports jacket, replied: "Yeah, my legs are killing me, but it was great. Paris is incredibly beautiful..."

He paused for a moment and took out a pack of cigarettes. He lit one and inhaled greedily. "I never remember churches, cathedrals, and monuments for very long anyway. But I never forget where I had good coffee and where I had a nice place to sit," he said and took a sip of coffee. "Unfortunately, they don't actually know how to make good coffee in Paris. I should have had a glass of wine."

Irena nodded in agreement: "I don't really like coffee either. But you can still make up for it with wine. You know what? I'll have one with you."

Hofman looked around for the waiter. After a moment, he waved to a young man in a black apron.

"Oui, monsieur, s'il vous plaît?" (Yes, sir, what would you like?)

"Deux verres de bordeaux, je vous prie." (Two glasses of Bordeaux, please.)

The young man smiled at his broken French and walked away.

Hofman couldn't resist, got up, took a few steps into the street, raised the camera hanging around his neck to his eye, and framed a shot of the Paris street with its blossoming trees. The Eiffel Tower rose majestically in distance.

A beautiful girl with a paper bag accidentally walked into the frame, and by coincidence, at that moment she ran her free hand through her hair, looked back at the lens, and smiled. Click. The camera shutter clicked. The gesture, like that of a model being photographed, was immortalized on celluloid film. Hofman checked that he had five shots left before he had to change the cartridge, returned to the table, and sat down.

Suddenly, he stopped, hearing something. The calm that had reigned all around was suddenly gone.

Irena also pricked up her ears: "Oto, what's going on?"

The noise was getting closer, even though the street still seemed empty from the café. A young boy, probably a student, ran past, looking about eighteen years old. The torn leg of his blue jeans flapped in the wind, and he had a bloody gash in his hair from which blood was trickling down.

Behind him, boys and girls of similar ages swarmed out of a side street and rushed past the café. In an attempt to shorten their route, they bumped into chairs and tables and jumped over seated guests. More and more came running, stumbling over overturned chairs. They were running like mad. Behind them, they could hear the sound of police whistles, the screeching of police sirens, and shouting.

Suddenly, seemingly out of nowhere, a paving stone flew through the air and smashed the café window. Shards flew across the pavement. Glasses and dishes shattered with a deafening crash. Hofman grabbed his wife by the hand, and they fled with the terrified crowd.

003 Prague, May 14, 1968

Jan Wagner, director of the sales department at the state-owned company Koh-i-noor, pulled back the curtains in the dining room and looked out the window of his fourth-floor apartment in an Art Nouveau apartment building at the Church of the Sacred Heart of Jesus. He never tired of the view of Prague's Jiřího z Poděbrad Square bathed in the slanting morning light. His wife, Marta, a petite, well-groomed woman in her forties, who had been struggling with being slightly overweight, had just begun serving breakfast.

Marta Wagnerová looked at her husband with red, tired eyes. "I didn't sleep all night. Do you know what could have happened?"

Wagner turned to her: "But in the end, everything went well. The girl did great. She takes after me! Rudé Právo newspaper wrote about the horrors yesterday as if they were student riots in Paris. They wrote about hundreds of injured people, the lunatics. Apparently, there were fierce battles with the police in the Latin Quarter, on the barricades. The worst was between the Pantheon and the Luxembourg Gardens. I know that area well. There was even a photo of burning cars, allegedly hundreds of them. They also wrote that more than sixty cars were completely burned out; it must have been a real mess there."

Marta Wagnerová brought plates with yesterday's rubber rolls, ham, cheese, and freshly brewed coffee to the table, accompanied by a flowered tablecloth. Klára Wagnerová shuffled wearily into the dining room, yawning, still half asleep, but she had heard what they were talking about. "Dad, Mom, I'm here, and I'm safe and sound. I told you yesterday, everything turned out fine in the end. Luckily, I made it to the train in Paris on time, but now I'm terribly hungry. I had to forget to take something in the cafeteria because of my limited foreign currency allowance, so I was starving for the whole exhausting trip home. Here, I brought you something, Dad." Klára pulled a tiny Eiffel Tower out of a paper bag.

Dad took it from Klára appreciatively and sang two words from a hit song by Suchý and Šlitr: "Souvenir, souvenir... I don't even deserve it." Both of them laughed with Klára.

"And here's something for you, Mom."

Mom unwrapped the scarf. "Thank you, sweetheart. It's beautiful..."

Wagner sat down at the table, changed the subject, and became serious: "Otherwise, I'm very proud of you, sweetheart."

Klára waved her hand: "Come on, Dad. It's just practice."

Wagner put some ham on his roll: "Practice, but what practice! Květy magazine, that's not just anything. You worked hard for it, and what's more, you achieved it on your own. Květy, it has a ring to it, and it's a tradition, I think, a hundred, maybe even a hundred and fifty years old. I'm very proud of you," he repeated. "When do you start?"

Klára sat down opposite him and ran her fingers through her hair in her favorite gesture: "Not until Monday. At least that way I'll have a chance to write down all my impressions of Paris. Maybe they'll take them and print them. I'll give it a try. But I know I'll just be making coffee and delivering the mail at first."

Wagner nodded: "Everyone has to start somewhere. But honestly, those who used to make coffee and deliver mail are now writing reports, aren't they? And don't underestimate yourself. That's an unfortunate trait we Czechs have. That's why you went to Paris, to understand that."

Klára paused: "I'm sorry, Dad, but I don't know if I fully understood it there. You know, the barricades, burning cars, and stuff."

Wagner looked at his watch: "I'm in a hurry, I have to be at work in a minute, your mother will tell you."

"But I'd really like to know what I was supposed to understand there, and I want to hear it from you, Dad."

"For example, the fact that you're asking about it now. The world is, how should I put it, multicolored. And you should get to know all its colors and shades. That's why I wanted you to go there."

"Okay, but I don't understand."

Wagner looked at her: "So, are you going to write? Just a moment, wait." Wagner went into his study and rummaged around for a moment. Then he returned to the table: "I'd really like you to take this." And he handed his daughter a Montblanc fountain pen. Klára Wagnerová was well aware of her father's passion for fountain pens.

"It's beautiful. The stones, they just sparkle."

"They're not just shiny. They're real diamonds."

Klára couldn't help herself: "Really, real diamonds?"

Her father continued: "This Montblanc fountain pen is unique. It cost a fortune; take good care of it," he said, carried away by his passion for his hobby. "It's a symbol of writing culture with a tradition dating back to 1906. It's not just an ordinary pen; it's a real tool of joy for anyone who can appreciate it, and above all, truly appreciate it. This particular pen features a 14-karat gold nib and requires over 45 handcrafted steps to produce. Other pens from Montblanc differ in the purity of the gold and the colors. During production, each step is checked under a magnifying glass. Precise work. Furthermore, this is a special edition pen, adorned with precious stones. Just take a closer look..."

Wagner looked humbly at his wife, who suddenly perked up: "They offered me a huge discount for my long-standing cooperation with Koh-i-noor, so I sold my mother's gold brooch for it. It also cost me a number of other pens from my collection. But I don't regret it at all, it's worth it, don't you think? It's completely unique in the world. A collector's rarity of unparalleled value."

Marta Wagnerová couldn't resist commenting: "Your collection is quite a financial burden, you know that, don't you? You don't want to ruin us completely, do you? Would you like some eggs and bacon, dear?"

Wagner was horrified: "Eggs? Are you kidding? You know fatty foods aren't good for me, and cholesterol isn't my friend either."

Klára Wagnerová had her mouth full of a cheese roll, but she mumbled: "But Dad, if you really feel sick, you can go to OUNZ. That's the advantage of our socialist healthcare system."

Wagner snapped at her: "OUNZ? Do you know what that abbreviation means? (Okamžitě uteč nebo zemřeš), Run away immediately or you'll die!"

Klára chuckled.

"You're still a child, darling. Use this pen for writing and interviews, make your dad proud, promise?" Wagner stood up, hugged his daughter, and held her close.

004 Prague, May 18, 1968

The apostles of the Old Town astronomical clock were busy. They turned in their stone windows as they did every hour of their centuries-old journey, glancing briefly at the small pub garden on Old Town Square. It was striking six o'clock. A semicircle of tourists, mostly from abroad, watched the procession with excitement, camera shutters clicking to capture the fleeting moment. The cock crowed. Death rang out one last time. The spectacle was over.

The beautiful, warm May evening magically enhanced the pleasant, relaxed atmosphere at the tables in the garden. Three interesting men had gathered here today: Ota Hofman, a forty-something Barrandov screenwriter, a tall, slim man with longer gray hair combed back, whose artistic fingers were perpetually clutching a cigarette, sipping Gruzignac; Jan Procházka, a more robust, gray-haired and still somewhat nervous but very confident head dramaturge of the Barrandov creative group, with a glass of slivovitz, and František Pavlíček, a film and radio screenwriter and artistic director of the Vinohrady Theater, a dandy with a permanent smile, mischievous eyes, and a glass of beer.

Hofman took a sip of cognac: "Gentlemen, I love Thursdays. Every week there are premieres in the cinemas and new books in the shops."

Pavlíček was intrigued: "Really? What did you get? I've been running around bookstores all day looking for the new Hemingway. No luck, it was gone in an hour."

A surprised girl's voice caught their attention: "Hey, isn't that Procházka from TV over there?"

Procházka turned toward the voice and stared at the girl, as did the other friends at the table. She was a young, barely legal high school student wearing a miniskirt so short it couldn't have been any shorter, which was quickly disproved by her friend, who wore an even shorter miniskirt, thanks to her longer, slender legs. The long-legged girl whispered something in her friend's ear. They both giggled and seemed to be gathering their courage.

Procházka turned his head and addressed them a little boldly: "And if I was?"

The two girls plucked up their courage and approached Procházka. One of them began: "We saw you on TV yesterday, talking about the end of censorship and freedom of the press. You know... well, you should know that we're big fans of yours."

Procházka smiled: "Thank you. Hopefully, something will change. If you have time, I'm having a discussion with students at Slovanský dům at seven tomorrow evening. Come along."

The girls plucked up their courage and each kissed him on the cheek. Then they ran away giggling.

Pavlíček said with an astonished expression, "You sure know how to surprise me."

All three friends laughed loudly, but this attracted the attention of the other guests, who, of course, hadn't missed what had just happened. One of the guests stood up and began to applaud, and the others joined in.

Procházka stood up and bowed like an actor in a theater. The applause moved him: "Thank you, my friends," he said loudly to the audience so that everyone could hear him. After a moment, the applause died down. The guests sat back down to their coffee, beer, or mineral water. The three friends at the table seemed to be lost in their thoughts for a moment.

Procházka broke the silence at the table with a cough: "So what did you get, Ota? You don't have the new Hemingway, do you?"

Hofman was happy to take up the renewed topic: "I go to the bookstore on Husitská street regularly and give the salesman free tickets to Světozor cinema for our group's premieres, so I consider that question completely unnecessary. We have an agreement that he always saves the interesting new titles for me, and once a month I choose the ones that catch my eye."

Pavlíček lit up: "Really? You have it? Or will you get it? Can't you get another one?"

Hofman replied modestly: "Of course...," he took a slow sip of his Gruzignac and put the glass back on the table, "...no."

Everyone laughed.

Pavlíček's eyes lit up: "Thanks, old friend."

The laughter intensified.

"When I finish reading it, I'll trade it for a new bike," Hofman told his friends about his plans.

Procházka took a sip from his glass and leaned toward Hofman: "I'm amazed, you and a bike? What do you need a new bike for?"

Hofman's face became serious. "My dad's turning eighty in a few days, and I recently asked him what he wanted for his birthday. That's why I'm looking for a new bike. But try finding a new bike without handlebars around here! I might be able to get a racing bike, but I guess the comrades in the Planning institute forgot about regular bikes in their so planned economy."

"You say eightieth birthday. And a new bike! Well, congratulations, but I don't know how to make one," Pavlíček chuckled.

Procházka thought for a moment: "He's good for a laugh, but I sense something in the air."

Pavlíček clearly didn't like the shift to a serious topic. He definitely didn't want to talk about politics right now. "How was Paris, Ota? Tell us all about it. I'm sure you went to see the hopping girls at the Moulin Rouge, or at least to a strip club..."

Hofman grimaced indignantly: "Why would I go to a strip club in Paris when they recently opened Beauty Unveiled just down the road in Vodičková street? But I can assure you, my friend, that I haven't even been there yet. Oh, and don't forget. Radio Yerevan reported that a strip club has opened in Moscow. It was packed on the first day. Half empty on the second day, and on the third day, not a soul showed up. They discussed it at a party meeting of the Moscow regional communist organization, where they asked the chairman how this was possible and whether the comrades had perhaps underestimated something, and above all, whether all the performers were also party members." And he said, of course. Since the founding of the Communist Party."

Pavlíček burst out laughing: "Yeah, funny, gentlemen. So how did you get on?"

Hofman leaned over again for his glass. "Well, what can I tell you. The Eiffel Tower is still standing. The French still don't know how to make good coffee, but otherwise... Broken shop windows, burning cars. Irena and I only just managed to avoid it. It was a close call; we could have lost our car. Ultimately, we decided to return home two days early. I have such bad luck, gentlemen! I feel like a magnet for trouble. In 1962, Irena and I were on vacation in Cuba, and we almost started World War III. Now I'm going to Paris, and there's chaos in the streets, people are setting cars on fire and building barricades. But wait, I've got some photos here, I just picked up the developed film." He handed the envelope to Pavlíček. "Take a look for yourself. I haven't had time to look at them yet."

"Once we reform our socialism, everything will be fine and excesses like these student riots in Paris will never happen here," Procházka assessed the situation.

Pavlíček looked fondly at one of the photos of a beautiful girl. Klára Wagnerová.

"She'd be worth a sin. Ah, those French women, no Czech woman can compare to them."

005 Prague, May 18, 1968

The Spořilov housing estate was certainly not beautiful. The simple eight-story cooperative apartment buildings were all identical, as if copied from the same template. With their characteristic socialist architecture, they looked like prefabricated buildings. Yet they were built of brick with the help of prisoners. And this was clearly evident in the quality of the buildings; crooked walls were just the tip of the iceberg. The leaky roofs had been repaired countless times.

This is where writer and screenwriter Ota Hofman and his family had just moved into a brick "prefabricated building." He settled in a fifth-floor apartment in a block of flats at one of the many entrances with an elevator that only worked sporadically, when it felt like it. The view from the apartment windows offered a glimpse of the drab façade of the same "prefabricated building" on one side and a view of the loggias of another equally unappealing building on the other.

However, the new apartment was larger than the one in Jarov, at the very end of Žižkov, which Hofman had just left. There, foxes still said good night. That is, until they built a housing estate there too.

What a surprise it was for Hofman, the new member of the housing cooperative, when he met Antonín Moskalyk, a film director at Czechoslovak Television, in the hallway! He lived with his family one floor above him on the sixth floor.

From the first day they moved in, Moskalyk's huge boxer, Adam, began to enliven the lives of both families. He immediately remembered that he could always find something good to eat one floor below. Hofman had known Moskalyk for many years. They sometimes played tennis together, but Antonín Moskalyk, the junior national champion, never lost a game. Ota Hofman took his losses in stride, knowing that he was no match for Tonda and that winning wasn't important to him.

The two knew each other very well, both professionally and personally. Ota Hofman and his wife, Irena, had recently written a scathing, ironic satire on socialist bureaucracy called **The Kissing time Ninety,** originally titled **Children, Children, Children.** It was a somewhat offbeat comedy about the birth of the first Czechoslovak quintuplets, and Tonda directed the film at Barrandov as his feature debut. But before that, they had already made a short film exploring the relationship between father and son, **Orange Moon**.

It didn't take long time after they moved in for the idea of quick communication to be born: two red children's telephones were connected between the floors by a thin string. The dog, Adam, was also good at barking for attention in the hallway when he felt like eating the Christmas cookies stored under the couch one floor below, which he knew about thanks to his reliable sense of smell.

006 Prague, May 20, 1968

At the end of Jindřišská Street in Prague stands a Gothic tower dating back to the 15th century. It was originally a free-standing bell tower for the Church of St. Henry and St. Kunhuta, which is just across the street. In front of the church is a small park with tall trees.

František Pavlíček was hurrying through here to the house behind the church. The Procházka–Švabík dramaturgy team at Barrandov Film Studios had their offices there. Bohunka Šourková, a kind and well-groomed lady with perfectly styled blonde hair, worked as the secretary for the dramaturgy team.

All the dramaturges were out, so she was enjoying a moment of peace and reading the newspaper. František Pavlíček entered the office and immediately asked, "Bohunka, please, that radio over there on the cabinet that no one ever turns on, does it work?"

Bohunka Šourková put down the newspaper: "Well, I think so. Do you want to try it?"

Pavlíček approached the radio and turned the knob. A faint crackling sound came from the speaker.

"It works," Pavlíček confirmed and began searching for a station by turning the second knob.

After a moment, he tuned in to Czechoslovak Radio, and Jiří Šlitr's current hit, sung by Suchý, began to play. "I'll hide a strand of hair secretly, I'm crazy under the pillow..."

Bohunka looked at Pavlíček in amazement: "Are we going to have this production here all the time now?"

Pavlíček remarked dryly: "It's about to start."

Bohunka looked at him questioningly again: "What's about to start?"

Pavlíček went to make himself a coffee: "Honza will be on the radio. They're going to broadcast a recording of yesterday's big discussion with students at the Slovanský dům , and I don't want to miss it."

Jiří Suchý finished singing, and the voice of the radio commentator filled the office:

"Slovanský dům is under siege," said the conductor of tram no. 5 yesterday at around 7 p.m. as he made his way through the crowds of girls and boys at the Prašná brána tram stop. A woman immediately added emphatically: 'What's going on, there are hundreds of them here, as if they were giving something away for free! But they're going dancing. And one day they'll go crazy from all that dancing.' She concluded her speech with the reflection: 'Well, yes, there must be some kind of ball here.' A young man in corduroy trousers and a dark blue jacket replied, "You're wrong, ma'am. There's a discussion going on."

Yesterday, the Slovanský dům was besieged by young Praguers from seven in the evening until late at night. According to official reports, three thousand young people were unable to get inside. It was a genuine political discussion. The hall of the Slovanský dům was filled to capacity. The organizers barely managed to secure a place on the podium for those who were to step up to the microphone and speak to the young people without prejudice or illusions, without embellishment, and truthfully, as only a human being can, about our past, present, and future. Judge for yourselves how they fared."

A female voice took the floor: "Speaking is Comrade Josef Smrkovský, Minister of Forestry and Water Management."

"As a comrade whom you have welcomed among you, I am truly delighted to be able to march in the same ranks as the younger generation, I tell you that."

This was followed by thunderous applause from the audience. Bohunka Šourková and František Pavlíček listened attentively as Josef Smrkovský's long-winded voice continued: "But at the same time, comrades, I tell you that at twenty years of age, you have the right to use your own minds and that you have the right and the duty to be more revolutionary and more radical than we, your fathers, were. And we older people, in turn, have a duty to keep an eye on everything! So that in the great, great transformation that our country, our state, is undergoing, nothing happens that could spell disaster." His words were again accompanied by loud applause from the audience. "And that is what I want to ask of you. You will be there, you will have your say, you will run your organizations. That is also part of the project. You will run everything, but please, let your actions take today and, in the days, to come be responsible actions. Nothing like yesterday or the day before yesterday in Warsaw, because if you allow that, if you allow something like that, you will deal a terrible blow to the tremendous efforts that the party's central committee is making. We must proceed cautiously, in our own way, but cautiously and responsibly. Why? Because in a few years, in ten years, in fifteen years, this state will pass into your hands. And we want you to take it over as a mature, culturally and industrially developed socialist republic with a socialist society, where the nation, the people themselves, rule, where the people are truly masters of their country and their destiny."

After a long round of applause, the female voice of the commentator spoke again on the radio: "Writer Jan Procházka."

Pavlíček and Bohunka Šourková looked at each other. Pavlíček thought: Now it begins.

"I would like to follow up on what Comrade Smrkovský said before me," Procházka began his speech in a much more forceful and convincing voice. "I also think that for us, for Czechoslovakia, Budapest," Procházka tried to correct Smrkovský's slip, "is not the way forward, because our cities are falling apart even without our help."

The hall erupted in cheers accompanied by thunderous, prolonged applause. "I have received a question about censorship," he said, as if reading from a piece of paper: "Abolition of censorship... Are there any measures being taken to abolish censorship? asks the questioner."

Procházka replied in a raised voice: "Censorship has ceased to exist, my friends."

"Hurrah!" The cheers from the hall were deafening, accompanied by long applause once again. Procházka continued after the applause died down.

"This is a huge step forward; the last time we achieved something like this was fifty years ago." The cheers and laughter from the hall were full of the enthusiasm of young people. "I think freedom of speech is fundamental in a civilized country. Because it is illogical for a person to learn to speak for so long and then not be allowed to speak. A free exchange of views will show us, how to get back to Europe."

The hall erupted again with laughter and cheers, which were then interrupted by Procházka's voice: "I have another question, whether I would like to be president. To that I must reply that it really does not depend on me."

After another round of applause, a female voice came on the radio and announced: "Zdeněk Hejzlar, first chairman of the youth union."

"In addition to a lot of questions, I'm very nervous because I haven't spoken in Prague for seventeen years." His words were accompanied by applause from the hall. "But if I'm afraid, then I'm not afraid..."

Pavlíček went over to the radio and looked at Bohunka: "Do you want to listen to this?"

Bohunka shook her head: "We heard the word of boss, we heard the word of God..." she paraphrased.

Pavlíček laughed and turned off the radio.

The door opened, and Jan Procházka entered.

"Speak of the devil," said Pavlíček. "Hi, Honza."

Procházka paused: "Hi Franta, Bohunka. What were you saying about the wolf?"

"I wanted to hear what you said yesterday at the Slovanský dům, and Bohunka and I just listened to it on the radio. Listen, Honza, you really know how to stir up a crowd."

007 Prague, May 21, 1968

Klára Wagnerová, already dressed for summer, got off the tram in front of the White Swan Mall in Prague, looked around the platform, and crossed the street onto the cobblestone sidewalk. On her way to her new job, she glanced at the window of a general store.

The queue stretched all the way outside. She made her way inside past the orderly queue and went to look at the sales counter. "There's a queue here, young lady," said elderly, strong woman with a strange bun on her head behind her.

Klára didn't respond to her call, but she managed to notice the rubber rolls in a crate behind the counter and then the potato salad with meatloaf of an indeterminate color behind the display case.

Disgusted, she turned around and ran along the line of shoppers out of the store. She thought to herself that the baker in Paris was actually right. In a way, it's hell on earth here.

As she walked out the door back onto the street, the lady with the bun gave her one last satisfied look. She was proud of her victory. Klára turned onto the cobblestone sidewalk and walked briskly toward her destination, the building with the bronze sign "Magazine Květy". I'd rather go without a snack than this, she said to herself.

008 Prague, May 21, 1968

Jan Zelenka, editor-in-chief of magazine Květy, walked into his office on Poříčí Street and refused to believe what he had just heard. He had been summoned by Fojtík, head of the cultural department of the Communist Party's central committee, and he had no idea why. Now he knew. He had been fired, fired on the spot. He, who had always faithfully carried out the tasks of the party, of which he had been a loyal member for many years. He couldn't understand it at all.

Květy was said to be out of step with the current trend of political liberalization, Zelenka's views were said to be incompatible with the modern concept of socialism, and who knows what other nonsense they would have used to justify the simple fact that on Friday, he would no longer be the editor-in-chief of the weekly magazine Květy. That was that. He could have stayed on as a regular editor. But what would the Central Committee of the Communist Party think of him? He certainly wouldn't give them the satisfaction of humiliating him like that! What's more, they didn't even bother to tell him who would be replacing him. "That's none of your business," they told him.

He refused to accept that on Monday someone new would be running magazine Květy, and that it wouldn't be him. Such humiliation! The words still rang in his ears: The party demands new and flexible approaches to the tasks ahead, requiring greater insight and flexibility. What nonsense! He walked like a zombie and, relying on memory, made his way to the entrance with the sign "Magazine Květy." What now? What would he say to the people in the editorial office? The editorial meeting was about to start...

He hesitated, but then reassured himself: I'm still the boss here, only until Friday, but I'm still me! What would I tell them? Let the new guy tell them. I won't say anything to them today. Until Friday, Květy is mine magazine, and until then, I'm the only one in charge.

With this decision and a determined expression on his face, he entered the building.

009 Prague, May 21, 1968

Two floors above, in the editorial office of magazine Květy, the sun shone brightly through the dirty, unwashed windows. On a gloomy day, the dirt could be overlooked, but today the sun was harsh and unforgiving. Klára Wagnerová looked at the worn floor and thought again that it must have taken a lot of work to come up with such an ugly pattern. She looked uncertainly around the editorial office where she was now to spend part of her life. She had been assigned a desk and chair on Monday. She had already prepared the articles she wanted to contribute to magazine Květy at home, so she didn't hesitate to hand them over to her colleague Borský, who had been assigned to train her.

He showed her the coffee pot and told her to bring her own mug and coffee. That was the extent of his activity as the new intern's mentor. Borský didn't even read her articles and put them straight into the new editorial submissions tray.

Klára looked up from her desk when she heard an older woman enter.

"Good morning, comrade. Comrade Wagnerová, if I'm not mistaken. We haven't met yet. My name is Černá, Miss Černá. I was in the field this week."

Klára greeted her loudly: "Good morning." She stood up and shook her hand. The others in the room ignored them and continued working or pretending to work.

The newcomer didn't find Klára very likable, but at least she greeted her politely. Klára thought a little maliciously that after so many years spent in the editorial office, they might even assign her an inventory number.

She noticed that every shabby desk and rickety chair in the editorial office was adorned with an unsightly inventory number. Klára looked around the bleak workplace again. Her eyes wandered to the motley collection of photographs of famous people from culture and social life that covered the walls.

Pop singers, Waldemar Matuška, Václav Neckář.

She glanced at the door, which was opening abruptly. Jan Zelenka burst into the editorial office with a grim face. Everyone in the room except Klára knew that he was returning from the Central Committee of the Communist Party.

Zelenka looked around, hesitating for a moment to see if anyone knew anything, but there was no sign of it; everything was as he had arranged it. A sporadic "Good morning" was heard. He did not answer. His chair at the head of the conference and executive table was empty.

Editor-in-Chief Zelenka put his briefcase on the table, took out some papers, and sat down in the empty chair. Quietly, as if with one voice, everyone else got up from their seats and headed for the meeting. He waited until everyone had sat down, leaving one chair for Wagnerová, who also sat down.

Jan Zelenka glanced at the new addition to the editorial team, and at that moment, his blood boiled again. He looked at her hatefully and thought to himself: So, these are the new ideas, the new approaches... But I'm still the boss here.

Then he began: "Well, comrades, welcome to today's editorial board meeting." He looked at Klára again. Their eyes met. "I've read your new proposed articles, and so," he cleared his throat, "first of all, I'd like to focus on the articles by our new addition, comrade intern Wagnerová. Interesting, interesting..." The editor-in-chief paused and looked down at the papers on his desk. "You write here about your visit to Paris and, in particular, about the achievements of capitalist society in the variety of pastries in a capitalist bakery. You write about the delicious taste of macaroons that melt in your mouth. And in particular, you compare these bourgeois luxuries with the range of pastries in our socialist homeland. As you say, the Parisian baker describes our society as hell on earth."

He put down the sheet of paper and cleared his throat again. He stared at the next sheet as if fascinated.

"In your next proposed contribution, you write about your accidental arrest during the student riots in Paris. And here you write how nice the police of a capitalist country were to you, allowing you to contact the embassy in Paris immediately. And when they realized their mistake, they then, allow me to quote: treated you to coffee with croi..., I can't read this," he looked at Klára.

"It's pronounced croissant, but it's spelled with a c at the beginning," Klára added.

Zelenka looked at her mockingly. "And what am I supposed to imagine?"

"A delicate, fluffy butter pastry," Klára replied timidly.

"And you think our readers know what that is? Who among you, apart from Comrade Wagnerová, knows what a croissant tastes like?" He looked back at the papers on the table.

He raised his head and looked around at the editors at the table. Everyone was silent as the grave.

"So, with croissant... croissant, and in the end, they apologized and invited you to lunch."

The editor-in-chief put down the paper, blushed, cleared his throat again, and looked at Klára. There was a moment of silence, and then, barely audible, he began: "You see, Comrade Wagnerová, if you wrote with the same fervor about police brutality in the bourgeois world, then yes. I would welcome that and understand it. That would be the right path for a conscious socialist journalist. And that's what our readers are waiting for," he gradually raised his voice, "however, comrade, you probably haven't realized yet that we have socialism here and that capitalism is definitely not a paradise on earth. This is evidenced by the student unrest, which expresses the class dissatisfaction of the younger generation with the capitalist system in an urgent manner. Certainly not the way you describe it, comrade!" Now he was shouting, his face red with anger. "Capitalism is an evil that must be defeated. Didn't they teach you that in school, comrade? Now we finally have an end to censorship and Comrade Dubček at the head of the party..." He paused, his adrenaline rising even more, and repeated to himself: I'm still in charge here. Then he continued slowly, in a whisper: "But, comrade, the way you write, in our magazine Květy, is definitely not the way forward, and we don't want to print such reports, and we won't."

I'll be completely honest with you, Comrade Wagnerová. I consider your appointment as an intern at magazine Květy to be a mistake. Therefore, after careful consideration, I think you should definitely look for work elsewhere." Klára turned pale as a ghost and couldn't utter a word.

The furious editor-in-chief added, looking at her: "Does anyone else have anything to say about Comrade Wagnerová's articles?"

The editors sat silently, staring at their hands clasped tightly on the tabletop, no one wanting to be the next victim of the furious editor-in-chief.

Jan Zelenka looked around at the stunned editors at the table. "No one? Well then, honor to your work, Comrade Wagnerová."

Klára got up and went to her desk to pack her things. Behind her, the editor-in-chief's voice rang out again:

"Now we will turn to Comrade Černá's article on the work of miners at the Družba coal mine..."

But Klára couldn't hear anything anymore; her head was spinning. She didn't understand what had happened and just kept thinking: Get out, get out, get out of here!

010 Prague, May 21, 1968

Martin Konopásek, a sergeant in the regional StB - State secrete Safety administration, knew these stairs like the back of his hand. He couldn't even count how many times he had climbed them in the Krátký film building in Prague to get to his superior's office. He didn't take the elevator; he didn't like confined spaces. He was meticulous, conscientious, and above all, absolutely loyal, which is why Kamil Pixa liked him so much. And, of course, because he didn't talk much, and the word "conscience" was not in his vocabulary. He carried out the tasks his superior gave him. He didn't ask questions or express doubts.

One more floor to go. He knocked on the unmarked door. A voice said, "Come in."

He entered. The secretary's small, dark room was very spartanly furnished. One desk with a lamp and a telephone, and one wardrobe. No decorations, flowers, or pictures.

The secretary, Eva, looked up: "He's been waiting for you. You should have been here ten minutes ago. Go on in."

He remained silent, made no comment, and did not apologize for his delay. He did not greet him.

Kamil Pixa, a slightly graying man in his forties, was lying on a sofa in an equally dark room, Rudé právo newspaper spread across his face, and said quietly, "Is that you, Martin?"

Constable Konopásek stopped in front of the desk and sat down: "Yes, boss."

"Have a seat." The guest chair at the desk was very worn and needed to be repainted or replaced. Constable Konopásek pulled a briefcase with files onto his lap.

"So what have you brought me today, Martin?"

"The usual weekly report."

"Anything interesting? But don't bother me with trivialities. I'm fed up with that nonsense. You know who I mean? Landovský. He's always getting drunk somewhere. He talks rubbish, and the whole Prague StB is having a field day with it. How many times has it been in the last month?"

"Three times."

"Everyone talks nonsense these days, but it can't go beyond a certain limit. Yeah, three times. We'll have to get rid of him."

Martin glanced at the files in front of him. He discreetly put the first one, labeled PAVEL LANDOVSKÝ back in the briefcase.

"What else do you have there? You know I'm mainly interested in people from Barrandov."

Martin presented the next item: "Ota Hofman," he read from the file label.

"What about Hofman?" muttered Pixa from under the newspaper.

Martin opened the file and began to read: "He was in Paris on a private trip. Crossed the border at Rozvadov on May 22 at 2:18 p.m. Returned to Rozvadov on May 28 at 9:17 p.m. Standard foreign currency allowance. No additional currency was declared in the customs declaration. No customs inspection was carried out at the border. Upon his return, he declared the purchase of gramophone records and a handbag for his wife."

"Anything else about the trip? You must have something, otherwise you wouldn't be bothering me with it."

"He went to Paris via Munich."

"Did we put him under surveillance?" Pixa perked up.

"No, we didn't. But our man in Munich happened to spot a Czechoslovakian license plate, so he took the initiative and tailed him. In the center of Munich, next to the clock tower, Hofman met with a Westdeutcher Rundfunk television employee. We've already found out his name, Gert Müntefering. Our man can't swear to it, but apparently an envelope was exchanged."

"To whom? Who?" asked Pixa.

Martin continued reading: "Münte... I can't pronounce it. Müntefering to Hofman. We already have a file on Müntefering. He has applied for a visa several times and has visited Prague on multiple occasions. On business. Meetings at Filmexport and Barrandov Film Studio. So far, just routine, nothing special."

"Anything else?"

Martin read for a moment and then said, "We lost sight of him in Munich. But no instructions were given, so they let it go. When he returned from abroad, he had the photos from his trip developed at Foto-kino in Štěpánská Street. I thought we should get copies made."

"And anything interesting?"

"I don't know. Just ordinary tourist photos. Hofman and the Eiffel Tower, his wife and the Eiffel Tower, and so on. Only about two photos are interesting," Martin continued.

Pixa took the Rudé Právo newspaper off his face: "Pass them to me." He reached out his hand, but remained lying down.

Martin walked around the table and handed the photos to Pixa: "The first one is his wife leaving the hotel."

"So what, a hotel?"

Martin returned to his place behind the desk: "If he got the foreign currency allowance he was permitted to apply for, it would only be enough for one bed and half a night in this hotel. I think the envelope he received in Munich explains it."

"Yeah, that's probably how it is. However, there are many people like that these days. Instead of an exit visa, all you need is a stamp in your ID book, and you can go wherever you want. Apparently, there's a law in the works to abolish even that. But we'll take a closer look at this Gert guy. When he comes back, we'll stick to him like glue. Take care of it."

Martin added dryly, "Then the second photo."

Pixa looked at the photo: "Pretty girl. I like her."

Martin continued, "She's pretty, that's for sure, so we looked her up in the database. Just to be on the safe side. I started wondering why Hofman was photographing Czech girls in Paris."

Pixa paused: "She's Czech?"

"Yeah, her name is Klára Wagnerová. And she was in Paris on a foreign exchange program."

Pixa thought for a moment: "How did we even find her? There are girls like that on every corner in Paris."

"Well, it's a bit of a coincidence. We received a message from our embassy in Paris stating that she had been arrested for sedition. Our colleague, who received it on his desk, compared her to a photo by Hofman and identified her by name. But then the arrest turned out to be a mistake, and she was released the same day."

Pixa looked at the photo with pleasure, his mind racing. "Aren't we being a little paranoid? We're always looking for class enemies. Always and everywhere. But she's a real piece of work." Then he returned to reality and answered himself:

"No, being paranoid is our job, and that's why we get such great results. So check her out. I want to know everything about her. And bring me the comrade who found this out, he works for you, right?"

"Yeah, he's new."

"He's smart, observant, and can put two and two together. I want to meet him. Anything else?" Pixa added, continuing to look at Wagner's photo with obvious pleasure.

Martin didn't interrupt him. He remained silent.

"If you don't have anything else, you can go."

011 Prague, May 21, 1968

Wagner sat in his study looking at his collection of fountain pens. He wore white gloves, and behind him stood an open safe. The painting that usually covered it, leaned against the wall. Suddenly, the study door opened and Klára Wagnerová spoke in a quiet voice:

"Am I disturbing you, Dad?"

She stood there looking dejected. Wagner put the pen in its case: "No, you're not disturbing me at all, I'm just looking at my new find." And he showed her the latest addition to his collection. "Don't tell your mother. I'll be lectured all evening."

Klára just smiled slightly. She thought to herself that her dad would never learn.

"I'll have to give you back that pen you gave me."

"Why's that?"

"I got fired."

Wagner perked up and put on an interested expression.

"I'm completely stupid. As a new intern, I was supposed just to make coffee and deliver the mail, like you advised me, but instead I wrote about the beauty of Paris and the taste of macarons, and I got fired."

"Politics again, right? You got into a fight with an idiot, I bet. What's his name?"

Wagner smiled: "Jan Zelenka."

"I don't know him," Wagner replied, "the name doesn't ring a bell."

"The editor-in-chief. When he was squeezing me like a piece of meat in a pressure cooker, he was really enjoying himself."

"But that's okay, every beginning is difficult. Times are changing. You'll definitely find something else where you can write what you like. Keep that pen, though. Wait, let me think for a moment. " He paused. " Now I'm thinking of Kino magazine. You'll write about films and actors. You often go to the cinema and enjoy it. Would you like to try it?"

Klára hesitated for a moment. "Yeah, I'd like that. I'll go there tomorrow, maybe there won't be such an idiot there..."

"Unfortunately, they're everywhere. Party than Party and again Party, nothing else is important."

"Thanks, Dad, I would could I do if I didn't have you..."

"Wait, wait. It won't be that easy. Girls like you, who enjoy movies, probably go there every week, at least five of them, I'd guess. And maybe even more guys. Watching movies and writing about movies are two very different things. Everyone can watch, but the latter is something else. Not everyone can do that. And you can't go there like one of those five. You wouldn't get very far."

"So, what do you advise me to do?" asked Klára.

Her father thought for a moment and picked up a pen from the table. He thought for a while. "You have to go there with something that will catch their attention, something that shows your genuine interest, that you're really serious about it. Bring them something, some kind of scoop, to get them interested. Avoid politics, so you don't get rejected again," advised Dad, playing with his pen.

"So, what do you think I should do? To write about movies, actors, I think I'd really enjoy that."

"They won't be interested in movie reviews; they write those all the time. Don't waste your time with that. Interview someone interesting from the film industry first, or bring in more interviews with interesting people, maybe from Barrandov. That way, you'll spark their interest and jump ahead of the other applicants. Then it'll depend on whether they like it and whether they have any openings. But if they like your work, they might even make a spot for you. Jan Procházka comes to mind, for example. He works at Barrandov, has written a few screenplays, and is now active on the forum; however, avoid discussing politics with him at all costs."

Klára gave him a kiss. "You're great, Dad. I'll get started."

012 Central Bohemia, Kostelní Lhota, June 7, 1968

Kostelní Lhota is a small village behind Sadská on the road from Prague to Poděbrady. The houses wind along the road in the flat Polabská lowlands like beads on a rosary. Kostelní Lhota has been mentioned in church records since 1354. Mr. Boček had the Church of the Assumption of the Virgin Mary built in this village and appointed Petr as its parish priest. The owners, the lords of Kunštát and Poděbrady, were highly respected in their time and always Czech-minded. In 1355, Mr. Boček was present at the coronation of Charles IV in Rome. His great-grandson, Jiří of Kunštát and Poděbrady, became the only Czech king in 1458 who did not come from a ruling dynasty, but from the domestic nobility.

Alois Linka got the farm from his father. His dad owned Linka's delicatessen, which is across from Masaryk Station in Prague. It's known for its Italian salad and even more famous ham. Alois was tasked with supplying Linka's delicatessen with meat and hard-to-find foods, such as asparagus, which was in short supply. The second son became a pastry chef and the third a greengrocer. Alois Linka married Stella, who is Ota Hofman's sister. They farmed the fields and forests near Kostelní Lhota. However, the local cooperative then took their land.

Ota Hofman's older brother, Evžen, bought a small house in Kostelní Lhota before the war, located in the middle of a pine forest, and left it to his father, Josef Hofman.

Ota Hofman and his wife were busy. They had just passed Sadská and were nearing the turn-off for the isolated house in Kostelní Lhota. A big party was set up for Ota's father's 80th birthday.

"Do you have it?" Stella asked Ota as soon as he managed to stop in front of the house after driving through the narrow forest road and opened gate.

"I've got it," Ota nodded from behind the wheel.

"He'll be so happy."

"But it was hard work," added Ota as he got out of the car and looked around. He saw the birthday boy with his mother, Anna, coming to greet him. Josef Hofman was much smaller than his son, but he was very energetic for his age and still had a sharp mind.

"Go keep him busy so I can unload the bike," Ota muttered hurriedly.

Stella nodded.

"It has to be a surprise!"

A friendly welcome followed between the son and his parents. Stella thought for a moment, but nothing clever came to mind: "Dad, I don't know if we have enough wine."

Her father snapped, "There's plenty of wine."

Stella wouldn't let it go: "Really, come check," she said emphatically, grabbing her father by the elbow and leading him away.

Otto, Ota Hofman's fourteen-year-old son, felt more at home at his grandfather's house in Lhota than anywhere else. Now, barefoot, wearing only shorts and a T-shirt, he shouted, "Hi, Dad, Mom. You're finally here." He headed for the car and asked conspiratorially, "So, did you get it?"

His mother, Irena, nodded. Fortunately, his grandfather, although still within earshot, had not heard Otto's question.

Irena managed to put her finger to her lips in warning and then opened the trunk of the car.

The bicycle had been dismantled and smelled new. Otto grabbed the rim and ran, using one wheel, to a nearby shed.

His father cautiously looked around to make sure the coast was clear, then quickly followed his son with the frame. Irena was left with the rear wheel.

Stella's husband, Alois, a short-haired, tanned man, didn't wait around and joined in: "Go on, go to the jubilant, I'll put the bike together."

Under the pine trees and a row of brick outbuildings, a long table had been set up with chairs of all shapes and materials.

The family celebration began. Gifts were handed to the jubilant. He was a little embarrassed, but happy to see his family together again. Finally, Alois brought the new bike. Josef Hofman took it and gave it a test ride.

To the applause of the well-wishers, he made a ceremonial circle and immediately sat down at the head of the table. After a moment, he looked at Ota and beckoned him with his finger. Ota stood up, walked over to the jubilant, and sat down on a chair next to him. So that no one could hear, his father leaned toward him and said, "Ota, Otík. I'm glad we got together. You see, I have something on my mind, and I'd like to talk to you. Come to the porch in a moment."

The porch was the little celebrant's kingdom in the small house in Kostelní Lhota. There, in an old carved bookcase, he kept his books and treasures, which he loved dearly. Opposite an old, worn wingback chair on a small table, a chessboard dominated the room, and next to it, on a shelf, stood a radio tuned to Radio Free Europe.

013 Central Bohemia, Kostelní Lhota, June 7, 1968

Josef Hofman lived with his wife Anna and her two sisters, Františka and Marie. During World War I, both sisters had promised to marry their fiancés, who had been drafted into the army, and wait for them to return. However, neither of them survived the war.

Both of their fiancés died in battle. So, faithful to their promise, they lived together in love for God and Jesus Christ. Unlike the women of the household, today's honoree was an atheist and never went to church. He loved books and chess, and lived in Kostelní Lhota, away from the village, in peace and quiet.

Ota smiled as he stepped onto the porch. He sat in a chair across from his father, who was waiting in the wingback chair.

He glanced at the chessboard, but didn't notice the arrangement of the pieces.

His father began without preamble: "You surely remember Honza Čermák, your uncle, who rose through the ranks in the army to become a major general and commander of the mobilization department of the 2nd military district. You also knew his friend Míla Zatřepálek. The former saved your life in Bohdašín when you fell into a cesspool as a toddler, and he jumped in after you in his smart uniform. The latter was dismissed from the army after February 1948, as he had served as a military attaché in London following the war. But then came 1956, and no one really knows what the two of them got mixed up in. At that time, the uprising against the Bolsheviks in Hungary was crushed by Russian tanks, but just before that, Honza was involved in a strange car accident in Slovakia, in which he broke his neck. Míla Zatřepálek was found a few days later with a bullet through his heart near the Liechtenstein Palace. Nothing was ever explained, you know, the KGB is very good at that. And even though you already know these stories, I wanted to remind you of them today. Just to remind you, because I would really hate for you to end up the same way."

Ota wanted to object, but his father's gesture silenced him.

Dad shifted in his armchair and continued: "Please let me finish what I have to say. Rest assured that our current ridiculous demonstration of freedom will not go unanswered. The Bolsheviks can't afford that. It could quickly spread to other colonies, and worse, even to Moscow. Be absolutely certain that they are already speculating on how to stop this... what they consider to be the mess that is happening here. You know, Ota, I listen to Radio Free Europe every day. These Dubček, Smrkovský, they are, between the lines, naive clowns to the West, whom Moscow neither sent nor approved. Out there in the West, they already know that this will have serious consequences. Are you following what I'm saying?"

Ota nodded and listened further.

"And I don't think I'm a naive fool, I've been through a lot. When something happens, no one will give a damn about us, the West will certainly not start World War III because of us. No one will lift a finger for fourteen million people in a vassal colony, because that's what it is on a global scale. I know that the world was already divided once in Yalta, and no one, no one in the world, except for our currently deluded idiots, wants to change that now, and above all, no one will. However, what I want to share with you today is a kind of request or advice, take it as you will. You know, I understand that you signed up with them before the coup when you were seventeen. You really upset me with that back then. Okay, I understand; they fooled you, just as they fooled many others. But as Churchill said, anyone who isn't a leftist at twenty has no heart, and anyone who is a leftist at forty has no brain. And you have a huge heart. I know that, and I know you, and based on your films and books, so do others. But now, now listen to me very carefully."

Dad paused, and Ota waited for what would follow, "You've always had a mind of your own and followed your heart. I could have had a heart attack back then when you secretly took the entrance exam for Film Academy at Prague - FAMU and dryly announced to Mom and me that you were throwing two semesters of law school in the trash. Screenwriting and writing are uncertain professions, especially in today's world, where politics influence everything. But when I talked my mom out of making you become a priest and told her that you would decide for yourself, I had to respect your decision. Law was the sensible choice, but you followed your heart. And today I admit that you made the right decision. But now, please," he paused for a moment, "Use your head and get rid of them as soon as possible and leave the party. It's much better to leave than to be kicked out. Now you have a chance to get rid of them; now it will definitely work. It's a good time for it. We both know you're a pragmatist, so listen to Churchill; he was a very smart man."

Ota thought for a moment. "Sure, you're right. However, the way I see it, the two hostile worlds, as they are today, are created by people. And only people. And they are similar people: stupid people, smart people, reasonable people, people in love, unhappy people, happy people. They are on both sides of the border, in these worlds that are so divided today. And I think that with what I can do, I have to try to bring those on one side together with those on the other. At the very least, bring them a little closer together, and above all, do it with a smile and understanding for both sides. What divides us is fear, and that is a terrible weapon. And that fear must be broken. That is the only way to overcome the Iron Curtain. So those behind the curtain stop fearing those in front of it. Then the curtain will lose its meaning. That's why I write the way I do."

"Ota, don't be silly, you'll never change. Like I said, your heart rules your life. Never mind. However, if you and Irena decide to run away, do so and don't hesitate. We might never see each other again. I don't know. But from what you say, you can continue your mission from the other side, and maybe it won't be so hard. Now I'm just waiting to see what happens, and when it does, it's going to be crazy, count on it. And it will be soon."

Ota really wasn't expecting such a serious conversation. He thought about his father's logic for a moment. It was relentless. And the urgency of his father's plea weighed heavily on him.

"Thanks, Dad, I'm sure you're right. Now I have to finish the *Pan Tau* scripts. I still have a few episodes to write.

And the Germans, those Germans behind the curtain and on the other side, are putting a lot of pressure on me, and I can't let them down. I must finish it by the end of the summer. So now I won't be able to think about anything else, but then, in September or October, I'll definitely quit the Communists. Do you really think the KGB killed Honza and Zatřepálek?"

"Well," sighed the birthday boy, "I don't think so, I know it. Honza rose too high in the army. I just don't know what our army got itself mixed up in back then. I believe that the Hungarian uprising was intended to spread to Slovakia and reach us. But the Bolsheviks put a stop to it. Besides, it wasn't a good time for us. All I know is that the car accident was very strange, and Zatřepálek wouldn't have shot himself right after that. No, no. There had to be a reason. He walks out onto the street in front of the ministry and shoots himself in the heart? No, he would never have done that. They simply killed him."

014 Central Bohemia, Kostelní Lhota, June 7, 1968

Stella entered the porch and immediately interrupted the discussion: "What are you two doing here? The guests want to celebrate!" Then she paused. "You can't be serious, you're not playing chess now!"

The jubilant quickly shifted gears. "No, we're not playing. I was just going over Spaskij's endgame with Fischer yesterday."

"Never mind. Where were we, Ota, ah yes... I would like to thank you very much for the new bike; the old one is really falling apart. But..." He paused, searching for words.

"But what?" asked Ota.

"Well, it's kind of... how can I put it... overengineered. I don't know how to use the derailleur, and when I step back, I can't stop; I just keep going."

Ota quickly changed the subject: "It has brakes on the handlebars and reflectors, you'll see when you ride it in the evening."

But Dad had made up his mind: "Okay, I'll save this for later and ride the pre-war bike to do the shopping until it falls apart completely."

Stella replied, "It was hard to find, and bikes like that aren't made anymore."

The birthday boy looked at her: "Isn't that a shame?"

Ota gave up and invited him: "Come join the well-wishers..."

They went outside to the table. Someone turned on the music, and the well-wishers demanded a dance. With little enthusiasm, Josef Hofman and his wife Anna began to dance clumsily under the twisted pine trees to the delight of everyone. The slightly drunk well-wishers clapped to the rhythm and gradually joined in.

015 Central Bohemia, Journey to Prague, June 7, 1971

Ota Hofman did not drink alcohol at the party; he was driving home. They left their son with his grandparents, where he always enjoyed spending time. In fact, he had spent half his childhood in Lhota. However, Irena noticed Ota's disappearance during the celebration, so on the way home, she began to probe discreetly: "That was a nice party, but where did you and Dad disappear to all of a sudden?"

Ota drove with a cigarette between his fingers, staring at the headlights on the empty road. "Dad invited me out on the porch. He wanted to talk. I've been thinking about what he said, and I think it must have been hard for him."

"Go on," Irena urged him.

Ota more or less recounted the conversation, not omitting the call to emigrate. Irena listened attentively. When he finished, she was silent for a moment. "Who actually won, Fischer or Spaskij?"

"Don't be silly. I can't stop thinking about what Dad said. The whole nation is euphoric and talking about freedom. Is it really like he says? Are we not in control of our own destiny, just blades of grass in the wind, at the mercy of the winds of change? Do you think Dad is right?"

Irena became serious: "I don't know, but I'm afraid. He's right about one thing: as long as the Bolsheviks don't fall in

Russia, they won't fall here either. We're a colony, whether we like it or not. And colonies don't control their own destiny; colonies are controlled by puppets."

After driving for a while, Ota added, "Yeah, I didn't get a chance to tell you that Jindra Polák got Jan Werich for the next episodes of *Pan Tau*. I already had a rough idea of how to approach it, and Werich is the key. Now I'll have to work, work, and work. With him, it'll be perfect. Werich, it's... It's indescribable, I'm so happy." Irena was taken aback by the change of subject. She knew Ota perfectly well. She knew that from now on, he wouldn't talk about anything other than *Pan Tau* and Jan Werich until he handed in his work.

So, she began to make a mental list of things she had to do in the near future: Tomorrow, take the car to the garage for an oil change, find a plumber, the tap in the bathroom is dripping, and I'll have to paint the walls, they're so gray. Otta could help me with that when he comes back from Lhota, but he's supposed to be there for the whole vacation. Oh well, I'll go pick him up. Then I'll wash the curtains and clean the windows. Oh, and the door on the kitchen cabinet is loose, so I'll have to fix that too.

016 Prague, June 12, 1968

Klára Wagnerová wandered back and forth along Jindřišská Street, unable to find the Barrandov studio offices. She had been told at the Barrandov studio that the offices were on Jindřišská Street, so that was where she went. She wandered around Jindřišská Tower and checked the signs on the buildings. Finally, she asked a newsagent: "Excuse me, I'm looking for the Barrandov studio offices and I can't find them. They're somewhere on Jindřišská Street."

The newsagent shook her head: "I can't help you, young lady. I don't know."

Klára didn't know what to do, so she sat down on a bench in the park next to St. Henry's Church. She sat there for a while and then decided to look in the phone book in a phone booth. She had just stood up when a man walked by. "Excuse me, do you know where the Barrandov Studios offices are?"

František Pavlíček appreciated Klára Wagnerová's beauty and smiled. "Of course I do, please come with me."

They set off together, and Pavlíček felt that the girl looked familiar. "Haven't we met before?"

Klára thought to herself, yeah, I know this line, but she replied aloud, "No, I don't remember meeting you anywhere."

"Who are you here to see?" asked Pavlíček, holding the door open for her gallantly.

"Jan Procházka."

"Come on in."

František Pavlíček entered Bohunka's office. "Hi Bohunka, is Honza here? I've brought a visitor."

Klára entered the room.

"Who should I announce?" asked Bohunka Šourková. "Do you have an appointment?"

"No, I don't. My name is Klára Wagnerová, and I'm here on behalf of Kino magazine. I'd like to ask Comrade Procházka for an interview," Klára lied.

"I see, I'll ask," said Bohunka and ran into the next room.

She came out a moment later. "I'm afraid Comrade Procházka is busy at the moment. How else can I help you?"

"That's a shame, I just wanted to talk to him about his films."

"I see. All right then."

Klára turned to leave, but Bohunka Šourková stopped her. "Wait a moment." She went into another office. Then she came back and left the door open. "Since you've come all this way, would you like to see the dramaturge and writer Ota Hofman? He has some time."

Klára hesitated, but then she thought, why not?

"Sure, thank you."

"Go on in," Bohunka urged her.

Klára entered the office and closed the door behind her. "Good morning, Comrade Hofman," she greeted him.

Ota Hofman looked up from the papers on his desk and invited her to sit down.

"My name is Klára Wagnerová, and I'm here on behalf of Kino magazine. I'd like to ask you for an interview."

Ota Hofman looked at the girl. She looked familiar. "Hello, I'm sorry, I'm not comfortable with journalists. But haven't we met somewhere before?" He had seen her face somewhere before and couldn't remember where...

Here we go again, thought Klára. Men in the film industry are all the same! "I'm really not aware that we know each other or have met before."

"What would the interview be about?" asked Hofman.

"Your work, what you're currently working on. What interesting films are you preparing?"

"I prefer a less formal setting for such interviews. So, shall we go for a drink?"

Klára was nervous as she bluffed, then it flashed through her mind: If he starts hitting on me, I'll run away. And she said aloud: "I'd love to."

017 Prague, June 12, 1968

Kamil Pixa thoroughly examined the young man who had just arrived. Martin Konopásek was sitting next to him and asked, "Can I have a light, boss?"

Kamil Pixa nodded but remained silent. Then he looked at the papers lying on the table in front of him. He raised his head. "Do you know why you're here?"

The young man was a little nervous. He didn't know why they had pulled him out of the office he shared with other new recruits recently recruited by the StB. Their job was to go through a pile of uninteresting documents assigned to them every day, find the more interesting ones, and set them aside.

"I don't know, comrade, did I do something wrong? Am I in trouble?"

Kamil Pixa smiled: "My name is Kamil Pixa and I'm your superior. Don't worry, you're not in trouble, quite the opposite. You're quite observant and, unlike the others in the office, you might actually have a brain. I'm looking for talented people for our work. The way you attached Wagner's photo to the report on her arrest, the photo from the embassy, you know? Was that a coincidence, or how did you think of it?"

The young man had clearly calmed down. "I don't even know. I saw this pretty girl in a photo this morning, and in the afternoon, I was going through reports from the embassy, where her photo was also, and it just occurred to me that it was the same girl. Did she do something?"

Pixa looked at the young man again. "We don't know yet, but I can appreciate a good job. Martin will take care of you now. I've decided to make you partners. You already know something about our work, but not everything. Martin will fill you in. You have no idea how much work it took to create a perfect human network. Everyone must cooperate with us. All public service employees are automatically included in our system without even knowing it. Every cop, soldier, medic, firefighter. They all report regularly on their work. That's a lot of people, hundreds of thousands of ordinary people in the field. Then we have all the members of the Communist Party under our control. One and a half million. They all play along. All we must do is ask. Our intelligence service alone has some 45,000 agents, and each of them has at least one informer. The system of so-called street informers has proven to be our best source. We have an informer on every street. All we have to do is call him to get his lazy ass off some piece of shit by Jaroslav Dietl, which we use to brainwash them, and he goes and checks out what's going on and what we need to know. In a system like this, not even a mouse can slip through. However, to put this system into operation, we need to thoroughly understand the terrain. Take car traffic leaving Prague, for example. Have you noticed how many towers Prague has? Our people sit there every day from midnight to midnight. Up there, in the church towers, they have a great view. They count the cars leaving Prague, randomly write down their license plate numbers, and always do so for expensive imported cars. Then they report the direction the suspicious car is going, and sometimes we get advance notice of who is going where. In any case, not even a mouse slips through our net. But what awaits you and Martin here is a slightly higher league of our work. I like you, so don't screw it up."

018 Netherlands, Noordwijk, August 23, 1968

The sea played its endless surfing song. This afternoon, it was just a gentle lullaby. Gert Müntefering, a children's program producer at Westdeutscher Rundfunk, had taken a few days off and was planning to spend them with his daughter at the seaside in Holland.

Even though the August sun was doing its best, the sea was still very cold. He dipped his toes in the water, and that was enough. He wanted to go back to the hotel reception. "Come out of the water. You're blue. Your mom will scold me for letting you catch a cold." "Just a minute, Dad."

The little girl's body splashed into the sea.

"Get out and no arguments." Gert prepared a towel to dry the girl off.

The annoyed child reluctantly obeyed, her body shivering with cold. Gert rubbed her with the towel to warm her up.

019 Netherlands, Noordwijk, August 23, 1968

Gert Müntefering approached the reception desk in the hotel lobby to ask for his room key. Still, before he could address the receptionist, the latter was slightly quicker: "Mr. Müntefering from German television?"

"Müntefering, yes. I'm from television."

The receptionist turned around and took a room key and an envelope from the mailbox: "You have an urgent message from Czechoslovakia from Mr. Polák."

Gert took the key and the envelope with the telegram and opened it: "Yes? Could you read it to me, please? I didn't bring my glasses with me to the beach." He handed the open envelope to the receptionist.

The receptionist began to read in fluent German: "Hello Gert, we're starting to shoot *Pan Tau* in September. We're expecting you in Prague."

The receptionist responded quickly: "Excuse me, sir, I don't mean to interfere, but didn't the newspapers say that Soviet tanks had arrived in Czechoslovakia?"

Gert looked him in the eye. "Yeah, I heard that too." Then he glanced at the TV screen in the reception area, where Russian tanks were crushing the cobblestones of Prague in a news report.

020 Netherlands, Noordwijk, August 23, 1968

So, what now? His mind was racing. Gert Müntefering had staked his career as a children's program producer at Westdeutscher Rundfunk on one card. His trump card, he firmly believed. Now he was staring out at the sea from the balcony of a hotel room in Holland, momentarily unsure of what to do next. He recalled that it had been five or six years since he had met Ota Hofman at a festival in Venice. Yes, it was in 1962. At the time, he had returned to Venice to search for films and programs for WDR's children's broadcasts. On that fateful afternoon, a competition film from socialist Czechoslovakia was being screened, called *Clown Ferdinand and the Rocket.* He remembered that he didn't really feel like going to the screening at the time. He didn't expect anything from a film from a communist country. In the end, he was glad he didn't give in to temptation, and he stared in amazement at the screen, where the story for children unfolded in the completely unreal setting of a spaceship. The sets looked like something out of Stanley Kubrick's *2001: A Space Odyssey*, but Kubrick didn't shoot his famous film until a few years later. However, these sets were designed for a children's film. You understand that correctly, for a children's film! No cheap cardboard, no amateur acting, nothing cheesy, something completely unreal and unthinkable in children's programs on West

German television or in films produced by East German DEFA film studio. These were real movie sets.

But! But, as always, there was this but. Nothing is as it seems at first glance. Ota Hofman immediately dampened Gert's enthusiasm in the café in Lido, but he didn't mind at all. Maybe it was just the opposite. It was precisely this clever move that won Ota over completely.

Gert looked out at the sea again. He remembered how Ota explained to him that the director of the film, Jindřich Polák, had not been approved for the huge costs of the sets for the sci-fi film *Ikarie XB 1*, and so he had been given a knife to his throat by the studio. He therefore approached Ota to write another film using the same sets. And Ota wrote the script within a fortnight. And Barrandov was the Hollywood of the Eastern Bloc at the time.

Gert really wanted the WDR management to agree to let him work with Ota and Jindra on other projects. However, before the management could make up its mind, Ota and Jindra Polák were snatched up by the competition, namely producers from Italy, the powerful Carlo Ponti, who needed to increase his expenses in order to stay below the tax threshold for his production company. Not only did he join the production of Miloš Forman's film *The Firemen's Ball*, but he also asked Ota and Jindra to come up with more episodes featuring the clown Ferdinand, thus snubbing WDR. Gert was very disappointed at the time. As Ota later told him, they couldn't do it. They racked their brains trying to figure out how to approach the clown character, but nothing came to mind. The character was too visually distinctive, limited in his means of expression. Therefore, they came up with a silent character, an elegant gentleman with a dandyish flower in his lapel, Pan Tau - a charming fellow with a bowler hat who is a friend to children and loves animals.

Carlo Ponti didn't hesitate and sent Barrandov money for the first pilot episode. Was it luck or bad luck for me? Gert wondered when Carlo Ponti finally backed out of the *Pan Tau* project. He didn't understand Ota at all. He wanted to add pretty girls to Charles Bridge and then shoot each episode in different locations around the world—New York, Tokyo, Sydney—and turn the series *Pan Tau* into a small travel agency.

But Ota didn't like that idea at all, and he and Jindra Polák both had their feet firmly on the ground and knew that the communists would never approve of it.

God, how happy I was, Gert recalled, when I could put my head on the chopping block and take over their project. But now what? The contracts are signed. What's more, now it's my, my personal huge mess. What am I going to do? WDR is going to shoot in Prague with their money, and Russian tanks will be driving around?

A girl's voice interrupted his train of thought from the hotel room: "Dad, what are you doing? I'm bored."

"I'm coming, sweetheart, let's go for a walk."

"Are we going to the beach again, Dad?"

"No, sweetie, let's go for a walk for a while, then we'll pack up and go home."

"No!!! But why? You promised we'd stay here for at least a week!"

"Something happened, sweetheart, you know? And I must go to work."

"What happened that's so important, Dad? Did someone die?"

"Sort of, sweetheart, not someone, but something died. I'm sorry. We have to leave."

021 West Germany, Cologne, August 26, 1968

Gert Müntefering was furious. On the way to Cologne, he kept explaining to his daughter why they had to go back home from Holland. She was disappointed because he had promised her a week at the beach. And now he would have to defend the indefensible. Russian tanks had rendered all his previous arguments obsolete. He took a deep breath in front of his boss's door.

Müller wasted no time: "Gert, I like you. You were right about **Pan Tau**, but the Soviet tanks won't just pull out of Czechoslovakia." We're not going to cooperate with those communists! It's dangerous."

"I know these people. They know their craft, and they are professionals. Czechoslovaks know how to make films. And it's cheap there. For the money we can offer them, we couldn't shoot even a third of it here in Cologne. And they shoot on film material, not on video technology that can't be played back in a year. Barrandov always had great sound. And the actors! First-rate!"

But Müller was cautious: "They're mainly communists. I'm not at all convinced that this is the right way to go. Maybe we should call it off. And if not, call it off, then wait a while until things clear up there."

Gert wouldn't give up: "You know, a few years ago, I went there to discuss the preparatory work for *Pan Tau*. I was an unknown dramaturge. And before I even got to the meeting, a dramaturge from the Barrandov creative group came up to me and shook my hand. It worked out...

You know, he didn't have to do that. He could have ignored me. He could have screwed me over. But he didn't. He wished me well, and his eyes sparkled with joy. I believe in the Czechs. I can't wait. It's not like you say. Like everyone says."

Müller grimaced and then gave in: "Okay... You probably have your reasons, Gert; you're an adventurer. But have it your way. I'll let you go, of course. But it's all on you. If something goes wrong, and I'm not sure what could go wrong, I'll have to let you take the fall. Deal?"

Gert didn't hesitate: "I accept."

"So, what do you want from me?"

Gert thought for a moment: "Pocket money in our currency. But it doesn't have to be that much, just enough to buy beer and sausages for everyone I meet there."

But Müller knew the risks: "You'll have to sign up with our secret service, are you prepared for that?"

After what had happened in Prague, Gert knew the answer even before he entered Müller's office. "Of course. I'm not an idiot."

022 Prague, September 14, 1968

The Russian tanks with white stripes had already left the center of Prague. Still, Brezhnev's signature, shot out on the facade of the National Museum at the head of Wenceslas Square, remained, as did the smudged inscriptions **GO HOME, IVAN**, and **FREEDOM**, but rain and time also took their toll on them in a short time.

Gert sat at a table in the Alcron Hotel on Štěpánská Street, not far from Wenceslas Square. He had a draft beer in front of him and plate with pieces of pork meat, cabbage, and four dumplings.

Ota Hofman sat down at the table in the hotel restaurant with a smile on his face. Gert started with his mouth full: "Moravian sparrow. Very good. With such a delicacy, one forgets that one is living under socialism."

Hofman shook his head sadly. "Hello, Gert, how was your flight?" Gert swallowed a bite: "Exciting. I wanted to buy something in the duty-free shop, but they didn't have anything."

The cigarette box in Hofman's hands opened. He took one out and lit it. "There's nothing here. The newspapers only started coming out a few days ago. So, it's a change."

Gert took a sip of beer. Hofman took a drag on his cigarette and swallowed the smoke with relish: "I'd like to thank you all for coming. We really appreciate it. No one knows what will happen, but the filming is ready and Jindra Polák is really looking forward to seeing you."

Gert's eyes lit up: "Me too."

Hofman leaned toward Gert: "Gert, to be honest, was it tough for you guys?"

Gert put down his cutlery: "To be honest, it was. It was very tough. Ota, I've got a knife at my throat right now."

Gert took another bite and added with his mouth full: "Ota, if things go completely down the drain here, you know I'll take good care of you. Keep that in mind."

Hofman looked Gert in the eye. "Should I take that as an offer?"

Gert replied without hesitation: "Yes."

"Thanks, I'll put it to the family council."

Gert finished his meal. "I've got a schedule of meetings and a list of people from Barrandov and Filmexport I'm supposed to meet."

Gert handed the paper to Hofman. Hofman shook his head.

"Is something wrong?" Gert asked.

"I don't know, Gert, I don't know most of these people."

Gert leaned closer to Hofman: "And don't talk too much, if you know what I mean."

Gert looked around. Hofman nodded in agreement.

023 Prague, October 2, 1968

The small cinema in Barrandov film studio was not bursting at the seams. A private screening of a recently completed film was on the program. The film **Marathon** about the liberation of Prague by the Red Army, based on a screenplay by Jan Procházka and starring leading Czechoslovak actors, was being shown. The credits began to roll on the screen. Starring: Jaromír Hanzlík, Jana Brejchová, Vladimír Menšík. The action on screen transported the audience back to May 1945, the time of the Prague Uprising.

During the screening, it seemed as if the entire Czechoslovak army must have been involved in the filming. The screenwriters Jan Procházka, director Ivo Novák, director Evald Schorm, Josef Škvorecký, and director Karel Kachyňa were sitting in the auditorium. The actors in the film spoke with a Russian accent. Most of the action on screen, despite the intimate story, was accompanied by gunfire, explosions, and pyrotechnic effects. The screening took place in complete silence. After the final credits rolled, the audience remained seated in awe.

After a moment, Evald Schorm came to his senses: "Gentlemen, apparently any nonsense can become a work of art if trained artists perform it."

Kachyňa added: "If we screen this film now, the audience will probably destroy all the cinemas. Honza, you're really lucky you sent your family to France."

Director Novák remarked: "I had planes and an entire tank division at my disposal."

Procházka suddenly realized the complete and utter bizarreness of his current situation: "It's completely fucked. Only Dubček can save me now."

024 Prague, September 28, 1969

Jan Procházka sat slightly hunched over his desk, a copy of a document in front of him on his typewriter. He thought about what to write next and reread what he had already written in a letter addressed to the Prague 5 district committee of the Communist Party of Czechoslovakia. The letter summoned him to disciplinary proceedings.

He did not even notice the voice of the television announcer, who calmly and coldly reported where, when, and how many renegade members had been expelled from the Communist Party and how the Communist Party was now dealing with revisionists. Shocked and silent, Procházka was completely focused and continued writing:

"... And so – to conclude – when I think about my political discussions, my book Politics for Everyone, my five-year series of articles in magazine MY, and my entire attitude toward human progress, I have nothing to revise. Except for that optimism, hope, and belief in common sense. My public appearances yesterday and the day before yesterday, as well as my private meditations today, are in such stark contrast to the current line of the Communist Party that any disciplinary committee would be obliged, without the slightest hesitation, to conclude that I should be expelled from the Communist Party."

He paused again, thought for a moment, and added: "But it seems to me that even then my socialist convictions would not change. I renounced God long ago, I was also expelled from the Sokol organisation, and so I will probably stick to my vision of civic and unattainable socialism…"

025 Prague, October 18, 1969

In the representative office of the Embassy of the Union of Soviet Socialist Republics, Soviet Ambassador Stepan Vasilyevich Chervonenko sat at the head of the table.

Also present in the room was Ludvík Toman, the newly appointed ideological dramaturge of the Barrandov Film Studio.

He was a short, overweight man with a penchant for alcohol, and Kamil Pixa, director of state Enterprise Krátký film, (Short Film) and a high-ranking officer of the StB, the Czechoslovak secret police, was a tall, energetic man with a commanding voice.

"Who is this Procházka? At first, he borrows tanks from us to shoot a film about the liberation by the Soviet army; he is almost licking our boots, and when we arrive, he yells at us from the revolutionary barricades."

The Soviet ambassador addressed the crew in Russian.

Toman, who had been raised in Moscow, did not need a translation and replied in fluent Russian: "Comrade Ambassador, we don't understand him either."

Chervonenko listened attentively and stated, "We need to take care of him."

Pixa knew Russian, but he stammered a little: "Comrade Ambassador, Comrade Procházka is a very prominent public figure. We allowed him to travel to the West. His family is already in France, and he was supposed to go too, but he didn't leave, even though he promised..."

Toman added, "He wrote a completely outrageous letter to his Communist party organization in Prague 5, and he's giving me his resignation at Barrandov. I haven't accepted it yet. The party organization had no choice but to expel him for his views. Allow me, Comrade Ambassador, here is a translation of his letter into Russian, along with a translation of the Communist Party statement."

Toman stood up and handed the documents to the ambassador.

"So, he defected?" asked the ambassador.

"No. We don't have confirmation of that," said Pixa. "It's a tricky business. My colleagues from counterintelligence have given me all the detailed reports. He doesn't strike me as a hero. More like a scaredy-cat..."

"But don't worry about it, comrades. Keep watching him, he'll give us an opportunity. I want to be kept informed," Chervonenko asked them.

"You can count on it, comrade," confirmed Pixa.

Chervonenko glanced at Toman, who nodded silently.

"You know what, I'll send a request to Moscow to send us a specialist in similar cases immediately," decided the ambassador.

026 Prague, October 5, 1969

In a darkened room at the Soviet Embassy in Prague, a team of Soviet advisors was preparing a slide show. Jiří Purš entered. "Good morning, comrades. You surely know me from the media. For those who don't, I am Dr. Jiří Purš, the new director of Czechoslovak Film. I would like to thank our friends for convening this meeting, as the Central Committee of the Party has tasked me with dealing with Comrade Procházka in an exemplary manner. And since Moscow is closely monitoring this matter, as I have already been informed, they have sent Comrade Kozlov to assist us, who has extensive experience in similar situations. Now, Comrade Decastelo, you have the floor."

Decastelo, a small, completely bald man in a poorly fitting jacket, asked the slide projector operator: "Please show photograph number 1."

A slide with a portrait of Jan Procházka appeared on the large screen. Decastelo began to speak emphatically about the photograph: "Jan Procházka comes from a peasant family. He graduated from a higher agricultural school in Olomouc, and after completing his studies, he began working in the border region as the head of the State Youth Farm in Ondrášov, in the Bruntál region.

He stayed there for only a year and then left for Prague to join the Central Committee of the Czechoslovak Youth Union, where he organized youth brigades for the border regions. As an employee of the Czechoslovak Youth Union, he initially worked in the agricultural department of the regional committee and subsequently in the Central Committee of the Czechoslovak Youth Union. In 1956, he wrote his first book.

In 1959, he became a dramaturge and screenwriter at Barrandov Film Studios. He was a reliable comrade, completely devoted to our cause, a member of the Central Committee of the Czechoslovak Youth Union, a candidate for the Central Committee of the Communist Party of Czechoslovakia, and a member of the Central Committee's ideological commission before he completely lost his way and broke with the party ideologically and politically. He became vice-chairman of the Writers' Union, which undoubtedly had a very harmful influence on developments in Czechoslovakia in recent times. His public appearances and journalistic activities were completely in the service of our enemies. He became one of the leading figures of the so-called Prague Spring, which was completely incompatible with our goals in terms of opinion and ideology.

Next slide, please. Purš interrupted him: "Thank you, comrade, there is certainly no need to introduce this traitor to the communist cause any further. However, this is not the 1950s, and a trial like that of Slánský and Horáková is out of the question now, given the reactions of the foreign and domestic public. Comrade Kozlov in the Soviet Union has already resolved several similar situations in a far more sophisticated manner. I now give the floor to our distinguished guest, Comrade Kozlov."

"Thank you for giving me the floor, comrade. As I have been informed, you have top experts in document production in your StB organisation. You will prepare one such defamatory documents for Comrade Procházka and inform the media about him. In Rudé právo newspaper, on Czechoslovak Television, and on Czechoslovak Radio. We have also requested the medical records of the traitor Procházka. We are aware of his health issues, and according to our experts, this can be leveraged. Comrade Pixa, who is, incidentally, very knowledgeable about cinema and will be a key figure in the upcoming normalization process, is a highly skilled expert in provocation."

Pixa smiled and nodded to Kozlov with a condescending smile.

Kozlov continued: "I leave you free rein here, Comrade Pixa. You will keep me informed of the results."

"You can count on me, Comrade Kozlov."

"After twelve months, we will evaluate the operation and decide on the next steps. In Moscow, the deadline for setting up the processes is August next year. I hope I don't have to emphasize that this is a party task of exceptional importance and that dealing with Jan Procházka must set an absolutely deterrent example for all other hostile forces."

027 Prague, October 6, 1969

Autumn Prague was shrouded in fog in the evening. In Jindřišská Street, the windows of the offices hidden behind St. Henry's Church gradually lit up as the members of the children's film dramaturgy group of the Barrandov Film Studio gathered for their weekly meeting.

At the agreed time of five o'clock in the afternoon, everyone gathered in the conference room according to a seating arrangement that no one had ever determined yet was always the same. The group's secretary, Bohunka Šourková, an attractive woman in her forties, always sat to the right of the group's crowned ruler. Ota Hofman, František Pavlíček, Marcela Pittermannová. The mood at the table was good; everyone was chatting and laughing casually.

At one point, Jan Procházka, the chief dramaturge, arrived and sat down at the head of the table. Without any formalities, he began the meeting immediately. "Hello everyone, what do we have here today? Bohunka, please pass me the agenda." It happened without a word. Procházka glanced at the paper handed to him, where the individual items on the meeting agenda were written by hand. Bohunka always thinks of everything, he thought to himself.

"First, let me officially confirm what you all probably already know. A new dramaturge has been appointed to the management of Barrandov to oversee the ideological aspect of our work," Procházka cleared his throat with a stony face.

"His name is Ludvík Toman, and he studied in Moscow. His role complements that of the studio's chief dramaturge, Vladimír Hanach. That's all I have to say on this point." Procházka cleared his throat again and continued: "I'm sure you've all seen my latest edits to the script for the film *On the Comet*. Does anyone have any comments? Any ideas I should discuss with Zeman before we start shooting?"

Pavlíček scratched his head: "It's fine, I don't have anything to add."

Procházka glanced sideways at Marcela Pittermannová: "We discussed your comments last time. Do you have anything else to add, Marcela?"

Marcela Pittermannová just shook her head: "No, I don't. I also think it's really good now."

Procházka ticked off the first item on the agenda with his pen. "So, approved? We're making good progress today. All right, let's move on to the next item, which is the new adaptation of Cinderella. I have the synopsis here on my desk. It's a completely modern take, with Cinderella riding a scooter and the story set in the present day. It was written by director Věra Plívová-Šimková. What do you think?" František Pavlíček joined the debate without being asked: "I don't know. It's a classic by Božena Němcová, and we shouldn't harm her. Well, I don't like it, so I've prepared my own version. It's just a rough draft at this point; it can't even be considered a film story. I gave it to you a few days ago as a counterproposal to what I consider to be a crazy modern solution. Cinderella, for sure, shouldn't ride a scooter, and the fairy tale should definitely be set in historical costumes. It will be more cinematic and richer that way. I wouldn't want to go down the well-trodden path, I mean, the one written for television adaptation by Mrs. Turnovská, but in my opinion, Cinderella shouldn't be a downtrodden girl who sits in a corner waiting to be found. She could be a little cheeky; she wouldn't have to just wait for the prince to discover her. She should act like a normal, active girl whom the audience will root for because of her rather modern way of thinking."

Procházka spoke up again: "What do you think, Oto?"

After a moment's hesitation, Ota Hofman joined the debate: "I know her well. I respect Vera's tremendous talent for directing child actors. As you surely know, she made her debut in my film *Kate and the Crocodile* when she excellently stood in for Jan Valášek, who felt ill. That's why she approached me. However, I think Franta is right about this. I had the honor of seeing his version and concept for Cinderella yesterday, and I really like it; I share the same sentiment. I suggest we go with a costume fairy tale, but with modern elements. By that, I certainly don't mean a scooter or a gramophone, but rather modern elements in the main character's behavior. However, I am concerned about one thing, it is a very ambitious concept, which will certainly not be inexpensive. After *Marketa Lazarova*, who, as we know, made a significant dent in Barrandov's budget, I'm unsure if the new management will approve it. They haven't even warmed up their chairs yet, and we haven't even had a chance to talk to them. It's nothing against you, Franta. Markéta's script was great; it's just that everywhere I go, I keep hearing about the huge costs that the film swallowed up. Apparently, you can't count, and neither can František Vláčil. But I have an idea. How about we throw it to Berlin, to our Comrades from DEFA for review? Maybe they'll take it. We'll share the costs."

Procházka nodded in agreement: "I also skimmed through it yesterday, and I agree that Cinderella on a scooter is wild, and classics are classics. Franta, let's have your synopsis translated into German and contact our colleagues at DEFA. Oto, you have our best contacts there. Can you arrange that? If we join forces with DEFA, maybe management will give us the green light. In the meantime, Franta, write the story, we'll pay you so that we're properly prepared for our German partners. How long will it take you?"

It was obvious at first glance that Pavlíček was very happy: "About two weeks, maybe three. I'll get started right away."

"All right," nodded Procházka. "If they like it, Ota will fly to Berlin with the story. He speaks German well, but first we'll wait for their response..."

Suddenly, the door opened without warning, and Procházka was interrupted by an uninvited guest. A bald, stocky man with a rude expression looked around at the meeting attendees. His greasy jacket smelled of sweat. His tie hung crookedly.

He immediately became the center of attention with his hoarse voice: "My name is Comrade Bartoníček, and I am now the chairman of the Communist Party organization at Barrandov Film Studios. For those who don't know, I was appointed to this position yesterday. I'm glad to have found all of you, comrades here. As you are surely aware, the Central Committee wishes to verify the loyalty of all members of the Communist Party, including those at the Barrandov Film Studio. Please note that on October 7 at 5 p.m., we will all be informed of the details regarding the exchange of party membership cards. We will meet in the conference hall at Barrandov. Attendance is mandatory. You all look healthy, so no excuses for absence will be accepted. I repeat, no excuses. And that goes for you, too, Comrade Procházka. Even though you have already been expelled from the party, you are still in a leading position. Honor to work, comrades."

He turned quickly. The door remained open behind him. The sudden change in the atmosphere in the room was palpable. Everyone was silent; the mood dropped to a freezing point. No one could utter a word. František Pavlíček got up and went to close the door. Then he sat down again.

Jan Procházka just stared blankly at his file on the table. There was a long, long silence.

Then Procházka suddenly snapped out of his stupor: "That's all for today."

He pushed back his chair, stood up, and left silently.

028 Prague, October 7, 1969

Jan Procházka could no longer bear to listen. Everything he had heard and had to listen to in the conference hall of the Barrandov Film Studios was completely beyond his comprehension. He did not know the speakers who took turns at the podium, nor did he want to know them. This was not the socialism with a human face he had dreamed of, to which he had committed himself, which he professed, and for which he had recently become so intensely involved in politics. From the lectern thundered the voice of demagoguery, Bolshevism, and unrelenting threats to all who would not comply with the new directives of the Communist Party whether it was the new director of Czechoslovak Film, Miroslav Fábera, some ideological functionary from Moscow, some Toman, or the new voice of culture from Rudé Právo newspaper, Jan Kliment, a man with a bandage over his eye.

He left the hall and saw Ota Hofman standing by the window, smoking a cigarette, as usual.

Procházka began: "Ota, do I understand this correctly? I am still an employee of Barrandov Film Studios in the position of head of the dramaturgy group. Today I received an official invitation from my superiors to attend an interview. The topic is clear. What is my opinion on the entry of Soviet troops and other Warsaw Pact armies into our territory? But on August 21 of this year, tanks rolled into Prague to trample our freedom! Back in October, I wrote a letter stating that I do not want to and cannot change my opinion."

Ota took a drag on his cigarette. "You summed it up well. But now it applies everywhere, not just to filmmakers at Barrandov."

"You're right. They've arranged it in Moscow so that everyone must express their opinion, employees, students, and simply everyone. The difference for those at Barrandov is that anyone who answers wrongly will be fired."

"And what is the wrong answer?" asked Ota.

"How should I know?" Procházka looked Hofman long and hard in the eyes and laughed bitterly.

029 Prague, October 12, 1969

Procházka sat against the wall in a wine bar, a glass of vodka on the table. Hofman took off his coat as he walked over to him.

"Hey, Ota, you'll never change, will you? Half an hour here, an hour there. I'm on my second shot, and I'll have a third, that'll be on you. What are you having? The usual?"

Hofman nodded.

"Waiter, vodka and cognac."

"Sorry, but I'm driving, I can't have a drink," Hofman stopped the waiter.

"You'll have one," Procházka insisted. "It'll be a long one today... Like me. I wanted a change, you know, Ota..." he smiled, "but your watch is still running strangely. Remember when I was appointed chief dramaturge of the group, and you came to the first meeting I called? You were an hour late. Everyone was waiting for you. So, I called the group an hour later for the next meeting because of you, but you kept us waiting for another hour. I can't forget that."

"That was a long time ago," said Hofman apologetically.

Procházka smiled again: "I know, I'm glad you came, Ota."

"Of course."

"Although this time I thought you were running late, like everyone else who has turned their back on me. Have you heard what they're calling me?"

"Honza, I really don't know."

Procházka leaned toward him, clearly already thinking, "Czech Danton."

"I see."

"That's why I used to see President Novotný," added Procházka.

Hofman was intrigued: "And how did you actually get to him?"

"You mean how I got my other nickname, P. K. Procházka, meaning Procházka kissed by the president?"

"I've heard something. There are legends about it."

"And what do they say?"

Hofman replied, "The milder one is that the president mistook you for another Procházka."

"That's very dull," Procházka frowned.

"And the other one is that you beat up an official at the Congress of Moravian Socialist Youth, whom Novotný wanted to get rid of. And that's why he wanted to meet you."

Procházka took another sip: "When filmmakers start spreading rumors, you can't help but wonder, can you?"

"I guess so."

Procházka paused for a moment: "When I wanted to become a candidate for the Central Committee of the Communist Party, I did what was necessary."

"Honza, you really don't have to justify yourself to me."

"Of course not, I wouldn't even think of it. But that article about the afternoon meeting with President Novotný in his summer residence Lány, that one was a hit."

Hofman knew he had to warn him: "They'll come after you. They really don't like you. For them you are a traitor of Communist ideas"

Procházka waved his hand: "They can't get rid of me. It's not the 1950s. I write a long letter to Alexander Dubček every week; they can't just dismiss me. If Jurij Gagarin hadn't killed himself last March, I'd write to him too."

Hofman's face stretched in amazement: "Why Gagarin?"

"He was really excited about the screening of my film *Long Live the Republic*, so I invited him home. We became friends. How are things going with Franta Pavlíček and Popelka?"

Hofman was glad that Procházka had changed the subject: "Popelka is beautiful, but it will be a long road."

"You have to help Franta, Ota, but I don't have to tell you that, do I?"

"What about you, Honza?"

"What can they do to me? They've already fired me from my job; at worst, they'll lock me up."

Hofman shook his head dismissively: "These people are different; we don't know them. I think they're capable of anything. It's perfectly natural to be really and truly afraid right now."

030 Prague, October 22, 1969

The television was on, glowing in the room, and the evening news continued with the topic that was currently the main driving force in society: the checking of Communist party membership cards.

Hofman had just thrown one of the cards into the pile in the middle of the table. It was a regular evening ritual: Ota, Irena, coffee, indispensable cigarettes, and cards on the table.

Hofman listened to the news, fully aware of the consequences of the television announcer's words.

Of course, he couldn't know how many people would lose their jobs or how many lives would be cruelly affected by what he had just heard, but he knew for sure that it would happen to someone.

Irena stared at the fan of cards and wondered which one to discard: "So, have you decided what you're going to tell them tomorrow?"

With a cigarette in his mouth, he replied, "You know, I don't think I can stomach the occupation. I just can't."

Irena finally chose a card and threw it away: "I don't blame you; I definitely wouldn't be able to control myself. You know what, do what you feel, so you don't have to be ashamed of yourself."

Ota put his cigarette in the ashtray so he could take a drag from the pack on the table: "I know. The Germans imprisoned my mom and dad during the war, and now the Russians and Germans are occupying us again. I can't agree with that. We'll see. I remember my dad's birthday and the advice he gave me then. I really didn't think it would happen so quickly. He was right, leaving is always better than being left. I wouldn't have these worries now."

Irena stared at the card he had thrown away: "You wouldn't have had time for that in two months. Yeah, Grandpa was right. You can't put spilled milk back in the udder. I wonder what will happen now. The boy was taking entrance exams for high school, and you do realize what could happen, right? Irena still has two years of journalism school ahead of her. They don't mess around with that stuff. I know you well, and that's why I care about you so much. And I also know that you realize that tomorrow could ruin your kids' lives."

Yeah, yeah. I got all that. I don't know what I'd do then either. Maybe it won't be so bad, but still... Gert made me an offer."

Irena perked up: "You mean what I think you have on mind? If they fire you, tell me straight up if I should start brushing up on my German or if I should start looking for a cleaning job or..." She trailed off.

"Can you think of anything else? But you know what, let's go to the cinema, it'll take our minds off things."

Hofman, with a cigarette in his hand again, asked, "What's on?"

"It doesn't matter. Come on, let's go. We'll choose something."

031 Prague, October 22, 1969

František Pavlíček, current artistic director of the Vinohrady Theater and dramaturge at Barrandov Film Studios, had just left his wife, leaving behind unpacked boxes and a mess in his apartment. He was now sitting on the sofa, embracing his new love, Czechoslovak Radio editor Eva Košlerová. Pavlíček was also watching television.

The announcer finished reading the news about the checks. This was followed by a report on the shortage of toilet paper on the market, stating that the current situation was once again the fault of reactionary and ideologically misguided people who needed to be dealt with decisively. Pavlíček stopped paying attention to his lover for a moment and pricked up his ears.

"Tanks invaded us because they didn't have enough toilet paper in Russia. I really don't understand that." he blurted out.

His current love was clearly not bothered by the news of the toilet paper shortage: "Darling, did you move in with me from your wife so you could watch TV?"

Pavlíček got up, walked over to the TV, and turned it off.

His girlfriend whispered, "Now pay attention to me, please."

Pavlíček turned off the light in the living room.

032 Prague, October 23, 1969

For the third day in a row, a commission consisting of six people and a clerk questioned filmmakers about their stance on the entry of Soviet troops. Party investigations were also underway. Invited employees entered one by one. Today, Menzel, Kachyňa, Vorlíček, and Hofman appeared before the commission.

Menzel, Oscar winner for Closely Watched Trains, disagreed. Jan Procházka, a key screenwriter and head of a large dramaturgical group, had already been expelled from the party. Karel Kachyňa, a prominent director and close friend of Jan Procházka, talked his way out of it as best he could to avoid giving a direct answer.

Vorlíček agreed with the entry of the troops: "They obviously had a reason, otherwise they wouldn't be here." Hofman was next to the agenda. He told them briefly that he could not agree with the entry of German troops, citing the arrest of his parents during the war as his reason.

After his speech, the clerk asked Hofman to leave the room, formally informing him that the commission would communicate its decision to all participants in writing.

As soon as the door closed behind Hofman, Toman turned to Pixa: "So what did your sheep find out about Hofman, Comrade Pixa?"

Pixa began leafing through the file: "A well-ordered married life, no mistress. No debts. His daughter Irena is studying journalism at Charles University; his son Otto is applying to a prestigious Prague high school..."

Toman interrupted him and cut him off: "Damn it, do you have anything on him or not? Cut it short, comrade, or we'll be here until Christmas..."

"We don't really know anything dirty about him, except that he recently went on a spree in Paris and his foreign currency allowance certainly couldn't have covered it."

Toman frowned and then leaned into Pixa with gusto: "What an organization you are," he said mockingly. "You have nothing on him. Remember, comrade, they taught us in Moscow that the sum of all vices is the same in every person."

Pixa defended himself: "Everyone knows he's on cigarettes drive, that doesn't help us much. But he still laughed at us with his statement. On the one hand, he's now making deals with the Germans on both sides of the border, and at the same time, he resents the Germans for coming to liberate us! I propose expelling him and firing him! I don't believe a word he says!"

Toman followed up and decided, "Let's just strike Hofman off the list of Party members. He should be given a chance, even if he is politically misguided. He speaks German well and has contacts both in the DEFA and with the West

Germans, and they could come in handy. The party will keep an eye on him. Comrade Pixa will see to that. And then, Comrade Pixa, if we are really thorough and fire all these misguided comrades, who will work for us? Will we close Barrandov? Didn't you say his son is applying to a prestigious high school? Then the boy is out of luck. I'll take care of that. Let's send in the next one. Whom do we have there? František Pavlíček..."

The clerk opened the door and called out, "Comrade František Pavlíček."

František Pavlíček did not mince his words; he was strongly opposed to the entry of Soviet troops. He concluded his appearance before the commission with the words:

"As a worker in the field of film and theater culture, I want above all to contribute to the revival of emotional culture. To the renaissance of fundamental human and national ideals. For if the world is becoming a marketplace and a backroom sale of values, I must and will speak out. Because in times like these, the most fundamental questions inevitably arise again and again in countless variations: what is the value of a human being, what is the value of human life, what is the value of trust, does a person have the right to happiness and freedom...".

"That's enough, Comrade Pavlíček," Toman interrupted him, "your views are completely incompatible with the current line of the Communist Party leadership and, therefore, with the ideological line of film production at Barrandov Film Studios. You are dismissed with immediate effect." Toman signed the document he had already prepared on his desk. He then stood up and handed it to Pavlíček.

At the end of the third day of interviews with Barrandov Film Studio employees, one member of the commission, who was appointed as the recording clerk, asked to speak: "Well, that's all, comrades. To summarize the minutes: We heard from all employees who were members of the Communist Party. One hundred and eighty-seven members handed in their membership cards (red books thrown on the table), we expelled thirty people from the party (crossed out in the book with a marker), and we revoked the membership of ninety people in the Communist Party. We said goodbye to seventeen employees and dismissed them. However, we will have to deal with the issue of directors, because after the checks, we only have nine left."

033 Prague, October 27, 1969

Kamil Pixa lay on the sofa in his office at Krátký film , mulling over the recent interviews at Barrandov. The one who really bothered him was that new ideological idiot, Toman. Was it his bluntness and bragging that bothered him more, or the fact that he contradicted him? But there was nothing he could do about it. They trained him in Moscow. How he rudely attacked me because of Hofman! And Hofman made fools of us all with his pathetic excuse about the German army. We should have taught him a lesson once and for all! Toman clearly considers him ideologically misguided. Why did he defend him? And why should the boy be unlucky? What did that perpetually greased moron mean by that? I'll have to watch out for Hofman.

Then he remembered Hofman's trip to Paris. He got money from that Kraut. And why is he photographing Czech girl in Paris? He went through Hofman's file again in his mind. His son had passed his high school exams; his daughter was studying journalism in Prague. Suddenly, something occurred to him. He quickly got up and called out loudly through the door: "Květa, bring me the file on that taxi driver we got to cooperate with last week. The one, what was his name, Šmejda, Milan Šmejda."

His secretary, Květa, entered the office and silently placed the file on the desk. Pixa took the file and turned on the desk lamp. He opened the file. A photograph of a young, rather handsome man peered out at him. Pixa picked up the phone: "Invite Comrade Šmejda, born in 1949, to come in tomorrow."

034 Prague, October 27, 1969

Ota Hofman was typing a review of a film short in his office on Jindřišská Street.

On the wall hung diplomas from Venice for *Johnny's Journey*, honorable mentions from Gottwaldov, and awards for the book *The Escape*. Three other people sat at their desks in the room with him. Hofman was interrupted by a knock. "Who is it?"

Procházka appeared in the doorway. He looked around the room. Everyone noticed his serious, gloomy face. Undoubtedly, various information about the party investigations was circulating in Barrandov, and the grapevine was buzzing in offices and corridors. Procházka did not speak, waiting for the others to hurriedly leave their work, gather their things, and leave, the last one closing the door behind him. Only now did Procházka relax a little and sit down at Hofman's desk. He took several folders out of his briefcase: "Ota, you liked these stories. I like them too, but I'll be out of a job very soon. I didn't even go to the checks; I just wrote a letter to the regional organization. As you probably already know, Franta Pavlíček is out too. He didn't even have time to take his things from his desk before they kicked him out during the checks. You're the only one left from our old gang. "There are no other copies," he said, pointing to the folders, "but I'd hate to see these end up in the boiler room."

Ota took the stories in his hands.

"Honza, you know I know all of them. We talked about them. All these stories were written by friends."

"And me," added Procházka.

"That's what I'm saying, friends."

Procházka smiled.

Hofman stared at the folders in his hand: "You're putting me in great danger, Honza. If anyone finds out who wrote them, it's the end of me. And my children, too. It's a risk."

"I know, Ota. But I can't afford to think that way."

Procházka paused for a moment and then asked, "So, have you decided if you'll take over for me?" "You're still my boss, Honza. This is actually a strange conversation. I really don't know what's going to happen now." Hofman reached for the paper lying on the table.

"This is a brief note informing me that I've been removed from the party. So, as my father predicted not long ago, I'm out."

Procházka urged him, "Now you have to be pragmatic."

"You know I probably can't do that," Hofman hesitated.

Procházka understood that Ota needed time to come to terms with his decision: "All right... Then do the right thing. Do what your heart tells you. Tomorrow I'm going for a beer with Franta Pavlíček."

Hofman nodded and said in a quieter voice, "Say hello to him. I'll do what I can if I stay. Neither the commission nor anyone else has sent me any consequences for this message."

Procházka smiled forcedly: "They can't fire us all. They'd have to shut down Barrandov." Then he got up and left without another word.

035 Prague, October 27, 1969

It was only a few minutes later when the chief dramaturge Toman entered the office on Jindřišská Street with an unknown man and immediately began: "Good day, Comrade Hofman. Has Procházka finally been dismissed?"

Hofman gave Toman a dirty look. He didn't like the loud, brash manner of the little Napoleon. He probably learned it in Moscow, Hofman thought.

Toman didn't let himself be thrown off balance and boomed again: "I've brought you some promising reinforcements. This is Mareček."

Hofman quickly grabbed the folder with the stories that Procházka had left on his desk and hurriedly put it away in a drawer. This gesture did not escape the watchful eyes of the newly arrived Mareček.

"Good morning, Comrade Toman, welcome, Comrade Mareček.

"Would you like some coffee, gentlemen?" Hofman called through the open door: "Bohunka, three coffees, please!"

Toman explained with a broad smile:" Comrade Mareček will be responsible for ensuring that the material is suitable for modern cinema. I am sure you will get along well and work together. Well, comrades, you two discuss things, I have to run."

Toman left without saying goodbye and left the door open. Hofman and Mareček were left alone.

Hofman suddenly realized that he must have passed the commission, even though they had crossed him off the list, since Toman now wanted him to work with Mareček. Otherwise, he wouldn't have brought his man here. Nevertheless, he was cautious: "So I must find you a desk to sit at. We don't have much space here. So, what have you written? Can I read it?"

Mareček paused and stammered: "Well, I just have some notes so far. I'll bring them to you when I'm done."

Hofman thought for a moment, unable to understand why Mareček was even there: "You see, it's not so much about whether you've finished it, but rather what you've got. This is a children's art group."

Mareček nodded in agreement: "Of course, I know that Comrade Toman informed me in detail."

Hofman was slowly beginning to understand Comrade Mareček's new role: "That's good. Our selection of material is specific and, above all, apolitical."

Mareček interrupted Hofman, apparently with the aim of making himself look even more foolish: "But even with that, something could certainly be done."

Hofman took out a pack of cigarettes and offered one to Mareček. He refused.

Hofman lit up and took a long drag on his cigarette. He formulated his response.

"That's not possible. We speak to people's souls and make films for children as if they were our friends. When they grow up, they will form their own opinions. That is not our job now."

"Says who?" Mareček objected.

"Karel Jaromír Erben, Božena Němcová, the Grimm brothers, and Daniel Dafoe, among others, said so long ago, Mr. Mareček."

Bohunka Šourková entered the office with a tray holding three coffees and asked, "Has Toman left?"

Hofman looked at her: "Then the third coffee is yours."

Bohunka placed two coffees on the table and left with the extra one. Mareček sweetened his coffee, stirred it, and took a sip. Hofman went to the cabinet, took out a stack of scripts and manuscripts.

"Read these, and if you come across anything interesting, let me know. You can work at home. And keep track of your hours. I look forward to seeing the results."

"But I'd rather work here, if you don't mind, Comrade Hofman."

Hofman gave Mareček a dirty look: "Can we drop the formalities, Comrade Mareček? I am no longer a Comrade by decision of the party." He paused, and at that moment, he decided to accept Procházka's offer. "As your superior, I would welcome it."

Bohunka Šourková peeked into the door: "I'm sorry to disturb you, gentlemen, but you have to go see Hanach immediately, Ota. He says it's urgent."

Hofman took a sip of coffee. "You see, Comrade Mareček, that's how things work here. Now I must go to Barrandov, and it's Friday afternoon."

Hofman got up from the table and turned the key in the drawer: "Finish your coffee, Comrade Mareček, but I must go. Bohunka, have a nice weekend, see you on Monday."

036 Prague, October 28, 1969

Irena Hofmanová was ironing when the doorbell rang. The red telephone dialed and rang.

"Oto, you've got a phone call!" Irena called from the ironing board.

"Is there a fire, Toníček?" Hofman asked the children's telephone speaker.

Antonín Moskalyk, one floor above, didn't let himself be put off: "Shall we have some coffee, Oťásek?"

"What's up, Toníček? Is something on your mind?"

"At your place or mine?"

"I'll be right there. Put the coffee on in the meantime," decided Hofman.

Irena, who was busy ironing, looked at him: "Should I come with you? I'd rather finish this..."

"I think I can handle it. I'll see what's going on. Bye, I'll be back in a minute." Hofman opened the door and headed up the stairs.

There, the door opened, and boxer Adam couldn't resist his usual welcome ritual and jumped on Hofman's chest. Ota already knew what to expect, so he scratched Adam behind the ear. With his other hand, he tried to pull his slobbery mouth away from his shirt.

"What's going on, Toníček?" Ota began when they sat down, and Adam buried his head in Ota's legs.

"I need your help, Ota," Tonda replied. "You know we have a new director."

"I read something in the newspaper. His name is Zelenka, right?"

"Yeah. And things are happening. Do you know his history?"

"I have no idea who he is. But things like that are happening everywhere these days..."

"Hi, Ota," said Jiřina, carrying two cups of coffee. She placed the cups on the table and said, "I won't disturb you," and left, closing the door behind her.

"Well, listen to this." And Tonda began: "He's a great music lover and organized music festivals in Ústí nad Orlicí. Then he was editor-in-chief of magazine Literární noviny, which was a huge mistake because he became an ideological mouthpiece for the regime, and no one took him seriously, so he quietly slipped away. But his career in the press continued to rise. He became editor-in-chief of magazine Květy. He was fired from Květy, but when Husák took the helm, he managed to get back in. However, his mess at Literární noviny was well known, and the editorial board turned against him and all the editors threatened to resign, so he was quickly dismissed again. Then he hung around Štrougal and Kempný for a while, until his comrades appointed him director of Czechoslovak Television. As soon as he took office, he immediately launched a harsh purge. Half of the employees have already been fired. No one knows how television will function now. He is replacing those who are missing with quick fixes. It doesn't affect me yet, but he canceled what I had at work. And I also don't know who I can count on the staff and whether they will even be there tomorrow. Among other things, Zelenka introduced a 30-day deadline for approving programs before they are broadcast to prevent disruptions to programming due to a program being deemed politically objectionable just before it is due to air, which has happened several times. You have a good reputation at our TV station. We still remember that beautiful production, the first drama production for young people in the history of Czechoslovak Television."

"You mean **Robinson Girl** ?"

"Yeah, *Robinson Girl*, the one filmed by, well, you know... I can't remember right now."

"Pleskot."

"Yeah, Pleskot."

"But the very first one was directed for television by Milan Vošmik, right?"

"So? What do you need? Do you want to do *Robinson Girl* again?"

"Not exactly, but I need something new and very quickly. It has to be neutral, if you know what I mean. I don't want anything politically engaged, really, and I assume you don't either."

"No, I really don't want that, and I can't do it, Tonda."

"In the current mess, I have to make an impression to stay relevant. I think I'm about halfway out of television, and I don't have any good material, so I could get fired tomorrow. But if I bring in something good from Hofman... you understand me?"

"Sure, I understand, but are you sure I'm the right person for the job? The last thing I wrote for television was *Transformation of a Knife*, directed by Sadková, and I have no idea if it's finished. There's a strange silence surrounding it. Pavel Landovský as an actor isn't very popular right now; they even stopped the selected episodes of *Pan Tau* because of him."

Ota thought for a moment and smiled. "Quite recently, though, I thought of František Hrubín and his theatre play *Beauty and the Beast*. Cocteau is strong competition, but Hrubín's text could easily be adapted for film or television."

"That's it!" Tonda exclaimed enthusiastically. "How long will it take you, Oto?"

"I think about two weeks."

"Really, Ota?"

"Yeah, it's a play, and I've already thought out how to adapt it for television. And you really need to think about whether I'm the right person for the job."

"I don't need to think about it. You're a real treasure, Ota. I'll never forget this."

"All right, I'll give you a two-page synopsis tomorrow, and you can submit it for approval. And before they approve it, if they approve it, you'll have the script on your desk."

"*Beauty and the Beast*, you say, so I need a good beauty and a great mask maker. The beast has to be scary, not some ridiculous masquerade. Hopefully, some idiot won't find some kind of innuendo or other reason to shut it down. They're completely paranoid. They cut Dumas' wife's line 'The Prussians are invading!' from the three-part play by Alexandre Dumas because the 'P' at the beginning of the word could be misheard by the audience."

"I'll try. But isn't it sad? Censorship was recently abolished, and now I have to think in advance about how not to offend anyone, so now we're basically writing with imposed self-censorship. In themes, dialogues, writing... It's a crazy time. Right now, for example, I'm working with Karel Kachyňa on a film called simply **Love**, about a writer who isn't allowed to write. I don't know if it will get through..."

"I know, you're a sweetheart. Procházka is on the list of banned authors now, so you've taken Kachyňa under your wing of children's film, so he has something to do. Is that right?"

Something like that. Karel is out of favor right now because of *The Ear*, so we're trying this route. *Loudryboy* was a huge success some years ago, and Karel is a sure thing. It's a pleasure to work with him. He knows exactly what he wants, and I appreciate that. "

"It would be a shame if his activity will be wasted in just rebuilding his house and will not continue filming."

"All right," Ota took a sip of coffee. "My coffee's gone cold. We got a bit carried away."

"How about we get some exercise, Oťásek?"

"You mean a few games of tennis, Toníček?"

"Yeah, that's exactly what I mean."

"We'll have to put that off for now. I have to write that play for you first."

"But then we'll get right on it. You promise? "

"Sure. I promise."

Adam, who had been dozing at Ota's feet, woke up and realized that the visitor was leaving.

"Come by tomorrow evening for that synopsis, Tonda." Ota Hofman stood up and headed for the door. "Take care, Toníček."

"Say hi to Irena. And thanks."

The door clicked shut, and Hofman headed downstairs. He unlocked the front door and began thinking about the story of the brave beauty and the cruel beast.

"So, what did he want?" asked Irena.

"A job."

"Will you give it to him?"

"I'll try. Please make me another coffee. We got so caught up talking at Tonda's that it got completely cold."

It wasn't long before he sat down to work with František Hrubín's book on the table beside him, and the clatter of the typewriter filled the study.

037 Prague, October 28, 1969

František Pavlíček was having a beer with Jan Procházka. Small pub at edge of Prague was half empty.

"Franta, I'm trying to put out the fire as best I can. I just hope I've persuaded Hofman to take over as chief dramaturge after me. I'm leaving, of course."

"That's sensible, Honza. They can't just get rid of us all at once, man."

Procházka therefore asked for reassurance: "Do you have a working stamp in your ID card?"

"Sure. They fired me from Vinohrady theatre, and they fired me from Barrandov as well. I'm still employed at the Czechoslovak Army Theater."

Pavlíček breathed a sigh of relief: "At least that's something. Honza, we've had our differences, but now it all seems completely trivial. No one knows what's going to happen now."

"Franta, you're a writer. It's fatal. It's something you have to expect."

"Yes, but I didn't expect to have to live with it."

"And I did? I went to see Ota Hofman today. I think he can help us."

Pavlíček crossed himself.

"Franta, don't do this to me. I don't like it."

038 Prague, October 28, 1969

Martin Konopásek picked up the phone and dialed a familiar number. On the other end, he heard the voice of Eva, the secretary of the director of Krátký film Praha: "Hello, who's calling, please?"

Martin Konopásek knew that she never told anyone who she was calling, so he asked briefly, "Put me the boss on."

He heard a short beep and waited for another beep: "Is that you, Martin?" said Kamil Pixa.

"Yes, boss. We've got everything ready. Can we start?" asked Konopásek.

"Yes, go ahead," confirmed Pixa and hung up.

Martin Konopásek dialed another number: "Jelen here," came the reply.

"We're starting," Konopásek said simply and briefly.

Two operatives were sitting with him in the room on Bartolomějská Street. They had tape recorders in front of them on the wall, and the room was filled with smoke from cheap cigarettes. On a narrow table, they had headphones and several other phones in different colors ready.

"Get to work," Martin Konopásek ordered them. Both operatives put on their headphones and looked at each other. The one on the left nodded, and the other dialed the number on the blue telephone.

Jan Procházka was sitting at his desk writing when the phone rang. He picked up the receiver.

"Procházka, please?"

The other operative, with his hand on the button, started the tape recorder. Karel Kachyňa's voice came through the phone: "Hi, Honza, please. Come to me right away. I'm at Husická Thirteen. Please hurry."

The operative turned off the tape recorder. He waited with his headphones on.

Procházka said nothing, and his eyes darted around.

The operative turned the tape recorder back on.

"Don't tell anyone about this."

The button was pressed, and the tape recorder stopped again.

Martin Konopásek dialed a number on his phone. "This is Jelen," came the answer.

"He's on his way," Konopásek said briefly and hung up.

039 Prague, October 29, 1969

Procházka ran out into the street. A taxi was driving by, and Procházka waved it down. He got into the Volga and gave the taxi driver the address in Žižkov quarter of Prague. The taxi stopped on Husická Street. Procházka got out and asked how much it was.

"Forty-five," replied the taxi driver. Procházka gave him fifty crowns.

It didn't take long to find the old, dilapidated apartment building. He went inside. The door was open. He heard noises coming from the basement. He descended the stairs toward the sound. Beads of sweat were running down his forehead. Suddenly, the door opened, and cigarette smoke billowed out. Procházka looked into the face of a soldier in a Soviet uniform. In an instant, he was also looking down at the barrel of a submachine gun. Procházka cried out, "Don't shoot, don't shoot!"

The Soviet soldier looked him over with a menacing gaze. Then he motioned with his head for him to leave immediately. Procházka nodded in agreement, turned around, and ran up the stairs, through the door in front of the house, and quickly away. He looked around to see if anyone was following him. No one was there. He spotted a phone booth. He nervously reached into his pocket. He took out some change. He dialed a number he knew by heart: "Hi, this is Honza Procházka. Please, is Karel there? What? The line is crackling... Is he there? Can you put him on the phone, please? Hi Karel, did you just call me?" Procházka looked back. A man in a trench coat emerged from the house he had just left.

Kachyňa replied in surprise: "No, I didn't. Is something wrong, Honza?"

Procházka felt a wave of heat wash over him again: "I don't know if there is anything's wrong... I have to go."

Procházka left the phone booth and walked away from the house, quickening his pace. The man in the trench coat stared intently at him and started walking after him. Procházka clutched his heart. Sweat was running down his forehead. The man in the trench coat stopped for a moment, reached into his pocket, and took out a pack of cigarettes. He grinned and lit one. Procházka, his face contorted with pain, tried desperately to disappear into a side street.

040 Prague, November 6, 1969

Young Irena Hofmanová, daughter of Ota Hofman, and Lenka Procházková, daughter of Jan Procházka, balanced on barstools in a student bar on the banks of the Vltava River near Charles University. Each had a cup of coffee and a glass of water in front of them. Lenka, red with anger, complained to Irena: "First, they gave my dad a hard time at his interviews at Barrandov, and then they fired him. He's completely devastated. Every day, he writes a letter to Dubček, which no one has ever answered. If Gagarin were still alive, he would write to him too.

Irena jumped in: "Why Gagarin, please?"

"Don't you know? He was Dad's friend. He visited us once. I still remember today that you couldn't see him at all behind a huge bouquet of flowers. You know, he was really short." Imagine that. The door opens, and there's a huge bouquet of flowers, and behind it is tiny Gagarin, and he immediately says, 'Eto dlja mami.'

It made us both laugh, but Lenka quickly became serious again. "Yeah, and to top it all, I was called to the University dean's office. He gave me a lecture because of my dad. I can still hear him yelling at me. He said that journalists today must be conscious comrades, and that Comrade Jan Procházka is an enemy of the people and a subversive element. Basically, he told me that if I continued to express myself in the same way, I would be expelled from journalism

137

school and fired immediately. However, it would be best if I left the faculty on my own. Yeah, Gagarin, yeah, Dubček, where are those snowflakes from last year..." She burst into tears.

Irena didn't know what to do to distract Lenka: "Yeah, my dad was expelled, but he hasn't been fired from his job yet..."

Suddenly, a handsome guy approached them. "Such beautiful ladies, and all alone. What's this I see, don't cry, miss! Can I buy you a drink?"

Irena looked at him and smiled a little.

Lenka immediately understood: "Thanks. I have to run. See you tomorrow at the lecture."

The man addressed Irena: "My name is Milan, Milan Šmejda. Can I offer you a drink?"

Irena laughed quietly. "How about a vodka martini, shaken, not stirred?"

Šmejda froze, turning pale.

"That was a joke. I'll have a Coke," Irena reassured him.

Šmejda smiled wanly and relaxed. He thought to himself: Now get to work, man. Get to work!

041 Prague, November 10, 1969

Šmejda, beaming with confidence, had just reported to his superior. It only took a few minutes for him to finish. Pixa looked at the papers spread out on his desk and remarked dryly, "So she took the bait. That's good news."

"No one can resist me."

Pixa immediately cut him off: "Save that crap for someone else. I chose you. I'll coach you personally. You report to me, and me only, and don't you dare say a word to anyone else, or I'll tear you to pieces. Now you get to work, I want to know everything about Hofman, understand? Absolutely everything."

Šmejda was replaced at the door by the secretary, who brought Pixa his coffee. Pixa took a sip, his lit cigarette resting on the edge of the ashtray. He reached into the pile of old magazines at random. He pulled one out and went to lie down on the couch.

He opened the magazine Kino and leafed through it. He was intrigued by an interview with Ota Hofman. He sat up straight. There was a photo of Otto Šimánek in Pan Tau costume. He looked at the author of the article. Klára Wagnerová. Pixa thought: Wagnerová, Wagnerová.

Yeah, right! That's the girl Hofman photographed in Paris! That's really strange. It can't be a coincidence, can it? He thought for a moment and then picked up the phone. Pixa barked into the receiver: "Hey, Vladimir, I mean Volodya, I still can't get used to you changing your name, man.

Hey, look for the Wagner file. He's from the Koh-i-noor business. And put it on Eva's desk. I'm in a meeting and don't want to be disturbed. Thanks."

Pixa returned to the sofa and covered his face with a copy of magazine Kino. He fell asleep shortly afterwards. When he woke up, Wagner's file was on the table.

Yeah, Jan Wagner. And sweet Paris. Now I'm going to have a little fun with you! The folder contained photos of Wagner, some from Koh-i-noor meetings in Paris, and some private ones with his family and his pretty daughter. Pixa had an idea. He walked over to the phone: "Comrade Kadeřábek, this is Pixa. I need to do a thorough check of the accounts in the sales department at Koh-i-noor. I'm particularly interested in Comrade Jan Wagner."

Whatever it is, I'll find out what you're hiding from me, you bastards! He thought.

042 Prague, December 1, 1969

It was a cloudy Monday morning. Hofman had just entered the office on Jindřišská Street, glanced briefly at the always well-groomed Bohunka Šourková, and announced, "Call everyone to an emergency meeting immediately. And the new guy, Mareček? Is he here yet?"

Bohunka Šourková replied, "He's at headquarters in Barrandov, signing his employment contract." Hofman looked around again and fixed his gaze on Marcela Pittermannová. "Ladies, watch your language from now on. Toman has planted a mole here."

He paused again, hesitated, then made up his mind and entered Jan Procházka's office. He turned at the door. "No interruptions now, please. When everyone is here, let me know, Bohunka.

Bohunka and Marcela looked at each other but said nothing.

Mareček burst through the door and immediately announced the news with a jubilant expression on his face: "Did you know that Barrandov's chief dramaturge Hanach was fired on the spot? As of today, Toman is our boss."

Bohunka Šourková ordered uncompromisingly: "Ota is calling an emergency meeting, everyone to the conference room." She opened the door to the head dramaturge's office: "Ota, everyone's here."

Ota Hofman looked at her: "Fine, I'm coming."

Hofman stood at the head of the table, his hands resting on the tabletop, surrounded by members of the dramaturgy team:

"On Friday afternoon, I received a decree from Chief dramaturg Vladimír Hanach appointing me head of our dramaturgy team."

Mareček interjected: "But Hanach was dismissed over the weekend and Toman was appointed."

Hofman continued: "That doesn't change anything. I already spoke with Toman this morning. He said that when I was appointed by the former director on Friday, it happened before Hanach was dismissed, so my appointment is valid."

Marcela Pittermannová raised her head: "And what about Honza Procházka?"

Ota sighed: "His employment was terminated with immediate effect."

Hofman stood with his head bowed and spoke at the table: "We have to keep going, whether we like it or not. And believe me, some decisions are very difficult to make. Although I hesitated, I finally accepted the appointment decree," he raised his head, "as far as the functioning of our group is concerned, I have no reason to change anything. Only Comrade Mareček has joined us as a new reinforcement for the ideological component of our work."

043 Prague, December 5, 1969

Hofman sat at his desk in his study at home, pounding away at the typewriter with two fingers. A cigarette, a glass of wine. A stack of papers lay on the table. Carbon paper was inserted between the sheets so that five copies would be made with each keystroke. There was a mess around the table and chair, and balls of crumpled paper. He was alone in the room, wearing slippers, with a cigarette in his mouth, trying to repeat the dialogue aloud. Always the same dialogue with subtle nuances of words.

A boy of about fifteen peeked into the room. "Dad, you have a visitor."

Hofman, startled, took a sip of wine. "Yeah, I'll be right in the living room. Ask Mom to make us some coffee, please."

Jan Procházka was already sitting in the living room with his coffee when Hofman joined him.

Procházka looked very worried. He glanced at Ota: "I'm finished. They're after me, and if they're not after me now, they will be soon. Today, Karel Zeman showed me a new design for the poster for the film *On the Comet*. My name disappeared overnight. This is the end for me."

Hofman poured two glasses of cognac and handed one to Procházka: "Is it really that bad?"

"Look, Ota, we've known each other for a long time, that's why I'm coming to you. I'm not entirely sure, but you can assume that if you call me, it's being tapped. There's a strange crackling on the phone, and sometimes the call gets cut off. I feel like I'm being watched all the time, and they probably know I'm here now. Still, I came to see you because I have a favor to ask. Could you cover for me with your name on the script? "

Hofman lit another cigarette: "Which one do you mean?"

"I'm jumping over puddles again."

"Honza, everyone knows you wrote it. You got paid for the idea. The accounts even show money paid out for a film story."

Procházka didn't give up and pressed on: "I wrote a letter saying I was giving up the material. I said I didn't feel up to it and someone else should do it."

Hofman looked Procházka in the eyes: "Now reach into your briefcase and take out the script."

Procházka reached into his briefcase and took out the script: "Ota, you must be clairvoyant."

Hofman stared at the table in front of him and hesitated, then whispered, "Did you see the guy who opened the door for you?"

Procházka blurted out, "Yeah."

Hofman continued, "Do you know what will happen if someone finds out that you wrote the script and not me?"

"I know, you already told me."

"I'll tell you fifty more times. I've known you for almost twenty years, and I know you'll say something, but you don't see the reality of the situation. What this could unleash could destroy us all. They'll lock us up, destroy us. Every evening, my wife and I discuss whether we should emigrate to Germany. Toman has now put a spy in my office, some guy named Mareček. When I want to discuss something, I must go somewhere else, maybe there's a bug in my office. I don't know, but I must be damn careful.

"Oto, it's a movie for kids."

"It's a movie for kids, but we don't live in a fairy tale."

Procházka raised his head: "So give me a clear yes or a clear no."

"Of course I'm giving you a clear yes... Yes, damn it." Hofman raised his glass and took a drink.

044 Prague, December 8, 1969

Dr. Jiří Purš was sitting in his office when Toman came in. He glanced at Toman: "Hello, Ludvik. Sit down."

Without any more comments he reached into the desk and threw a thin stack of papers on the table. "I hope you can explain this to me."

Toman picked up the folder. It was a film script called *The Ear*.

145

Purš put on an angry expression: "What is this reactionary crap? The main character is a communist persecuted by the secret police? What the fuck are you doing as the head dramaturge?"

Toman began to stammer: "I... I'm seeing this for the first time."

Purš continued: "What?"

Beads of sweat appeared on Toman's forehead: "I don't know what it is."

Purš was relentless: "You're not telling me that Procházka bypassed you?"

Toman shrugged.

"What kind of bastard is he? I went to see *the Ear*. This film can't be released!"

Toman tried to defend himself: "He must have bypassed me..."

"Get rid of him already. I'm sick of him. That's all. Leave," added Purš angrily.

045 Prague, February 8, 1970

"I have called you here today, comrades, because we have an operation of extraordinary importance ahead of us." Kamil Pixa stood on the blackboard in the StB operations room. "We have intercepted a letter sent by Jan Procházka via the Czechoslovak postal service to Paris, addressed to Professor Černý, confirming the date and time of Jan Procházka's planned visit to Paris. We have been monitoring Professor Černý's activities in exile for some time, but our priority target is Jan Procházka, so we will not prevent him from traveling to a capitalist foreign country.

Our task will be to make an audio recording from Professor Černý's apartment. We have prepared a cover for our operation through a film delegation at the Paris Film Festival, which I will also attend under my own name. I will thus be in Paris to direct the entire operation."

Several trained StB agents sat around the table, not taking notes but listening attentively to Kamil Pixa's explanation. Kamil Pixa continued his explanation.

"The plan is to use screenwriter Jan Procházka's visit for a targeted provocation. Our plan is clear: to secure manuscripts and materials damaging to the Czechoslovak Republic and to film all enemies of Czechoslovakia who appear at Černý's apartment. It has already been agreed that the secured materials will be given to our agents working in the press, who will prepare a series of articles and television reports.

Now for the individual tasks. Comrades Kolář and Mráček will go into the house. They will unlock the door with a special key so that no damage to the lock is visible. We have already had our agent, who visited Professor Černý under the cover of being a journalist, briefly inspect the apartment.

It consists of a living room, bathroom, hallway, pantry, and bedroom. From the outset, it must be clear that the apartment is inhabited by an intellectual who has problems keeping things tidy. Our agents' task will be to photograph the items on the tables. Check diaries and handwritten notes.

Place the listening devices in the lamp on the table, in the vase, in the mirror, in the desk, or wherever you deem appropriate. We estimate that you will have about three hours.

Comrades Nový and Mládek will provide security; they will be on the street and in radio contact with you.

Žalud and Macek will provide the cars. You all have extensive experience with similar operations.

There are envelopes on the table with documents, instructions, and train tickets. Comrade Bartoníček has prepared everything thoroughly for you."

None of them expected things to go so badly.

046 France, Paris, February 23, 1970

Kamil Pixa sat in a car not far from the scene of the action in Paris. He was extremely satisfied; his plan was going smoothly. The radio on the passenger seat crackled: "Done, Procházka just left the house."

Pixa pressed the button on the radio: "Excellent."

At that moment, the car door opened, a black hood was pulled over Pixa's head, and two men dragged him into the back of a van. The van drove off.

047 France, Paris, February 23, 1970

Kamil Pixa sat in a bare interrogation room. Jean Victor, a tall agent of the Service de documentation extérieure et de contre-espionnage (SDECE), sat behind a desk. He was in charge of Service 23 and was responsible for counterintelligence and protecting the SDECE from infiltration by foreign intelligence agents in France. A Czech interpreter stood with him. Victor smiled: "Well, Comrade Pixa. We finally met. You haven't learned French yet, so we'll interpret for you."

The interpreter nodded and translated the words into Czech. Victor began again in French: "It is absolutely unacceptable for your secret service to operate in Paris."

Pixa waited for the translation and replied: "We only deal with our own citizens."

Victor knew what he was going to say before the interpreter had finished the last word. "No. Your citizens are also under French protection. They asked for protection and assistance, and we granted it. And don't forget that we know very well who you are. And I'm sure you know who I am."

Pixa listened to the interpreter and lowered his eyes.

"Look me in the eye, Tovarisch Pixa."

Pixa waited for the interpreter to finish. "It has been several years since you killed our agent during interrogation on your territory."

"It was an accident. I didn't even touch him."

"No. You poured ice water on him, then stripped him down to his underwear and left him by an open window in the freezing cold all night."

Pixa began to feel afraid: "He wasn't even French."

Victor toughened his tone: "You can't be serious! You're also working for the Soviet Union, and how would you like it if a colleague left you in the lurch during an operation, comrade?"

Pixa went on the counterattack: "You're a tough guy, huh?"

Victor smiled: "I'd like you to take a little souvenir with you from your last visit to Paris."

Victor commanded, "Left hand on the table," and reached into the table for a hunting knife.

Pixa's eyes widened. The interpreter emphasized the words. Pixa shook his head. Victor repeated, "Left hand." One of the people in the room grabbed Pixa under his arms and pinned him to the back of the chair. Another grabbed his left wrist and pressed his palm with his fingers spread out on the table.

Victor then quickly cut off the last joint of Pixa's left little finger and two joints of his ring finger. Pixa screamed. The grip loosened. Pixa instinctively pulled his left hand toward his body, blood spurting from his stumps. He stared at the finger joints on the table.

151

Victor shouted, "Don't scream, they're not even whole fingers, you pig!" Then he went over to the iron door and banged on it. "Take this bastard straight to the airport. He's persona non grata in France."

The interpreter did not translate this into Czech for Pixa.

048 Prague, February 27, 1970

It was a freezing February morning, and Jan Procházka left his apartment to buy a newspaper at a nearby newsstand. A Volga pulled up beside him with a screech of brakes, and two men jumped out. They grabbed Procházka by the armpits and dragged him to the car. "You're coming with us," they ordered, pushing him into the Volha.

Procházka asked, "Where are you taking me?"

Silence. No one answered.

They drove on through the freezing morning toward the center of Prague.

The Volha stopped on Bartolomějská Street, and one of the men opened the door. The other grabbed Procházka by the arms and dragged him out.

Outside, without a word, they grabbed him again and led him inside. They walked all the way to the StB interrogation room. They pushed him inside, and a voice ordered him, "Sit down."

Inside, there was a single chair illuminated by a lamp, and Procházka obeyed the voice. He sat down. There was a lamp and a typewriter on the table. He waited for about an hour before two investigators entered.

They both stared at him for a moment before one of them spoke: "Let's begin, Comrade Procházka."

The second one asked in a mild voice, "Do you know why we summoned you?"

Procházka was afraid. Who wouldn't be? "I don't know."

"Now listen to me carefully, comrade. We are preparing new political trials against enemies of the state, and to behold, you are on the list as one of the leading defendants. What do you have to say about that?"

"I have not committed any crime, and I am not aware of having done anything illegal."

"Until recently, you acted and continue to act as a traitor to the nation. You have associated and continue to associate with foreign enemies of the state, such as exiles. That is treason, Comrade Procházka. Do you admit your guilt?"

"I don't know what I would admit. I haven't done anything; I don't associate with enemies."

"Comrade Procházka, you probably don't understand your current position very well. You are accused, and we have enough evidence to fill Wenceslas Square. It would certainly be better for you to confess and avoid what will undoubtedly be very unpleasant consequences. Understand that this is not fun for us, and the longer it takes, the worse it will be for you. So please start talking and tell us about the steps you took that were supposed to lead to the subversion of the republic. Who directed you from abroad? Who led you to this goal?"

"I really don't know what to say."

"Comrade Procházka, you probably don't understand that the prosecutor has already proposed a sentence for you, and it is up to you whether we help you reduce it. To do so, you must make a full and truthful confession."

The door opened, and Kamil Pixa entered with a hateful expression and a scarf over his shoulder, on which his bandaged arm was hanging. "So, how's it going, comrades?"

"He's denying it," said one of the investigators.

"So, Comrade Procházka is denying it," Pixa said, moving close to Procházka. "So, you thought the fifties were over, didn't you, you piece of trash."

Procházka watched him but said nothing.

"You don't even know how wrong you are. Now we're going to lock you up here and interrogate you until you're completely broken and you tell us everything you know, you bastard."

The investigator began again: "Do you admit that you associated with imperialist subversives of our state? Do you admit treason? Do you admit that your actions were intended to deliberately and purposefully damage our socialist system?"

"I admit nothing of the sort," Procházka replied with his head bowed.

155

The investigator placed a bundle of documents on the table and pulled out a few sheets. "As you can see, we have a pile of evidence here. Let's start with this piece of shit. You can't deny that your signature is on it," he waved the Two Thousand Words statement in front of Procházka's eyes.

"Shall I continue? Are you going to keep denying it? I have your public statements here, which are more than enough evidence of your anti-state activities."

"Then you will bear the consequences of your stubborn denial alone, all by yourself. And don't think you'll get out of this with your head on your shoulders. I'll make sure of that myself," Pixa interjected again.

Procházka glanced at Pixa and lowered his eyes again.

"Go on, comrades, you have all night, then all day, and then all night again."

A tall man in a leather jacket entered the interrogation room. He leaned toward Pixa: "You have an urgent call."

Pixa headed for the door.

"Comrade Pixa?" Pixa heard the receiver of the telephone in the next room.

"Who's calling?"

"This is Müller from the Central Committee. We've received a report that you're interrogating Jan Procházka, and we're aware of your sometimes rather hasty investigative methods."

"They're not hasty. They're effective, though..."

"Nevertheless, we know that sometimes, comrade, suspects tend to have accidents when they're in your hands."

"Nothing we caused with our methods. Those were innocent accidents."

"We don't want any innocent accidents right now. Palach is enough of a martyr for us, and we've got enough media and other chaos surrounding him. We don't want another martyr as fodder for foreign journalists. Do you understand our position, Comrade Pixa?"

"Yes, but..."

"No buts, that's an order we have from the Soviet embassy, short and clear. No more martyrs. Comrade Procházka will be free tomorrow. Feel free to continue with actions and provocations that could discredit Comrade Procházka in the eyes of the public and further affect his already fragile health. You have our approval to complete your, to put it mildly, unsuccessful operation in Paris. As we understand, the materials obtained have been successfully recovered, and your counterintelligence specialists are working hard on them, so please take great care. But we do not want a solution, as you call it, comrade, i.e., an innocent accident. Honor to the work, comrade."

Pixa stood there stunned, the receiver in his hand.

049 Prague, April 21, 1970

Karel Kachyňa liked his peace and quiet, and now he was enjoying it to the fullest. He was lying on the sofa in his living room, thinking about shots for his film. Filming has been going quite well so far. Tomorrow, he was supposed to meet with Ester Krumbachová to discuss costumes again. He knew what only a very small group of people knew. The film ***I'm Jumping Over Puddles Again*** was written by Jan Procházka, and not by the person whose name appeared on the first page of the script. It rest on the conference table now, covered with notes.

He had the TV muted, but suddenly he perked up when he heard his wife sitting in the studio.

"We have received a recording from the television station from Barrandov screenwriter and writer Jan Procházka. He visited the current exile, university professor Václav Černý, in Paris."

Kachyňa stood up and quickly turned up the volume. It's telepathy or something, he thought. Something else about Jan Procházka.

The television began broadcasting the documentary: "Yes, let's travel to the famous metropolis of the West, to Paris. Encounters here can be varied, curious, and admired, driven by an interest in the historical, artistic, and political values and contradictions that have made Paris a part of world history. Encounters that can delight us but also sadden us under the weight of loneliness. In recent years, many Czechoslovak citizens, especially cultural workers, have visited Paris. After all, as we know, travel broadens the mind.

However, some encounters had a premeditated purpose. These were meetings of old friends, if the term friendship was at all filled with the noble meaning of the word.

Nevertheless, they had not seen each other for almost two decades, mostly since 1948.

Part of our post-February emigration lives in Paris, and those who left our common homeland after August 1968 are also eagerly offering their services in a ruthless, competitive struggle.

Some of the current political figures are concentrated around Pavel Tigrid and the magazine Svědectví...

Karel Kachyňa grabbed the receiver on the side table and quickly dialed the number. He kept watching the television.

He heard the phone ring.

"Hello, Hofman speaking."

"Ota, don't wait for anything, turn on the television. There's a program about Honza Procházka, and it's really bad."

"Is that you, Karel?"

"Yeah, but don't call him. You'll understand why later," and he hung up.

In silent amazement, they both stared at the documentary about Procházka, who was cursing President Novotný and all the personalities of the Prague Spring. The documentary had been recorded at Professor Černý's apartment and edited by the StB.

050 Prague, May 10, 1970

Klára Wagnerová had a difficult day, running around libraries looking for everything related to Karel Zeman. She had seen his films *A Journey into the Primeval Times*, *The Outrageous Baron Munchausen*, and *The Deadly Invention* while she was still a student. She had her notes and a stack of magazines in front of her. She was reading a laudatory article in Rudé právo newspaper written by someone named Jan Kliment, congratulating Karel Zeman on his newly awarded title of National Artist. Klára had been invited to the approval screening of his new film *On the Comet* the next day. She was determined to thoroughly interview Karel Zeman.

Now she was sitting at the kitchen table, taking notes and preparing questions. She noted: Karel Zeman was a director, special effects artist, master of visual effects, but also a boxer, adventurer, and perfectionist. His films had been sold to countless countries.

On the one hand, she was excited, but on the other, she was afraid. Interviewing such a personality and then writing about it for Kino magazine was a challenge and a responsibility. Then something occurred to her. She got up and walked over to the study door. She knocked quietly. "May I come in?"

Wagner was sitting at his desk again, his collection of pens spread out in front of him. He was taking notes. "Come in, young lady, I'm just getting ready for an auction and on Friday I'm going to Gottwaldov to see my grandfather. The auction is on Saturday, would you like to come with me?"

"Well, you know, probably not. But I came to ask you something. Tomorrow I have to write about Karel Zeman and his new film *On the Comet*. And you're from Gottwaldov. Do you know anything about him?" Wagner turned his chair toward his daughter. "From Zlín, girl, from Zlín. When I left there, it was still Zlín. Communists rename it to Gottwaldov recently." Wagner thought for a while.

"So, you're going to write about Karel. Of course, I know something. But be careful, keep it to yourself. Grandpa would probably know more. Our families know each other. Few people piss off the communists as much as Karel Zeman. They were always after him and wanted him on their side, but he's a stubborn old man. So, they kind of tolerate each other; they need him because he's good at what he does. I think now that the Russians are occupying us, he's going to have a really hard time. He's a nice guy, fair, but don't talk to him about politics.

051 Prague, May 11, 1970

Today, the screening room 4 of the Barrandov Studios was unusually crowded. The anticipation for Karel Zeman's new film was really high, and no one in Barrandov wanted to miss it. The room was filled with the murmur of quiet conversations. Klára Wagnerová stood and tried to figure out who the people entering the screening room were. Over there is Ota Hofman, whom I have already interviewed. She also recognized Karel Kachyňa. But who could that bald man with a patch over his eye be? In front of her, she was struck by the raucous laughter of a man talking to the bald man. Is he drunk? she wondered.

Then she saw Karel Zeman coming. She recognized him from the photos in the magazines she had looked through beforehand. The room was completely full. Without hesitation, Zeman walked straight up the stairs to the screen.

The hall immediately fell silent. Karel Zeman waited a moment: "Good evening. Allow me to say a few words before the screening of my new film, **_On the Comet_**. Jules Verne's work has always fascinated me; it is full of magical fantasy, and I would like to bring it back to life with my moving images. I'm sure you know The Fabulous World of Jules Verne and my previous films, which I think... were successful, to say the least, even abroad. I hope you will enjoy my new film, but first... I would like to thank all my colleagues for their extraordinary dedication, from writing the script to the final take. Thank you for your attention."

The applause in the hall had not yet subsided when a bald, middle-aged man with an eye patch rushed up to Zeman on the stage.

"Comrades, allow me to take this opportunity. My name is Jan Kliment, and those who do not know me yet will soon get to know me." He paused and watched Karel Zeman leave the stage. Then he looked around the hall possessively: "Nice speech, Comrade Zeman. But I would now like to remind you, comrades, that you will all soon be familiar with my text on socialist realism and the new ideological concept of filmmaking. Your supervisor will distribute it to all of you. In the current situation, it is necessary to establish a new and progressive methodology. We are facing a period of new challenges, which I am sure you will all meet with excellence and conscious commitment. I understand that you already have some films in the works, and let's say that I won't be so strict with those, I'll turn a blind eye."

From the darkened hall came the reply: "If you turn a blind eye, you'll see shit."

Kliment looked around the hall, hesitated for a moment, but then pretended he hadn't heard.

"We will set up new special commissions, and the people will also decide with us on the suitability of films that have already been made. We have some films that are almost finished, but their authors have been emphatically labeled by Comrade Dr. Purš as right-wing revisionists, and I will definitely not turn a blind eye to them. We, comrades, will deal with such comrades decisively."

Then Jan Kliment paused and said dryly, "I was expecting applause."

Nothing. Silence.

Kliment looked around the hall again: "I'll teach you how to behave towards members of the Communist Party."

Hofman, Zeman, Kachyňa, all sat frozen. They really hadn't expected this. Kliment left the stage in complete silence. There was no whisper in the hall.

In the deathly silence, a drunken Toman shouted loudly: "Come on, Comrade Zeman. Start it!"

The screen lit up with the title "**ON THE COMET**". Other titles appeared, until the title "Screenplay: Jan Procházka, winner of the Klement Gottwald Prize, and Karel Zeman" gleamed on the screen.

Toman shouted, "Stop! That traitor must go!"

The film stopped. The lights in the hall came on.

Zeman and Hofman looked at each other. They stood up. Without a word, they made their way to the exit. Other guests also began to push their way through the rows of seats and out of the hall. There was no sound, not even a whisper, only the creaking of chairs as people stood up and quickly left.

The hall was completely silent, and Klára Wagnerová remained seated for a moment, staring at the white screen, her mind blank. She didn't understand. My God, what was this supposed to mean? And now she had nothing. No interview with Zeman, no review of the film. She had no idea how she was going to explain this to the editors.

052 Prague, May 11, 1970

Hofman, once again with a cigarette in his hand, stared at the papers spread out on the coffee table in his living room. His wife, Irena, brought two cups of coffee.

"So, how was your day, Oto? Shall we play a game?" she suggested briefly.

Hofman put the papers in a pile: "Don't even mention it. Toman shot down Honza Procházka during the approval process for *On the Komet* between the headlines in such a way that it makes me shiver. Now they must quickly edit the film's headlines and remove name of Jan Procházka from them. And that performance of new chief critic from Rudé právo, Kliment? He was really terrible."

An unopened envelope lay on the table. Irena noticed her husband's glance. "That's for Otto; we have to wait for him."

Hofman gave the order: "Hand them out." And so began the peaceful daily ritual of a card game over coffee and cigarettes.

He sipped his hot coffee: "I can't get Honza Procházka out of my head. The situation at home is getting worse, and it's going to get even worse. Now I'm really surprised they didn't get rid of me too."

A key rattled in the door. His son had just come home from school. His father went to meet him with the envelope:

"Don't keep us in suspense, Otto. Come sit down and open the envelope."

Otta tore open the envelope and read: "Although you passed the entrance exams, due to the excessive number of applicants, you have not been accepted to study at our secondary High education school."

All three were silent, sitting as if stunned.

Irena was the first to recover: "What are we going to do, write an appeal?"

Hofman thought for a moment and hesitantly said, "I don't think that makes sense. Toman hinted at something yesterday."

Irena: "That they rejected you?"

"No, something about Otto's entrance exams. He wished him good luck. I didn't understand why at all. And how does he even know? "

Irena quickly added," Maybe he knows something we don't."

Hofman thought for a moment: "Yeah, that's what I'm thinking, and I've been thinking about it a bit, and that's why..."

Irena was curious: "And that's why, what?"

"It's time for the backup plan."

"Please, what backup plan, Otto?"

His son Otto also looked at his father in amazement: "Yeah, what backup plan?"

Their conversation was interrupted by the ringing of a children's telephone, from which a thin cord led through the window to the apartment one floor above.

Hofman just sighed, glanced hatefully at the ringing device, and remarked, "That Tonda always knows how to pick a time..." He got up from the table and picked up the receiver. Tonda Moskalyk on the other end was in a very playful mood: "Hey, Otík, I was thinking we should go out somewhere together again.

"How about tennis?"

"Tonda, I'm not in the mood at all, my son didn't get into high school, so I'm going to Poděbrady tomorrow."

But Tonda wouldn't take no for an answer: "Come on, you're a genius, they just opened a new Chinese restaurant there, let's go there together, we'll chat and at least you'll take your mind off things."

"But I'm not going there for fun, I have to talk to someone."

Irena glanced at Ota and immediately understood what the backup plan was. Their daughter Irena had graduated from high school in Poděbrady a year ago.

"Well, you see, you can combine business with pleasure," Tonda wouldn't give up.

"A new Chinese restaurant, you say? All right," Hofman finally decided.

"Okay, what time shall we leave? How about half past ten?"

"I need to be there by half past eleven at the latest." Ota glanced at Irena. She just nodded in agreement.

"All right, ten o'clock downstairs then."

053 Prague, May 12, 1970

A white Saab was parked in front of an eight-story apartment building in Spořilov. The Moskalyks arrived and sat down neatly in the back seats.

Irena was the last to arrive and was about to open the front door. Suddenly, something caught her eye.

"Hey, Ota, there's a scratch here."

Hofman was already getting in but stopped halfway. He took off his sunglasses and placed them on the roof of the car.

With a worried expression, he hurried to look at the spot Irena was pointing to.

"It's nothing." Ota wiped the dirt off the paint. Irena got in and closed the door.

Hofman got in too. He started the engine and drove off. The bright sun shone in his eyes. He stopped.

He started looking for something. "I put my sunglasses somewhere."

Irena looked at him. "Didn't you put them on the roof?"

Hofman grabbed the door handle.

At that moment, the sunglasses fell from the roof of the car onto the ground.

Hofman opened the door and stepped on the glasses on the road with all his weight.

There was a loud crack.

"Damn it," he cursed.

Mom chuckled in the car. So did Tonda and Jiřina.

054 Central Bohemia, Poděbrady, May 12, 1970

The furnishings of the Chinese restaurant on the first floor of the building next to the castle square in Poděbrady seemed brand new. New revolving tables, new chairs. Everything was Chinese in design.

Hofman sat down and looked around with pleasure: "I can't understand why we only have one Chinese restaurant in Prague, on Vodičkova Street. It looks good here."

Moskalyk, as an expert, responded: "Yeah, you have to order an hour in advance, the phone is always off, and when we were a little late last time, the waiter was breathing down our necks with the bill and the other guests were giving us dirty looks."

The waiter brought the menus and handed them out to everyone. The study of the menu began.

"So, what have you chosen, Irena?" asked Hofman.

Irena looked up from the menu: "I like the classics, I don't even know what the other things are, let alone what they taste like, so I'll have the kung pao, but we'll wait for you to come back before we order. In the meantime, let's have an appetizer and something to drink."

Hofman, already impatient, got up from the table. "I'll leave you for a moment."

Jiřina Moskalyková asked, "Are you going to skip the appetizer, Ota?"

"I'd rather not, but I have to run out and take care of something. That's why I'm here today."

Irena wished him luck: "Good luck, Ota."

No one asked any further questions.

Hofman quickly glanced around to see if anything was coming down the street, then hurried across the square.

He entered a large building with a sign next to the door: **Secondary General Education School**.

055 Prague, May 12, 1970

Irena took off her shoes in the hall and slipped into her slippers. "Don't keep me in suspense, I understand you didn't want to talk in front of Tonda and Jiřina."

Ota closed the front door behind him: "The Director will call me tomorrow to confirm whether they'll take him. But apparently it shouldn't be a problem. He passed the entrance exams, they'll ask for them now, and they have places available. Miloš Forman, whom I know from the faculty, studied there, among others." Irena remarked, "But Otto isn't very good at writing, he's better at science, and anyway, it's all very strange."

"That's true. Tell me about it."

Otto peeked out of his room. "Hi, how was the Chinese food?"

Irena replied, "Yeah, it was good, and if you don't know, you'll probably be going to high school in Poděbrady. That is, unless you have something better lined up."

Otto looked at her blankly: "I really don't have anything else right now." Then he turned to his dad: "So that's your secret backup plan? I'll live with Stella in Kostelní Lhota. I'm in!"

"I have to go to Lhota with them to work it out. But since Irena was already there, then..."

"That's great, Dad."

056 Prague, May 12, 1970

A car stopped at Jiřího z Poděbrad Square with its headlights off. Two men in light-colored raincoats got out. They opened the door of an apartment building. They climbed the stairs to the second floor, taking two steps at a time, hurrying. They read the sign on the door, looked at each other, and then one of them banged loudly on the door. The other rang the doorbell until it rang loudly in the empty hallway. He held the button down continuously. The second man shouted in a rough voice, trying to drown out the doorbell: "Security, open up!"

A key rattled in the lock. The door opened. Klára Wagnerová stood there in her bathrobe. The man let go of the doorbell and asked, "Comrade Wagnerová?"

Klára replied timidly, "Yes."

"Get dressed, you're coming with us," ordered the man in the trench coat.

057 Prague, May 13, 1970

The StB interrogation room was small, lit by a light bulb above a table with an interrogation chair bolted to the floor. There were no windows, and the only light came from the single bulb in the middle of the room. The interrogator sat comfortably on the other side of the table and began: "So what can you tell us about your father, Comrade Wagnerová? Last year he was in Paris. Do you know who he met there? Then you went to Paris too and brought back some nice shoes..."

The investigator stood up and leaned over the table. "Oh, you're even wearing them now. And those pants, too? Elegant, aren't they? As the French say, chic."

Klára had no idea what he was talking about: "I don't know what you're talking about. Yesterday you arrested my dad and put him in custody, and now I'm here. I don't know anything, I haven't done anything, and my dad is innocent too. He definitely didn't do anything. "

In a dark corner of the room sat a man whom no one noticed, Kamil Pixa.

Pixa now joined the interrogation: "I love American westerns, I don't understand why we don't shoot them in Barrandov."

Klára still didn't know what was going on: "Excuse me?"

But Pixa continued: "We should make more westerns. We filmmakers, you know? I haven't introduced myself yet. I'm Pixa."

"Pixa? Should that mean something to me?"

"Certainly, young lady. You probably know my company, it's called State Secret Security. We know that your father met a man in Paris who studied history. He sent us a report about it."

Klára was surprised: "José works for you? My father spoke of him as a friend."

Pixa, still standing in the dark corner of the room, replied, "I don't want to brag, but we're the most efficient secret service in the world in terms of the number of agents per capita. And as you can see, we have convincing arguments even for foreign nationals. For example, a week ago, the boys killed a guy in a restaurant in Hradčany. He disappeared. That's what we do. Weiter closed the pub, we cleaned up the mess, and it was done."

Klára stared at him blankly, still not understanding:" What do you want from me? "

Pixa stood up and sat down on the table in front of her:" We know you did an internship at Květy magazine."

Klára thought to herself: Finally, something meaningful! "They fired me."

Pixa feigned surprise: "I'm surprised, I thought you were still working there, but the editorial office of magazine Kino isn't bad either, is it? But I have a better offer for you. How would you like to go back there?"

Klára paused: "To magazine Květy? Do you really want to punish me that much? You can do whatever you want with me, but I'm not going back there."

Pixa perked up: "What's the matter, girl, were they mean to you there? You know, before Jan Zelenka fired you, he was already on his way out. They fired him even before you. But now he's the director of Czechoslovak Television, and you wouldn't want to work there, would you? Seriously, though. It's a fair offer. The press department of Barrandov Film Studios and, of course, a nice little side job for us? Festivals, screenings, foreign currency, foreign countries, even capitalist ones."

Klára calmed down a little: "Why me?"

Pixa, still with his ass on the table, leaned toward her: "We'll get rid of your dad. Because of you, if you don't help us. But you have a chance. A beautiful girl like you. Why did you get involved with that French guy? I'll tell you why. Either you wanted to get some new boots, or you thought he'd help you get out, right? I'm right, aren't I?"

Klára shook her head. "But I don't even know him."

Pixa laughed: "Really? Don't play dumb. We know what's going on."

Klára swallowed hard: "What else would I do there besides my job?"

Pixa got up from his chair, leaned both hands on the table, and stared Wagnerová straight in the face: "Cooperate, of course, and you'll report directly to me. If they find out about you, especially that bastard Toman, I'll beat your face so badly that your own mother won't recognize you. And I'd really hate that, because I really like looking at that cute face of yours. Jarda will finish you off."

The investigator joined the conversation and caught Klára's attention: "I'll be honest with you: whether your father is guilty or innocent will now depend solely on you. So, we're going to play with him for a while. How long that will be, we'll see. It all starts with this signature."

Klára glanced at the paper he had placed in front of her.

058 Prague, May 19, 1970

Hofman spoke at a regular meeting with chief dramaturge Toman about the material he would like to put into production. He mentioned the films *Prince Bajaja*, *Three Nuts for Cinderella*, and *I´m Jumping Over Puddles Again.* He was acting as the new head of the children's film group, but the nagging question of what Toman had to do with Otto's high school entrance exams was still running through his head. He didn't know Toman at all. So, he hesitated whether to ask him about it or to ignore the nagging question.

After his introduction, Toman took the floor: "Listen, comrade, in children's films, it doesn't matter what you shoot. We're not idiots, we're not going to turn Snow White into a communist, but think about whether children's heroes could be communists. You should be progressive. They like that in Moscow. Basically, the point is that only trusted people should write the scripts."

Someone knocked on the door.

Toman invited the visitor in: "Come in."

A beautiful young girl in a summer dress entered, Klára Wagnerová.

Toman melted: "I forgot. Comrade Hofman, this is our new addition to the press department, she also writes for magazine Kino, Miss Wagnerová."

Klára approached Hofman: "Good morning, Mr. Hofman."

Hofman smiled at her: "Good morning. It's nice to see you again, Miss Wagnerová."

Toman was glad that he could quickly end the work meeting: "Well, I'll leave you to it. I have to go see Comrade Dr. Purš." And he left.

"Do you have a lot to do?" asked Hofman.

Klára shook her head: "Just you."

"So shall we go for a drink again?"

Klára agreed: "I'd love to. Our last conversation was very interesting and very engaging for the readers of Kino. The editorial staff loved it."

The wine bar U Sudu was usually half-empty in this afternoon time. No one paid any attention to anyone else over a glass of wine: "Press department?"

Klára replied timidly, "I'm here, but only for a very short time."

Hofman then asked, "Do you know Toman well?"

"I saw him for the first time today."

"So, a big double premiere. You'll see for yourself how things work here at Barrandov. You've jumped on a moving train. Karlovy Vary will happen this year, that's already been decided, but there are also a number of other festivals. We have plenty of screenings in our children's group, but I think it will certainly be better for us to help out here than where they're filming the correct interpretation of history, if you know what I mean."

Klára Wágnerová understood the hint: "There's probably something to that."

059 Prague, May 19, 1970

On the bed in a poorly furnished room in a hostel, a young girl named Irena Hofmanová was passionately kissing a taxi driver named Milan Šmejda. Šmejda, overcome with desire, reached between Irena's legs, but she stopped him and squeezed his hand.

"Won't it hurt our baby?"

"Of course not, my love."

Irena let go of his hand and Milan continued with the foreplay.

After making love, Šmejda lit a cigarette in bed. Irena lay next to him, catching her breath.

"Do you think your dad could get me a better car? He drives a Saab, and mine is a rusty old wreck."

Irena felt great after making love. "Ask him yourself. We're invited to lunch on Saturday. By the way, Dad doesn't know about us yet. Don't worry. He's cool."

Milan Šmejda took another drag on his cigarette.

060 Prague, May 20, 1970

Bohunka Šourková, perfectly made up and dressed as always, peeked into Hofman's office: "Oto, you have a visitor, he says it's important, from Toman." She motioned to the visitor to come in.

Bureš, a man around thirty-five in a suit and a grubby jacket, burst into Hofman's office. He was brimming with self-confidence and impertinence. He was holding a folder with manuscripts in his hand. "Comrade Toman sent me to see you. You have to read my work."

Hofman looked at the unknown man. He assessed him briefly but waited to see what he would say. "Do we know each other? What is your name, please?"

"Bureš, of course. Toman didn't call you? He promised me he would. He was enthusiastic about my ideas. He recommended you."

Hofman paused: "I really don't know anything about that. He didn't say anything to me or call me."

Bureš continued confidently: "I have some great ideas, it's going to be a hell of a movie, Comrade Hofman." He couldn't be stopped: "A total blockbuster. I have to tell you what it's about. It's about Váňa, the pioneer with the red scarf..."

Hofman stopped him with an uncompromising gesture: "Leave it here, Comrade Bureš, Comrade Mareček will take a look at it."

Hofman stood up and went to open the door. "Bohunka, call Mareček..."

Bureš interrupted him. "Comrade Toman told me to deal only with you and to agree on an advance payment with you."

Hofman swallowed incredulously: "On what, please?"

"On the advance payment, I'm not going to write for free."

Hofman responded irritably: "Come back in two weeks. Comrade Mareček will read it, and if it's as great as you say, we'll consider the advance payment."

Bureš insisted again: "But I need the advance payment right now."

"Then you'll have to take it up with Comrade Toman. Excuse me, I'm busy." Hofman stood up and pushed Bureš out of the office.

061 Prague, May 21, 1970

Irena Hofmanová and her daughter sat silently at the table in the dining room. The front door opened, and Ota Hofman entered. He looked around and saw them sitting there, looking dejected.

"Hello, girls. Is something wrong?"

His daughter stared at her hands on the table: "Hello, Dad."

Her mother looked at her: "Come on, spill it."

Irena blurted out without looking up: "I'm pregnant."

Hofman said casually: "With the taxi driver?"

"I came to invite you to the wedding. It's on July 6."

Hofman sat down next to her: "That's very nice, sweetheart, but Irena and I will be at the festival in Vary. So, you'll have to manage without us. And what about school, how are you going to manage with a baby? How long do you have left, a year? And by the way, where are you going to stay? Irena, please pour me a drink, we're going to have a long talk..."

062 Prague, May 28, 1970

Bohunka peeked into Hofman's office with a slightly apologetic expression:" Ota, Comrade Bureš is here for you, again..."

Hofman gave her a meaningful, annoyed look and sighed: "Please call Mareček in."

Bureš rudely pushed his way through the door as Bohunka was leaving. "I'm here, as agreed, Comrade Hofman. That's a great idea. Everything's in there. Loyalty to the party, class struggle. Will I get the promised advance? "

Mareček entered the office. Hofman looked at him with a broad smile. "Well, Comrade Mareček, have you read Comrade Bureš's work? What do you think?"

Mareček blushed and began to stammer:" Well... Well..."

Hofman added with a smile: "Comrade Mareček was obviously very busy and clearly didn't have time to read your work. So, Comrade Mareček, get to work and I want evaluation of Comrade Bureš on my desk the day after tomorrow. You can go, Comrade Mareček."

Mareček turned and disappeared.

Bureš persisted: "So what about the advance?"

Hofman stood up, put his arm around Bureš's shoulders, and slowly accompanied him to the door. "Comrade Bureš, please don't forget to say hello to Comrade Toman." With his free hand, he pulled 3 pieces of hundred Crowns notes out of his pocket.

"In the meantime, allow me to give you a personal loan."

Bureš took the money and his eyes lit up. Bohunka waited until Bureš left: "Ota, what are you doing, you fool, lending him money? Such a jerk!"

Ota smiled again: "Bohunka, I know I won't see him for at least a year. Want to bet?"

063 Prague, May 28, 1970

After being interrogated at Bartolomějská, he knew that the fact that they had released him after questioning was only temporary. He hailed a taxi in front of Lucerna. He had himself driven home. After a while, the taxi driver remarked, "It's interesting, sir, but someone is following us."

Procházka turned around and saw the outline of headlights. He turned to the taxi driver: "Are you sure?"

The taxi driver replied calmly, "I've been driving for a long time, and that car has been following us for quite a while."

Procházka looked at the taxi driver. Sweat beaded on his forehead. His heart began to race. The taxi stopped in front of Procházka's house. Procházka got out and looked at the meter. "Forty-eight," said the taxi driver.

Procházka took out a fifty-Crown bill and paid. "Keep the change."

The driver grinned: "Thank you, Mr. Procházka."

Procházka paused and looked through the open window: "Do you know me?"

"Everyone at the Ninth Department of the StB knows you. Have a nice evening."

The taxi driver closed the window, stepped on the gas pedal, and disappeared into the night.

064 Prague, May 28, 1970

When he got home, Procházka sat in his living room for a while, unable to get the incident with the taxi driver out of his head. He sat and stared into space. Suddenly, the phone rang. Procházka picked it up. Kachyňa's voice came through the receiver: "We can't shoot together anymore, Honza. *The Ear* will be our last film. And I seriously doubt they'll let it be released."

Procházka whispered, "Karel, is that really you, or is this another provocation?"

Karel Kachyňa didn't understand what Procházka was talking about: "Honza, I don't understand what you're talking about. What provocation? It's just the way it is. We can't work together anymore."

Procházka replied sadly, "Okay."

Kachyňa managed to add: "I'm sorry, my friend."

065 West Bohemia, Karlovy Vary, June 30, 1970

The Hotel Pupp on the colonnade in Karlovy Vary was fully booked long before the start of the film festival. That is, once every two years. Our Czechoslovak comrades had agreed in Moscow that the long-standing festival would be held in Moscow. In a city with no tradition of film festivals whatsoever.

A Mercedes limousine stopped in front of the Pupp Hotel. Gert Müntefering and two other gentlemen in tailor-made suits got out.

The hotel bellboy in livery opened the doors for them and the gentlemen immediately headed for the reserved lounge. They sat down on chairs on one side of the table, with Gert Müntefering in the middle. The chairs opposite them remained empty. The standing clock showed 2:10 p.m. You didn't have to be Einstein to understand that someone was expected.

The clock now showed 2:20 p.m. Gert finished his coffee and looked at the man sitting next to him. He shrugged his shoulders. For a precise German, this was incomprehensible. Then the door opened and Klára Wagnerová caught their attention. She immediately launched into fluent German: "Good afternoon, I'm sorry to disturb you, my name is Klára Wagnerová and I'm from the press department of Barrandov

Film Studios. May I speak to Mr. Müntefering, Mr. Gert Müntefering?"

Gert, pleased by the beautiful young woman's interest, replied: "Good afternoon, yes, Gert Müntefering, nice to meet you."

"Would I be able to ask you for an interview?"

Gert smiled at her: "I'd love to, I used to be a journalist myself, but not right now. Our meeting hasn't even started yet, so I don't know what I'd tell you."

Klára wouldn't take no for an answer: "Would you like to join me for a drink?"

"Of course."

Pixa and Toman were already approaching. Toman snapped at Klára: "What are you doing here, comrade?"

"I came to ask the gentlemen for an interview."

"That's definitely not appropriate right now," Toman replied angrily.

Pixa also snapped at Toman, not liking his tone, which was also noticed by the foreign guests: "It's not appropriate, but you can say it politely, comrade."

Toman backed down: "Excuse us."

Klára noticed the smell of alcohol on his breath. "Nothing happened."

Pixa, in a good mood, wanted to remedy the situation: "And you, comrade?"

Klára turned around.

Pixa added with a broad smile: "Don't be discouraged by your initial failure. A pretty girl like you has a lot ahead of her. So that your father can be proud of you."

Klára shot him a withering glance and walked out of the lounge with her head held high.

Toman sat down first, poured himself some mineral water from a bottle on the table, and then spoke: "Good afternoon, gentlemen. Have you had your coffee?"

The interpreter next to him translated his words into German.

Gert didn't like the delay: "We've already had about three each."

The interpreter remained silent, but Toman understood the meaning and laughed. Not a word of apology was uttered. His expression made it clear to Gert that he could literally wipe his ass with him.

So Toman began: "And you think you can just come here whenever you feel like it?"

Pixa gestured to the interpreter to be quiet and addressed Toman: "Leave it to me, okay?"

Toman looked at Pixa and shook his head.

Pixa spoke in fluent German: "Comrade Toman would prefer to work only with the East German DEFA."

"We'd rather not," Gert replied.

The interpreter whispered the translated words into Toman's ear.

Pixa continued in German: "The collaboration on *Pan Tau* has proven fruitful. In terms of foreign currency, of course. Would you be interested in any other projects? "

Gert was glad to be able to respond specifically:" Of course, that's why we're here. But we want to have a say in the scripts, and we're only interested in non-political material. There's no point arguing about topics we disagree on."

"I understand," replied Pixa. "But trust has to be built. You can take a look at what we're preparing for a children's film. I'm sure we'll find common ground there."

Gert added: "I'm interested in the material from Mr. Hofman and Mr. Polák. I've known them for a long time, and we get along well."

"In that case, you'll find it with Mr. Hanibal too," suggested Pixa.

Gert thought for a moment and remarked diplomatically, "We can try, but I trust our judgment. And I would also very much like to finance Mr. Juraj Herz's project."

The interpreter finished translating the sentence.

Drunk Toman lost his temper again: "What?"

Gert finished his thought: "Mr. Herz is a great filmmaker."

"And you don't mind working with a Jew?" Toman snapped, long known for his very strong anti-Semitic views.

The interpreter hesitated, but Toman nodded at him.

Gert waited for the translation: "What? Is that supposed to be some kind of provocation? Why should we mind?"

Pixa spoke German again, completely ignoring Toman: "Don't mind him. Let's just say that cooperation with Mr. Herz is undesirable at this time. He must earn our trust again."

Gert replied diplomatically: "Fine, when he earns it, I'd like to be the first to know."

Pixa glanced angrily at Toman: "You can count on it."

066 West Bohemia, Karlovy Vary, July 1, 1970

The reception at the Pupp Hotel in Karlovy Vary on the occasion of the film festival was already in full swing. Vodka was flowing freely. Guests could choose from a rich selection of sausages with bread and sliced melons. Toman arrogantly walked among the guests, sipping vodka. He spoke only Czech and Russian, so he looked around for someone with whom he could exchange a few words.

Gert took a glass of vodka from the tray, somewhat reluctantly and out of obligation, and took a sip. He looked around to see if he recognized anyone.

Klára Wagnerová recognized Gert at the other end of the hall immediately and headed towards him.

Gert perked up: "Finally, a familiar face!"

Klára addressed Gert: "You don't know anyone else here? Then you might have time for that interview now?"

"Of course, but I'm sorry, not here, everyone is listening, if you know what I mean," Gert remarked.

Klára immediately suggested, "We could slip away."

"You know what, just give me a moment," Gert accepted the offer.

Karel Kachyňa looked around the hall. When someone tried to strike up a conversation with him, he didn't respond.

Toman fixed his cloudy gaze on Kachyňa, but didn't want to talk to him because he had nothing to say: "That Kachyňa pisses me off. He's a stubborn old man."

Kachyňa spotted a new arrival at the door and hurried after him. "Ota, come have some wine."

Hofman asked, "Am I late? They never have wine here, only vodka."

Kachyňa: "I wouldn't drink anything here either. Melons, sausages, and vodka, that's a terrible combination. Let them shit themselves." He leaned toward Hofman and whispered in his ear: "Every waiter here is a cop; you can't talk here. Let's go to a wine bar."

Gert Müntefering approached Ota and muttered, "Hi, Ota, sorry, I'm in a bit of a hurry today, but I need to discuss something with you."

Kachyňa leaned toward Ota: "Let's meet at the wine bar in a little while, you can sort things out here in peace."

He turned and walked ahead. Gert waited until Kachyňa had left, looked around to see if anyone was listening. "Ota, I would like to offer you an official invitation from my boss. He would like to meet you. We will cover all the costs of your trip to Cologne. We need to discuss *Pan Tau*. Will you come?"

Hofman smiled. "If it were up to me..."

Gert persisted: "I need you there, I really need you there," he looked around the hall, "and we could have something good to eat, not just vodka and sausages."

This embarrassed Hofman. "Of course, I accept the invitation, but I have to get approval from management."

Gert smiled: "All right, see you in Cologne."

"Gert, I don't want to disappoint you, but if it were that easy..."

"Oh, one more thing, it's not official yet, but three episodes of **Pan Tau** will be screened in Venice. Do you think you'll be able to make it?"

Hofman shrugged again. Gert shook his hand and Hofman hurried to the door, where Kachyňa was still lingering. Ota waved to him that he was on his way.

Suddenly, Karel Zeman walked past Hofman. Hofman stopped: "Mr. Zeman?"

Zeman beamed: "Good evening, Ota Hofman, isn't that, right?"

"Yes. Pleased to meet you."

Zeman shook his outstretched hand. "I've been following your work for a long time. It's interesting. Maybe we should do something together, what do you think?"

Hofman seized on the topic: "I've been thinking about that too. I thought of a sequel to *A Journey into the Primeval Times.*" Zeman became serious: "Are you serious?"

"I've already thought about it a little. This time, teenagers would travel to prehistoric times, maybe even an entire high school class.

"I see, and what would happen then?"

"They would return to the present, but with dinosaurs."

Zeman laughed: "That's an excellent idea! And the dinosaurs would raze Gottwaldov to the ground, and it could be called Zlín again. Write it, it'll be fun." He shook Hofman's hand. "When you've finished, come to Gottwaldov."

067 West Bohemia, Karlovy Vary, July 1, 1970

Gert came out of the Pupp Hotel with Klára Wagnerová. He looked around. Seeing no one, he suggested, "Would you mind going for a drive? I have some Moët, delicious pâté, prosciutto, and Belgian chocolate. We could talk..."

"Now, now, Mr. Fairy Tale, are you making advances toward me?"

Gert grinned: "Would you mind?"

Klára sighed: "I like men who know how to ask for what they want. Life is too short to always speak in riddles."

"You'll certainly get your fill of that under communism."

Klára laughed. "Let's go then."

Gert drove his Mercedes, constantly looking in the rearview mirrors. For a while, there was actually a car behind him, but then it was empty. He headed for the lake. It wasn't his first time in Vary, and he knew the area. Gert took a blanket out of the car. The night was beautiful and balmy.

Klára lay down on the blanket and Gert prepared the promised refreshments.

"It's beautiful here," Klára sighed.

Gert replied, "We filmed *Pan Tau* here. I love the Czech countryside. You're probably wondering why I like coming here so much."

"Yes, why?"

Gert began to talk: "For me, Czechoslovakia is an adventure and an experience. And today, it's also my livelihood. When I signed the contract for **Pan Tau**, I had no idea if it would go through. When they told me in Prague, even before the official meeting, that it was going to be filmed, I was completely thrilled. I immediately called Cologne, and lo and behold, they gave me free rein. It was a wonderful feeling. I had achieved something, and I knew it. A wonderful feeling."

Klára lay down on her back: "Beautiful. So many stars."

Gert opened the Moët and poured it into Czech cut crystal glasses. "The best crystal in the world," he remarked.

Klára nodded.

Gert added: "And the most beautiful women in the world."

Klára turned and kissed him. Then she caressed his cheek: "Let's forget everything for tonight."

"Carpe diem."

"Carpe diem."

Gert began kissing Klára and laid her down on the blanket. He completely forgot to be careful, but not for long. Suddenly he stopped: "Did you hear that?"

Klára didn't let herself be disturbed: "There's no one here, calm down, Mr. Fairy Tale."

068 West Bohemia, Karlovy Vary, July 1, 1970

Kachyňa and Hofman had just clinked their wine glasses in a wine bar in Karlovy Vary. Karel Gott was singing on the radio, and Kachyňa began to reminisce: "Two years ago, we were here with Honza Procházka. That young Menzel won here back then. Do you remember how angry Frič was with him?"

Hofman added: "Yeah, he shook his hand and disappeared."

Kachyňa thought for a moment: "Miloš Forman was here then, wasn't he?"

Hofman replied immediately: "He came to the Pupp, found out that none of his friends were here except Menzel, and so he left again."

"And Forman. I think we'll be hearing more about him," added Kachyňa, than took a drink.

Hofman also took a drink: "I used to mind a little that I was making children's films and not films for adults, but today I'm glad I did."

"I'm glad you took me in, Ota." Kachyňa leaned forward and raised his glass again for a toast.

The glasses clinked together.

069 West Bohemia, Karlovy Vary, July 1, 1970

Gert lay next to Klára by the lake in Karlovy Vary, both breathing heavily. Gert looked up at the stars in the sky: "That was beautiful, but..."

Klára paused: "But? But what?"

Gert lay down on his side: "I'm nervous. Whenever I come to Czechoslovakia, the secret police put agents on me. When we left the hotel, we had one following us. He must be around here somewhere."

Klára lay on her back, hesitating for a moment, but then she made up her mind: "Calm down, Mr. Fairy Tale, you just slept with a secret police agent."

Gert looked at her blankly.

Klára also rolled onto her side: "Not every secret police agent has a scar on his face and looks like Ivan. Sometimes they're just people who have no way out."

Gert was clearly taken aback: "You mean you have no other way out?"

Klára reacted irritably: "I don't want to talk about it, and I definitely don't want to confess."

Gert looked at her for a moment. She's beautiful, he thought, but he didn't want to ask any more questions. "Shall we do the interview?"

Klára was glad he changed the subject: "Although I can't promise it will be published."

Gert relented: "Let's just talk, we have more in common than you think. And the pâté is delicious; it might go bad."

Klára blurted out with tears in her eyes: "Do you understand that sometimes people have no other choice? That they fear for their loved ones and, selfishly, for themselves too?"

"I understand it more than you think."

070 West Bohemia, Karlovy Vary, July 2, 1970

Early in the morning, the area in front of the Pupp Hotel was deserted, and the only man in livery at the door was clearly bored. A van pulled up and the doorman perked up. Some men began taking things out of the van to roast pork legs. The doorman received no instructions. They lit a fire. They were directed by a man with lively eyes, the composer Zdeněk Liška. He was a man about whom many legends circulated.

His world was music, especially film music. He could compose music for fairy tales, historical epics, crime dramas, but he also wrote the national anthem of Kuwait. He was a man outside of time and space, a true musical genius.

Liška was in a hurry: "Just do it, guys, do it right."

The doorman approached them: "What are you doing here, comrade?"

Liška snapped at him: "Do you know who I am?"

"I have no idea."

Liška, pretending to be angry, continued: "This is scandalous! He doesn't know who I am? Then find out."

The doorman knew his duties, and his job was to remove anything that would disrupt the dignity of the hotel, so he ordered, "You can't be here."

Outraged, Liška lashed out at him, "You're wrong, I have the right to be here! I have five of my films in the competition, so who else could roast pork leg here but me?"

Angry, Liška turned to the passers-by: "Ladies and gentlemen, in protest against the injustice of this festival, which didn't bother to invite me, I will be handing out roast pork leg here, free of charge! I'm not as stingy as these misers here!"

071 West Bohemia, Karlovy Vary, July 2, 1970

Gert woke up in his room at the Pupp Hotel and went to breakfast.

Jan Werich was sitting in the hotel restaurant and greeted Gert with a broad smile: "Hello, colleague." Werich was having champagne and caviar for breakfast. Gert went over to say hello. They shook hands. Jan Werich remarked dryly, "My fellow filmmakers and I had breakfast on you. And a little something last night." Gert looked at him in alarm, said nothing, and went to the reception desk. He asked the receptionist with a smile, "Good morning, a few friends of mine seem to have had some fun at my expense.

How much is my bill? "

The receptionist replied with a smile: "That's about three thousand marks, Mr. Müntefering."

Gert's smile froze. "Three thousand, three thousand marks?" he asked incredulously.

The receptionist replied to Gert, "Three thousand one hundred and fourty seven West German marks. To be exact Mr. Müntefering. Is that a problem?"

The red-faced Gert just blurted out, "A problem, you say?"

Enraged, Gert had not had breakfast and decided to get some fresh air. He left the Pupp and walked to the colonnade. At one of the cafés, he met Ota Hofman drinking coffee and reading the festival newspaper. Angry, Gert snapped at him, "Is that supposed to be a joke, Ota?"

Hofman stared at him in confusion. "What happened, Gert?"

"I just met Jan Werich, and he said that the Czechs drank and ate three thousand marks worth of food here!"

Hofman replied, taken aback, "That can't be true."

Gert realized that Hofman knew nothing and that he was barking up the wrong tree. "I don't have that kind of money, Ota. I got the same allowance as you receive for business trip. Do you know how much that is for me?"

Hofman was so ashamed he wanted the ground to swallow him up: "That's a terrible disgrace, Gert. Of course I'll pay for it."

Gert calmed down a little: "What about the fee we gave you for *Pan Tau*? We'll find out who it was. And I'll make them pay!"

"You're not in Cologne, Gert. These people don't have that kind of money. They just think you're some big shot from the West who lights his cigars with thousand-mark bills. It's an unfortunate trait of our national character. I'll pay for it. Don't worry about it. I've lost more than that before, and I'm sure I will again. Come have breakfast with me."

Gert stopped him: "No way, I'll send the bill to WDR, I'll find a way to justify it to Müller. Anyway, I can hear his comments."

An elegantly dressed elderly gentleman in a camel coat with a scarf around his neck passed by and greeted him politely: "Good morning, Mr. Hofman."

Hofman stood up politely and greeted him in return. "Good morning, Mr. Brousil. Would you like to join us?"

"I'd love to, Mr. Hofman, but I have some work to do. I'm sure we'll see each other again."

Gert was curious. "Who was that, please? It's hot outside, almost thirty degrees, how can he stand it?"

"You don't know the greatest ambassador of Czechoslovak film?" replied Hofman.

"He taught me at university. I remember when he first came to a seminar on contemporary film and asked all of us aspiring film stars a seemingly nonsensical question: 'Who here speaks English well? Russian? Italian? Can you communicate in French? Spanish? German?' Here and there, a hand went up. Some were older students who had to learn German during the war. And then there were a few younger ones who were just struggling with the pitfalls of the Cyrillic alphabet. 'Before you graduate from this school, you will have to master these languages,' he told us. It was as if he had overlooked the reality of our times, when it was impossible to travel to East Germany or Hungary. And

Moscow was terribly far away. So that's him. A. M. Brousil. A coat and scarf, even though it's thirty degrees in the shade. A personality who travels to the world's hotels attending film festivals and, instead of fine wine, asks for clean water heated to a temperature that suits his bronchitis. You know, only a millionaire from Texas or Professor A. M. Brousil from Prague would ask for something like that. A hotel guest, who, shortly before, had criticized three rooms at the local Hilton and chosen the fourth, with a few pennies in his pocket for a generous tip when he left. That's A. M. Brousil."

Gert was enjoying himself and didn't interrupt the talkative Ota. Ota continued: "But you surely remember Venice, Clown Ferdinand, where we met. Brousil was a member of our Czechoslovak delegation, and Trnka, the puppeteer, was with us at the time. We stayed at the Hotel Des Bains, which Thomas Mann used as the setting for his book Death in Venice. I remember it as if it were yesterday. The ceremoniously lit entrance. The gardens. The terraces. The arriving limousines. Ladies in evening gowns, tuxedos."

Hofman recounted, gesturing with his hands. "And there was A. M. Brousil in his camel coat, waiting for me and Josef Pinkava to tell us: I took two bottles of slivovitz from your room; that's all you had, but it's enough. I promised the hotel manager that we would supply the alcohol, and the hotel would provide the other refreshments, terraces, and waiters.' Italian television broadcast live from the hotel terraces at the time. A. M. Brousil was beaming, switching smoothly from

211

Italian to French to English. In the morning, the most important Italian newspapers and magazines carried long articles about the meeting with Jiří Trnka, the greatest puppeteer of the time. About the wonderful reception organized by the Czechoslovak delegation. That's A. M. Brousil. And the next day, it was you who invited me for wine, and now here we are sitting together. "Ota paused." I'm rambling. Am I keeping you?"

Gert smiled: "Not at all. You've really cheered me up. And thanks for offering to pay, but I really can't accept. I'll go and sort it out." He turned to leave. Then he added: "Thanks also for the tip about the screening of the film *On the Comet*. I saw it last night. We'll buy it. Ota, you know what I find strange? The credits didn't mention who wrote it, no screenwriter. It just said it was based on Jules Verne. Is there some politics behind it again?"

"Yes, politics."

072 West Bohemia, Karlovy Vary, July 2, 1970

It was busy in front of the Pupp in the afternoon. Liška was grilling a leg of pork and drinking beer. He laughed with people and signed everything they asked him to, even beer coasters. Liška was in a great mood and waved to Hofman, who was just passing by.

"Good afternoon, Mr. Liška, not composing today?" Hofman asked cheerfully.

"Ah, we have guests! Have a piece of roast, Mr. Hofman. Aren't you writing today?"

"Mr. Liška, I hope you will remain loyal to us and that I will be able to turn to you again."

Hofman, as usual, stubbed out his cigarette and accepted a piece of the roast.

"Of course I will, Mr. Hofman," the composer winked slyly and added, "Something nice in the works?"

"I'm finishing a script for Karel Kachyňa, it's called *The Train to Heaven*, I'm counting on you, Mr. Liška."

"I'm looking forward to it, you know, the basis of everything is a funeral march. I have one in every one of my films. My dad played at funerals, and you know, a funeral march like that makes everyone cry."

"It makes them cry because someone close to them has died, doesn't it?"

But Liška was uncompromising:" You know what the problem with this country is? Everyone here is too smart. Have another piece of meat and stop philosophizing."

073 East Bohemia, Ratibořice, July 12, 1970

Pavlíček was already quite tired from riding his bike. But he was getting closer to his destination, and that gave him more strength to pedal. Finally, he saw a film crew in the distance below the hill. The destination of his long journey from Pečky. He stopped, got off his bike, leaned it against the ditch, and sat down on the ground. He pulled a blade of grass and began to chew on it. He looked down at the film crew bustling about. He could hear Moskalyk's voice coming from a megaphone: "Ready. Action!"

The actors were dressed in historical costumes, and Pavlíček thought that they must be boiling in them under the summer sun. Down the road, a carriage passed by, probably carrying the princess from Ratibořice Castle.

Pavlíček smiled, completely forgetting his sore legs, and basked in the bright sunshine.

At the bottom of the hill, the crew with director Antonín Moskalyk began preparing the next scene. Moskalyk suddenly noticed a figure on the slope above.

He remarked angrily to the cameraman, "Look at that gawker over there. Don't let him get in the shot. Don't these people have anything better to do?"

074 East Bohemia, Žernov, July 12, 1970

A knock on the door brought Antonín Moskalyk to his feet. He was enjoying the peace and quiet of his newly purchased cottage in Žernov, not far from Grandmother's Valley, and thought to himself: What the hell do they want from the crew now?

He opened the door and was very surprised to see František Pavlíček standing there.

"Hello, Toníček."

"What are you doing here, Franta? We weren't supposed to meet until Thursday."

"I'm here on the fly. I came to see if you weren't messing things up for me."

"Come on in."

"Hi, Jiřina. Where can I park my bike?"

Jiřina Moskalyková joined them. Pavlíček handed Jiřina a bouquet of wildflowers.

"Oh, they're beautiful, thank you. Leave your bike there, where you left it. Did you ride your bike all the way here?"

"Yeah. The working class can't afford to be wasteful. I was watching you from the hill above the road this afternoon, Toníček, seeing how you were doing."

"So, you were the peeping Tom who almost got in the shot?" Moskalyk laughed.

"I'll make some coffee." Jiřina ran off.

Tonda Moskalyk went to the cupboard and took out an envelope.

Pavlíček took it and sighed: "Thanks for signing it for me. Stupid times."

Tonda Moskalyk: "Thanks for writing it so nicely. A script like that is a joy to shoot."

Jiřina looked at Pavlíček: "Franta, you won't be able to walk home today, I'll go make your bed. And you, Tonda, open a bottle of wine. We have a special guest."

075 Prague, July 14, 1970

Pavlíček heard the doorbell ring. He jumped over the boxes in his new apartment to open the door. Boxes were scattered everywhere. He had left his family. He was currently alone, but in love with his new girlfriend, radio editor Eva Košlerová. He opened the door and greeted, "Hi, Oto, what are you doing here?" In addition to Pavlíček, Hofman was greeted by the furious barking of Cinda, a cocker spaniel. He sniffed Hofman and then wagged his tail in welcome, demanding attention.

Hofman saw the mess and smiled: "Hi Franta, I'm not here to visit, I'm here for work." He stood in the doorway and asked, "How are you?"

Cinda felt neglected by the visitor, so he went to his bed.

Pavlíček replied, "I'd like to say that now I'll have time to write, since I got fired and left my family, but considering that now I can only write for my drawer, I'm pretty torn about it."

Hofman reached into his briefcase and pulled out a short story. "Honza Procházka took a short story from the Barrandov archives. He choose some other stories too. There are no records of these stories being written, and more importantly, who wrote them."

Pavlíček took the manuscript in his hand: "***Three Nuts for Cinderella**. The most beautiful fairy tale Božena Němcová ever wrote.*"

"DEFA is in on it with us, they want the script as soon as possible, and you should write it," Hofman remarked.

"I'd love to, Ota, but no one will ever allow it to be filmed under my name."

"Is it that important to have your name on it? You'll always know you wrote it. And I'll know too."

Pavlíček shrugged: "You've made me happy."

"Franta, I can't understand why you're sitting here worrying like this. We've known each other for years. It's not fair."

Pavlíček stood and looked sadly at Hofman, then leaned against the doorframe: "That's not true, Ota. I haven't done anything to anyone. And you're wrong, I'm not just sitting here. I run around wherever I can, and I need to get a working stamp for my ID card to prove that I'm working. Otherwise, they'll lock me up as a parasite. And you know what the worst part is? When I introduce myself, everyone stops talking to me. They won't even hire me as a laborer at the train station. I'm sinking lower and lower, and I don't know where the bottom is."

Hofman knew what he was talking about: "I know, Franta, times are really tough."

Then Pavlíček had an idea: "Could you sign my script for *Prince Bajaja*? I worked really hard on it and the new management will reject it otherwise."

Hofman put his hand on his shoulder: "Franta, I just signed Honza Procházka's *I'm Jumping Over Puddles* Again, and I'm trying to get his other material into production too. I can't sign everything for everyone. But don't worry, we'll think of something."

076 Prague, July 28, 1970

It was already dark, so when Hofman got out of the elevator on the fifth floor, he had to turn on the light in the hallway to unlock the door. "Hi, Irenka, I'm home," he called out from the doorway. Irena already had a warm dinner ready.

"It's good you're home. Tonda Moskalyk was here, and we're supposed to go over for a drink. He said he wants to talk to you about something important."

Ota frowned: "I think we both know what he wants to talk about. He bought a bottle and wants to chat about how someone on TV is throwing a wrench in his plans again. I'm pretty tired today."

"Going up one floor won't kill you."

"That's not the point, I can't go there looking like a tramp after work."

Irena looked at him: "Why not?"

"Jiřina would tell on us," replied Ota.

"Are you kidding? Tonda comes to our place in his underpants."

Their son Otto came into the kitchen. "What's for dinner?"

"Lentils with smoked meat, it's on the stove, help yourself," his mother smiled at him. "Would you like some?" she asked her husband.

"I'm not hungry, maybe later."

Hofman actually didn't want to go to meet Tonda Moskalyk today. "I wanted to write some more," he protested.

"You can do that later, we won't be there long."

"Are you going somewhere?" asked Otto.

Irena decided: "We're going to Tonda and Jiřina's."

Otto remarked in surprise, "Again?"

Irena sought a compromise: "Then take that clean shirt. It's on the hanger over there."

"I'll also take that jacket and tie I got for Christmas. I can't wear it to work anyway because it has the British royal colors on it."

"I won't be taking my evening dress tonight, if you don't mind," Irena remarked.

Hofman was amused: "That's the difference between us. You look good in everything."

Irena laughed.

Ota and Irena left the apartment and climbed the stairs one floor higher. Irena rang the doorbell. The door opened, and Tonda stood there in his boxer shorts. Ota and Irena burst out laughing.

Tonda didn't understand: "Hi, what are you laughing at?"

Their laughter was cut short by huge, ill-mannered boxer Adam, who burst out of the door and performed his obligatory welcome ritual. He jumped on Ota and tried to give him a hug.

Ota defended himself with his hands and took a step back: "It's unbelievable how ill-mannered your dog is."

Tonda was amused by the dog's actions: "He takes after his owner. He's not only ill-mannered, he's also unteachable. Unteachable as his master."

Ota looked at Tonda: "Tonda, I believe that if that dog had any sense, he would at least wear pants."

Tonda didn't understand the rebuke: "Why? I don't wear them either."

Ota looked at Irena and shook his head. They sat down in the Moskalyk living room. Jiřina brought coffee.

"So, how's it going at Barrandov?" asked Tonda.

Hofman looked at him and shrugged. "Could you start with a simplier question? Don't you have any other in your repertoire? But since you're asking so nicely, Toman put a cop in my group. He sits there all day, writing down who comes in and who they talk to. He's been pretending to read a story for a week. What a jerk. He just sits there snooping around. I try to spend time at work as little as possible. When I need to arrange something, we meet somewhere else. Most of the time, my stomach knots up as soon as I get close to Jindřišská street. It's a strange pressure in my gut. Before I go in, I have to have a cigarette to calm down. When I see that slimy bastard, it gets even worse. I guess it can't be any different for you at TV. Strange times. But let's leave it at that. How's it going with **Granny** shooting?"

"Don't let it give you ulcers. Listen, a Volha is bringing two guys to the set in the morning, they say they're from production. They hang around there all day. I thought they were keeping an eye on the film budget, but I guess I didn't understand it right. The other day, one of those smart alecks even got in the shot and I had to reshoot the scene. How I yelled at him! Let's not talk about it. But I already told you, Oto, how beautiful it is in Ratibořice. It's a divine place. It's gorgeous. I just couldn't resist and bought a cottage there. Not far from Ratibořice, in Žernov. You and Irena have to come visit us."

"I know that area very well, Tonda. I spent my childhood in Bohdašín, which is not far from Ratibořice and Grandmother's Valley."

"Well, you see, you'll come, take a look at Bohdašín, it'll be nice."

"Thanks for the invitation, we'll definitely come," Ota looked at Irena.

Moskalyk's eyes lit up: "But what really makes me happy is that we managed to find a great girl to play Barunka."

"Do I know her? Who is she?" asked Hofman with sudden interest.

"She's a completely new girl with big eyes. Her name is Libuška Šafránková. Wait, I have a photo. I'll show you." Tonda stood up and handed the photo to Hofman, which showed a close-up of the actress's face.

Hofman looked at the photo carefully and liked it: "Well, she was born to be a princess."

Tonda was puzzled: "Why a princess? Are you writing a fairy tale now?"

"Why shouldn't I write a fairy tale? Božena Němcová and Karel Jaromír Erben wrote them, by the way, our most brilliant screenwriter I know, he just hasn't found an equally brilliant director yet. That's up to you now, Tonda, so get to work," he looked at Tonda and continued: "Everything has already been done. Dragons, princesses, magic and sorcery, greed, evil, good. But I don't want to just modernize the classics."

Tonda put on a dreamy expression: "You know, Ota, I actually enjoy the classics, maybe that's why I'm filming *Granny*, which was published in 1855. By the way, the script for it is really great."

Hofman took a sip of coffee and looked around the room.

Tonda looked at Irena: "I told Jiřina that I just signed it and that Franta Pavlíček is the author. Pavlíček is for sure the best for Božena Němcová."

"But now he's on ice, or rather, on the back burner, to be precise. It's terrible what's happening around us! You don't know how much I'd like to ask him to finish the screenplay for his beautiful story about Cinderella, but I don't have anyone else to turn to, I don't know who to ask so that it wouldn't be too obvious and would be at least somewhat believable. I already have scripts from people who aren't allowed to work right now, signed by all my friends from Barrandov and the radio, everyone who can write and who I can trust. At least, I hope I can," Hofman grinned.

"Then look around here, find someone from television," Tonda suggested.

"And how am I supposed to do that, Toníček? I don't know anyone there. Am I supposed to go there and ask the receptionist if someone would sign a script for me from an author who isn't allowed to film? You won't get anything for it, and if it gets out, your life will be hell, and mine too, by the way."

Tonda wouldn't give up: "Good material is hard to come by, Ota, and the really good stuff needs to be pushed forward. But I don't have to tell you that. You need someone who won't ask any questions."

Hofman asked sarcastically, "How about the new TV director, Jan Zelenka?"

Jiřina joined the conversation, "You want them to lock you both up and throw away the key, don't you?"

"Don't even mention that" Tonda grumbled. "You know he was fired from Květy magazine before August? After August, he went back, but everyone in the editorial office quit, so they approved him as TV director in Moscow. He got right to work and fired everyone from the basement to the attic who knew anything, so now there's almost no one left to work with us. Screenwriters, directors, technicians, and even the cleaning ladies, if they didn't have the right view of August."

"You're repeating yourself, Tonda, you already told me that," Hofman stated.

Tonda wouldn't be silenced; he was on a roll. "A TV drama play about the Thirty Years' War can't be broadcast because someone could easily mistake the Jesuits for communists."

"But... now I'm thinking of something... Zelenka, Zelenka, he's not the only Zelenka in the world, is he?"

Tonda and Hofman looked at each other.

"Ota, are you thinking what I'm thinking?"

"Tonda, I don't know what you're thinking, but if you're thinking the same thing that just occurred to me, then we're both thinking the same thing."

Irena looked at Jiřina: "Those two have lost their minds."

Jiřina Moskalyková agreed: "Completely."

Tonda turned to Jiřina, who looked at him blankly.

"I'm not going to say it. And please don't ask, it'll be better if it stays between us."

Ota Hofman got up to leave: "Well, Toníček, I'll give it a try," he said to Tonda.

After a moment, they said goodbye, and Ota and Irena headed downstairs. At home, Hofman immediately went to the table with the telephone. He leafed through the address book and found František Pavlíček's crossed-out phone number, which had been replaced by a new one.

"Pavlíček, who's calling?"

"Ota."

"Hey, Ota, good to hear from you."

"Franta, we should meet up."

"Sure, when and where?"

"Not at my place, but how about tomorrow at three, maybe in the garden under the astronomical clock?"

"Okay, I'll be there," confirmed Pavlíček.

Hofman hung up.

Meanwhile, Irena had made two coffees and was carrying them into the living room. "Shall we play another game?"

"Why not, Irenka."

"Otta Zelenka," said Irena briefly. "Yes?"

Hofman looked at Irena: "We've known each other for years, he's a decent guy."

They reached the coffee table, Irena placed the coffees on it, and they sat down. "Please be careful," she urged him.

"I can't do any better than that," Hofman nodded, "it just occurs to me that hiding, covering up, conspiracy somehow belong to our family's destiny.

I think about how our parents hid English airmen during the war. Honza Čermák, Zatřepálek, and others would come to our house illegally to sleep and wash."

"You see," added Irena," and they almost got them."

"Yeah, they almost did. Honza and Zatřepálek were staying with us when the German police raided the apartment. Evžen, as you know, my brother, was a representative of the Baťa company in Romania and stayed there during the war, and because food was cheap and readily available there, he sent a package to our parents in Zlín every month in a Baťa wagon. From there, the package, like other packages, was sent secretly to the addressee. The Germans found out and tracked down the recipients based on the addresses. Fortunately, it was only the economic police. They checked the resistance fighters' IDs and took them away. As they were being led down the stairs from the house, Honza Čermák took out a cigarette on the first step and asked the Germans for a light. They must have agreed on this beforehand, because Zatřepálek continued down the stairs without speeding up. Only when the door slammed behind him did the Germans start running, but they didn't catch him."

Irena took a sip of coffee. She liked listening to Ota when he told stories. She didn't mind that she already knew the story.

"So, my dad and mom ended up in prison in Pankrác, and Honza Čermák was sent to a concentration camp. Stella was already married to Lojza at that time, and they had a farm in Kostelní Lhota. After the arrest, she immediately came to Prague, picked me up from school—I was fifteen at the time—and signed me up for agricultural work, otherwise I would have been sent to the Reich. Our parents were imprisoned for about nine months. When we go back to Lhota, my dad will show you the certificate they received from the Queen of England for hiding English airmen. "

"Go on, hand it over," ordered Irena.

077 Central Bohemia, Strašín, August 2, 1970

"Hello," called Ota Hofman at the gate of one of the cottages in Strašín close to Říčany near Prague. He hoped he had understood the directions correctly, as they had been given to him over the phone. No one came, so he began to have doubts.

He tried again: "Hello, is anyone there?"

He tried the door handle. It was open. He entered the garden and was suddenly attacked by a dachshund barking furiously. He kept his distance from the intruder but defended his territory and barked to signal the rest of his human pack.

"Hi, Otto. You found it after all. I'm glad. Come on in. Bax, be quiet, he's a friend."

Bax understood that this was not an uninvited guest and stopped barking.

"Good dog," Hofman greeted the beast first. Only then did he look up at Otto Zelenka.

"Hello, Otto, I'm glad to see you too. I was beginning to have my doubts."

They entered the garden behind the brick cottage, accompanied by the proud defender of the property.

Chairs were set up at a table. The sun was beating down. It was a beautiful summer afternoon. Ota took a bottle of wine out of his briefcase and handed it to Zelenka. He was still holding the bouquet in his other hand.

"Bohumila will be here soon. When she heard Bax barking, she went to make coffee."

They sat down at the table. "So, what else have you brought us, Otto?" Zelenka asked directly. "It must be important, otherwise you wouldn't be here.

Bohumila Zelenková greeted the visitors with a tray in her hands. "Hello, Ota."

Ota stood up, waited for her to put the tray on the table, and handed her the flowers.

"Oh, they're beautiful. Thank you."

She set the coffee and cookies on the table and sat down as well.

"I'll get straight to the point," Ota Hofman began, and both listened attentively. "Franta Pavlíček has written a beautiful fairy tale about Cinderella. Everyone loves it, and I've even arranged to work with DEFA, but there's one problem."

"That it's Franta Pavlíček," Otta Zelenka guessed correctly.

"Exactly. We need someone to sign it for him. And I thought you could do it."

"Why don't you sign it, Ota?"

"To be honest, I thought of that too, but it would be very obvious, and I can't sign everything for everyone."

"Puddles, right?"

"No comment, Otto."

"Otto, you said Cinderella, a fairy tale," asked Otta Zelenka. Bohumila listened attentively to the conversation.

Meanwhile, Bax the dachshund curled up at the Hofmans' feet and closed his eyes.

"That's not a good idea, Oto. It's not for me. I'm sorry. I've never written a fairy tale before. I have to say no. It's not that I'm afraid, but as you say, it would be too obvious."

"Well, I tried," replied Hofman sadly.

"What if I wrote it?" asked Bohumila Zelenková. "I've written some fairy tales before. What do you think, Ota?"

Hofman was taken aback: "I'm speechless. You'd really do that?"

"Why not? If the fairy tale is as nice as you say, it would be a shame not to film it."

"All right then, I'll take you at your word. I'll tell Franta and we'll go ahead with it. Thank you. I have a meeting with him tomorrow, so I'll suggest it to him.

But Bohumila Zelenková gazed at the sky for a moment, thinking: "Ota, please remember that I'll have to rewrite the whole thing. I know Franta's flowery style, and I write

233

differently. And then I'll have to rewrite the whole thing on my typewriter. You know that even this is checked at our TV station to make sure it wasn't written on the wrong machine. But those are details, and I'll talk to Franta. So please let me know or have Franta contact me himself."

"You can count on me, Bohumil. No one knows about this, just the three of us, well, four, I have to include Irena. Franta will get in touch with you, if necessary, but I don't want to interfere in any way in what you agree, and I won't."

"It's a deal, Ota."

Otta Zelenka picked up his coffee cup and took a sip.

078 Prague, August 26, 1970

A few lazy summer weeks passed, and Hofman was once again sitting at his typewriter in his office on Jindřišská Street. There was a knock at the door. "Come in."

The door opened. Bohunka muttered, "Ota, you have a visitor."

Director Karel Kachyňa entered, clearly in a good mood: "Hi, Ota, how are the rabbits doing?"

Hofman greeted his long-time friend with pleasure: "Fine, I should be asking you that. How's it going with Kalužem?"

"Great, that's why I'm here. Would you like to see today's work?"

Hofman replied without hesitation: "Sure."

Kachyňa was brief and to the point, as always. Hofman liked this style. No long speeches, just straight to the point. "I've booked a screening at Barrandov for Thursday at four. Will you be there? It's scheduled for three o'clock."

Hofman was clearly looking forward to seeing the results of the shoot: "Great, see you there, and we'll discuss it."

"All right, take care. You too, Bohunka."

079 Prague, August 26, 1970

Kachyňa left, Hofman tidied up his desk, and said goodbye to Bohunka at the door. He looked around and got on tram 21. He was pleased to find a free seat and sat down. Behind him, he heard the quiet voice of Procházka in his hat and glasses.

"Hi, Oto, they're watching me day and night. I can't even call you anymore; they're always listening in on me. I'm completely broke, Ota. The money you gave me for Puddles is saving me; otherwise, I'd be begging. But I mainly want to ask how things are going?"

"What do you mean, Honza? You wrote Puddles so don't thank me."

"Well, how's Puddles going? Karel is filming, isn't he?" Procházka insisted.

"He's almost done. I just spoke to him; he invited me to work on set tomorrow."

"That's great. I'd like to see it too, where is it?" asked Procházka.

"At Barrandov in studio four on Thursday at three in the afternoon, but you can't go there, Honza, or do you want it to be exposed?"

Outside on the street, a strange guy in a trench coat raised a camera to his eye. Click.

A boy of about twenty stood behind him with a girl. The girl just turned and whispered in the boy's ear, "Isn't it weird, taking pictures of a tram just like that? Why is he doing that?"

The boy looked at the man in the trench coat. "I really don't know, maybe he likes trams."

The girl laughed. "You always have an answer for everything. That's why I love you." And she kissed him on the cheek.

080 Prague, September 2, 1970

The staff of the Barrandov film studios slowly gathered for the screening of the day's work on the film *I'm Jumping Over Puddles Again.* Hofman and Karel Kachyňa entered projection room together. In the still-lit screening hall, Hofman spotted a figure sitting alone in a hat. He recognized him, so he hurried over.

"Honza, what are you doing here?" whispered Hofman excitedly.

Jan Procházka replied in a whisper: "You know, Ota, I had to see it. My health isn't very good now. I'm running around to doctors; it's probably cancer. I'm here on leave, then I have to go back to the hospital, and I probably won't live to see the premiere."

"Please, Honza, what are you talking about?"

Hofman turned, and his eyes widened. Toman and Kliment were approaching.

Hofman managed to utter a remark: "Honza, whatever it is, you have to get out of here now. Otherwise, it's bad."

To save the situation, Hofman rushed toward Toman, blocking the view of Procházka as he left, while thinking about how to address Toman. A saving idea occurred to him: "Hello, Comrade Toman. Do you happen to know a Comrade Bureš? He keeps referring to you."

Toman, apparently drunk again, burst out with his hoarse laugh: "Oh yes, hello, Comrade Hofman. Pixa sent him to me, saying he was a relative, someone from the Central Committee, I really don't know who." Toman laughed heartily. "You know, Comrade Hofman, I didn't know how to get rid of him, so I sent him to you."

Hofman sneered: "Thank you very much, Comrade Toman."

Toman remarked confidentially to Hofman: "I don't usually come to work, but I've heard nothing but praise for you, Comrade Hofman, for how beautifully you wrote it. I really couldn't miss it, so I invited Comrade Kliment here as well."

He turned to Kliment: "So that we'll get a nice review in Rudé Právo, right, Comrade Kliment?"

Meanwhile, Jan Procházka managed to cover his face with his hat and headed out of the hall.

Hofman noticed Procházka's departure and apologized: "Excuse me, comrades, I'm a little nervous right now and I need to calm down."

Toman leaned toward Kliment: "Comrade Hofman can't stand being without a cigarette for even a moment. Let's excuse him, shall we? They say he runs on cigarettes."

Outside in the foyer of the screening room, Hofman caught up with Procházka.

Procházka stopped and waited for Hofman: "But the workers never go to work during the day."

239

Hofman bit back his anger: "Yeah, I understand, but... You know how it is. I have to get back. It was good to see you, Honza."

081 Prague, October 5, 1970

The hospital room on Charles Square was not exactly luxurious. Eight metal beds in a small space did not offer much comfort. Jan Procházka occupied one of them, the one by the window. He hadn't slept well during the night because the snoring of his neighbor, separated from him by a simple metal hospital table, was persistent and quite loud. That morning, he had had an X-ray of his lungs. He felt weak and very tired. He had the impression that he would hardly make it to the bathroom, located three doors down the hall. He had undergone surgery two days ago, so he lay there bored.

A nurse came to his bed with a stand and a bottle of solution. "Mr. Procházka, can you hear me?"

"Yes, I can hear you..."

"I need to insert an IV. Can you move your arm, please?"

Procházka turned his head toward her. She was wearing a white cap and seemed quite nice. He obediently stretched his arm and then placed it on the edge of the bed. He turned his head away.

"I'm going to give you a little prick now," the nurse apologized. She felt around Procházka's arm with her left hand and found a vein. She inserted the needle.

"It worked," she announced. She adjusted the flow of fluid from the IV, turned around, and was about to leave when two men in plain clothes blocked the narrow aisle between the beds. Both were wearing leather jackets and tesil trousers. They were pushing a wheelchair in front of them.

"Can I help you, gentlemen?" asked the nurse.

One of them pulled out a piece of paper. "We have permission to transport Comrade Procházka," he said and handed the document to the nurse. The nurse took it and asked the men, "Please let me through. The attending physician must decide. I have not been informed of any transfer."

The nurse squeezed between the men and ran out. A moment later, she returned with the attending physician, to whom she had already handed over the transfer document.

"Comrades, Mr. Procházka is now stable after a difficult operation, and his transfer is definitely not possible or desirable at this time. As the attending physician, I am responsible for the patient," the attending physician informed the men.

One of the men pulled out his State Security ID.

"Dear Doc, we are overtaking responsibility now, and if you prevent us, you will come with us, but I really wouldn't advise that. So," he added, pulling the wheelchair up to Procházka's head, "please kindly make way for us.

Our ambulance is waiting downstairs. "

The second man took the bottle from the stand and held it in his hand. With his other hand, he helped Procházka climb out of bed and into the wheelchair. He was wearing only a hospital gown.

"We're taking you on a trip, Comrade Procházka," one of the men announced cheerfully to the patient.

Procházka realized that they were from the StB, so he kept quiet. He just wondered what Pixa had in store for him this time.

082 Central Bohemia, Slaný, October 11, 1970

František Pavlíček learned about Jan Procházka's transfer to the hospital in the town of Slaný completely by accident.

He ran into Lenka Procházková on the street near the National Theater. Lenka was in tears, complaining about how they were moving her father around and that he was getting worse and worse. Pavlíček took a bus from Florence to town Slaný, and the trip took about an hour.

He found the hospital quite easily, and soon he was sitting on a metal chair with a bent plywood seat, and Jan Procházka gave him a very depressing feeling. He was very emaciated and pale.

"How are you?" Pavlíček asked the obligatory question.

"I brought you some bananas. I happened to come across them on the way," Pavlíček lied bravely. He had been looking for them all day yesterday, and it was only a bottle of rum that finally worked on a greengrocer, who brought the bananas from the warehouse to his otherwise almost empty shop with three commodities – potatoes, onions, and apples.

Procházka tried to smile, but it didn't come out very well: "They won't get me. I won't give them that satisfaction. You believe in God, Franta, and if I survive all this, I promise you I'll start believing too."

244

The door opened and two orderlies entered with a hospital chair.

"So where are we going this time, gentlemen?" asked Procházka, trying again to smile at his friend. "We didn't have time to discuss it, Franta. I'm sorry." And obediently, with the help of the orderlies, who didn't say a word, he transferred to the wheelchair, and the orderlies wheeled him out.

František Pavlíček remained sitting by the empty bed, feeling like crying.

083 Prague, October 14, 1970

Pixa took the elevator to the fourth floor of the Short Film building. He walked past the desk of his secretary, Eva. "Good morning, boss," she greeted him. Pixa slipped into his office without a word and closed the door. Then he returned.

"Call me..."

The secretary looked at him.

He looked at her for a moment: "Or don't. Don't call anyone, I'll call myself... Haven't I told you that I think it's unnecessary for you to dress up for work? I'd prefer it if you sat here naked and everyone could look at your beautiful tits. You've got nice tits, haven't you? Show me."

The secretary didn't understand what was going on: "Excuse me?"

Pixa continued to eye her: "Show me your tits," he ordered her.

The secretary stood up and walked over to Pixa, unbuttoned a few buttons on her blouse, and showed him her breasts in her bra.

"Nice. I made a good choice." Pixa silently assessed her breasts. "What size are they? I think we're about the same height."

The secretary replied, already familiar with her boss's mood: "I don't know, but I'd say so."

"Come here," Pixa ordered her.

The secretary stood still. When she saw that Pixa wasn't looking away, she walked over to him.

Pixa took off his shirt.

Now he was standing there in a white undershirt and commanded, "Now take off your blouse."

Without a word, the secretary unbuttoned her blouse completely and handed it to Pixa. He put it on, but didn't button it up.

"I need a slightly larger one."

"... Shall I get one for you?"

"That would be very kind of you, Eva. I wouldn't forget."

Pixa went to his office. He opened the door and took out a bottle of vodka. He took a deep drink and then laughed loudly.

084 Prague, October 15, 1970

The smell of a hospital room is almost the same in every hospital. The smell of disinfectants mixes with the smell of feces and unwashed bodies of patients. Jan Procházka could no longer tell the hospital rooms apart. This time he was lying alone in the room.

"Mr. Procházka, how are you feeling? Can you hear me?"

Procházka focused on the doctor in the white coat and replied weakly, "Yes."

"You've had another heart attack, but the worst is behind you. Now just stay calm and get yourself back together."

Procházka stared blankly at the doctor but said nothing.

The doctor left, and Procházka closed his eyes and tried to fall asleep.

He was awakened by noises. A wheelchair with two attendants stood by the bed. Pixa entered the hospital room between them.

Procházka focused on him, and at that moment his insides clenched.

"Well, look at you, you piece of trash. Now I'm going to take you to the detention center in Ruzyně. And if they manage to cure you in that state, you'll be on trial, and your address will be the Ruzyně prison for the rest of your life."

Procházka didn't have the strength to respond to Pixa's words. The two guards lifted him up and sat him in a wheelchair. One of them had to hold him steadily so he wouldn't tip over.

085 Prague, February 24, 1971

Martin Konopásek was sitting in Pixa's office waiting for his boss. The door opened and Jan Pixa entered. "Hello, Martin, what have you brought me?"

Martin Konopásek took a bundle of documents out of his briefcase. "I have photos from Procházka's funeral. As you instructed, we took security measures and there were no incidents. We secured everything. I put everyone I had on the job. The photos are divided into individual phases. The transfer of the coffin to the cemetery and then the lowering of the coffin into the grave. The analysis department recorded in detail who attended the funeral; those are the numbers next to the photos of the individual faces circled. Then there are photos of Procházka's movements before he died, when he asked to be released from the hospital; that's in this separate folder."

Pixa took this folder from the table and began looking through the photos. "I don't recognize anything here, what is this, please?" he asked Konopásek, handing him the open folder with an unclear photo.

"Ah, document number thousand two hundred four," he looked into another folder. "That was a bit of a nut to crack, but then we figured it out. That's Ota Hofman in the front seat of tram twenty-one, with Jan Procházka trying to hide behind him. It was August twenty-six, nineteen seventy, at the Jindřišská station in Prague."

Pixa ordered, "Give me back that folder." He leafed through it again. "What's this list?"

Konopásek peered over the table: "It's a list of everyone who attended the funeral. Phase two, that is, the burial."

Pixa leafed through the folder again. He looked at the photograph of the coffin, behind which Karel Kachyňa was standing in close-up. "Thanks, Martin, you can go now and leave the folder here."

Martin got up from his chair and left. Pixa sat for a moment and then also went out into the front room.

"Eva," he addressed the secretary, "please put six sheets of paper in the typewriter, I'll dictate."

The secretary obediently stacked the papers and placed them in the typewriter.

"Final report." Pixa began dictating. "Title: The Final Solution of Jan Procházka."

Slowly and monotonously Pixa dictated, so that his secretary Květa could write everything down. He described the operation in Paris in detail, deliberately omitting his arrest and severed fingers. He thought that the damned Procházka was to blame for the incident anyway. He described the media articles that his department had prepared to sway public opinion about the traitor Procházka in Rudé právo. He emphasized that it took less than two weeks after their publication for Procházka to no longer be asked for his

251

autograph on the street and for his books to be withdrawn from stores. His name was removed from projects that had already been filmed. Pixa gradually leafed through the folder from which he was quoting.

The secretary wrote and wrote... When she finished, Pixa ordered, "Mark the document as top secret. Send it immediately for translation into Russian, then send it by our courier directly to the Soviet ambassador, Chervonenko."

Then he smiled and said to his secretary, "I think I've earned myself a medal."

086 Prague, February 26, 1971

Soviet Ambassador Chervonenko sat in his opulent office in Prague-Dejvice, accompanied by Toman and Pixa.

Chervonenko nodded approvingly as he looked up from reading the report on Procházka's final solution: "Comrades, I have invited you here to thank you for your exemplary work with that traitor Procházka. Just as we agreed, Procházka has been removed in an entirely exemplary manner. Really good work, and believe me, comrades, I don't use words like that lightly."

Toman replied in accordance with protocol: "Comrade Ambassador. My colleague and I greatly appreciate your appreciation."

Chervonenko then continued: "And what about his closest associates?"

Toman took the floor: "We took care of that with party checks and surveillance. We eliminated the loudest voices, and some even started cooperating with our state intelligence service."

It was Chervonenko who added to the discussion: "To be honest, we have found that some are still actively involved in children's films, but they can't do any harm there. I would be particularly interested in Kachyňa."

"But Kachyňa isn't causing any trouble," Pixa now took the floor. "Sure, he met with Procházka at a time when

Procházka was no longer an employee of our state structures, but there's no need to impose any restrictions because of that."

Chervonenko chuckled, clearly in a good mood: "Let's say I'm in a good mood today, but we're not going to let him out of our sight, are we, comrades?"

Chervonenko looked at Toman, who nodded eagerly. Pixa just gave Toman a long look.

087 Prague, March 10, 1971

After a meeting with Jan Fojtík at the Cultural Committee of the Central Committee of the Communist Party of Czechoslovakia on the "Report on the situation and proposed further consolidation of Czechoslovak film industry," Pixa and Toman left satisfied. Their footsteps echoed through the corridors of the Central Committee building in Prague's Těšnov district. The document they had prepared had been approved.

"So, we finally got rid of that bastard Procházka," Toman muttered.

"It was about time," replied Pixa. He certainly didn't want to discuss with Toman the fact that it had cost him two fingers on one hand.

Toman still remembered the last meeting at Purš's, so he asked Pixa, "Why did you hire almost all the filmmakers I fired from Barrandov?"

Pixa appreciated Toman's momentary honesty and responded with honesty of his own: "You know how it was during the war? When the tide turned, every smart Nazi had a Jew he had taken care of during the war. None of them was executed."

Toman was still in a good mood: "I see you're not afraid of microphones?"

"There aren't any here," Pixa whispered in Toman's ear. "They're in the hallway across the hall. Who do you think had them installed here, Comrade Toman?

"I keep a close eye on my people, too."

Pixa chuckled: "You mean Mareček, the one you put on Hofman? You really won with that one. I got quite a few reports on him. He writes reports with an unsharpened pencil, and apparently, he asked if we also employ lumberjacks."

"And what will you do if the unreliable ones turn against you?"

"I'll wring their necks too," Pixa replied succinctly.

088 Prague, March 15, 1971

The telephone directory, Rudé Právo, and the other daily newspaper Práce were the three sources that František Pavlíček pored over every evening. He had now been out of work for four months, four months since he was dismissed from his job at the Vinohrady Theater. He had worked there as an artistic director since 1965, and then they fired him overnight. This search brought him no joy. However, being unemployed, i.e., without an employer's stamp on his identity card, was a criminal offense under Section 203. Since 1965, he had been facing an increased prison sentence of up to three years. Pavlíček knew this very well. He had no choice but to familiarize himself with this section of the law. In Czechoslovakia, since 1957, those who systematically avoided "honest work" and allowed themselves to be supported by others or obtained their livelihood by other "unfair means" were punished. This included those who, for example, wanted to earn a living independently without the appropriate permits, which were mandatory for self-employment. Now, Pavlíček was also facing trial. He first tried to find work with friends and acquaintances. However, his friends and acquaintances worked in editorial offices, theaters, and the official cultural sphere. So, he received very vague answers such as "Franta, I'll ask around" or "Franta, I'll let you know." Or "I'll definitely get back to you." Only in a few cases did he receive a direct answer. "Franta, with your personnel file, it's completely hopeless."

So, he tried to lower his expectations a little and thought he could work as a salesman. But wherever he went, they didn't even want to talk to him. A greengrocer or a butcher was the best he could hope for. Everyone wanted bananas from under the counter or had a craving for scarce liver, and it was expected that such goods would be provided in exchange for a small or large favor, a small or large non-cash remuneration in the form of other otherwise unavailable goods, or a small or large financial reward on the side. However, they did not like to let outsiders into this select circle, lest they not be completely loyal.

After a short time, Pavlíček gave up this option and started compiling a list of socialist enterprises in the telephone directory that he planned to visit the next day to ask about job opportunities. One of the companies he picked out that evening was Koh-i-noor in Prague, which manufactured, among other things, press studs for clothing, pencils, and writing implements.

The next morning, he entered the gatehouse of the socialist enterprise Koh-i-noor in Prague Vršovice quoter and asked the gatekeeper who could help him, a job seeker. He was already familiar with the procedure from his previous visits to socialist enterprises. He called it a fairy tale about a hen and a rooster.

The lady in the accounting department sent him to the planning department. There, he was told again that he had to go to the deputy production manager, whom he did not speak to, but his secretary sent him to the foreman in production. The foreman told him that he did not make the decisions, and when he asked who did, the foreman refused to talk to him any further, saying that it was none of his business. So he went back to the gatehouse, where he started all over again and tried to give the gatekeeper a pack of cigarettes. The gatekeeper looked around to see if anyone was watching, took the pack, and whispered in his ear: "Second floor, room two hundred twenty-four."

František Pavlíček knocked on the door marked 224. "Come in," came the reply.

"Hello, I'm here, please, is that right, comrade? I'm applying for a job at your socialist enterprise."

The fat woman ruling the room 224 looked him over for a moment, then motioned for him to sit down. "I need to fill out a few forms with you first," she told him. She prepared the first form, which Pavlíček already knew, having filled it out several times in various places.

She began to ask: "Name?"

"František Pavlíček."

She wrote the name in the box.

"Date of birth?"

"November 20, 1923."

"Highest level of education?"

Pavlíček answered truthfully: "Doctor of Literature."

The clerk looked at him again, sizing him up, but wrote down the information.

"Last place of employment?"

"Artistic director of the Vinohrady Theater."

This time, she did not write the information on the form. Instead, she asked another question: "Before that?"

"Screenwriter and dramaturge at the Barrandov Film Studio."

"Highest political position?" she continued with her questions. But she did not write anything down.

"Candidate for the Central Committee of the Communist Party of Czechoslovakia."

She put down her pencil and asked, "And what, pray tell, do you do here?"

Pavlíček replied, "I told you at the beginning. I'm looking for work."

"Dear Comrade Pavlíček," the woman began, "there are plenty of intellectuals like you around these days, but we need people to work, especially now that we're behind schedule."

Pavlíček wanted to protest, but the clerk waved him away. "We'll be in touch."

"But you didn't write down your phone number or address."

"Well, you see, that's probably because we won't need them."
And she looked at him mockingly.

089 West Germany, Cologne, March 18, 1971

Gert was not looking forward to going to the office of WDR boss Müller. He was waiting to hear what had happened on the other side of the barricade. He hoped it was nothing important that he didn't already know about, but he still had a knot in his stomach. He entered the office, sat down, and waited. Müller was on the phone, saw Gert, and nodded in greeting. "Okay, let's meet at the café by the cathedral tomorrow at three in the afternoon, bye," he ended the call and hung up. "Hi, Gert, take a seat."

Gert tried not to provoke him and find out what mood his boss was in today: "Good morning, boss."

Müller started: "Hey, Gert, the comrades in Prague are making fun of you, aren't they?"

Gert's uneasy feeling immediately intensified: "What's going on?" he asked innocently.

Müller looked him in the eye and leaned toward him. Gert groaned inwardly, knowing he was in trouble again. Müller began: "Some political officer from Prague, some idiot, wrote to me. Wait. His name is Toman. He has reservations about Hofman's script. They've already redubbed it at DEFA."

Gert tried to look uninterested: "Oh dear."

Müller continued: "He literally writes here that it is out of the question for a line by some Werich to remain in the script."

Gert replied: "But he's a great actor. You know he played Blofeld in a Bond movie? But to avoid any trouble, the camera wasn't allowed to show his face. "

Müller wouldn't let it go: "Those Americans have gone crazy."

"Well, the producer of the American studio is originally from Barrandov," Gert added.

Müller burst out laughing: "What a surprise." He returned to the letter on the table: "Look, this sentence is... I'll read it to you, listen carefully: 'I can't forget it to my red brother.'"

Gert smiled. "Ah, the comrades probably think it's a reference to Soviet tanks."

"Is it?" Müller asked inquiringly.

Gert shrugged: "What do I know... Communists stick to the well-known slogan – just because I'm paranoid doesn't mean they're not after me."

"What are we going to do about it?" Müller pierced Gert with his eyes.

Gert just shrugged again: "What do I know, I'd leave it there. What can they do to us?"

"Yeah, what can they do to us. I agree. We won't forget our red brothers in the West. Let that asshole come here and kiss my ass," Müller said, relieving the tension.

090 Prague, May 12, 1971

The neon sign "Kino Světozor" on one of the buildings on Wenceslas Square in Prague was impossible to miss. It was an unusually warm May evening, and the invited guests and journalists still had a few minutes before the premiere screening began. Ota Hofman kept two tickets but came alone.

He had saved the second ticket for someone who couldn't make it. He didn't feel like talking to anyone. He had arrived a little early, but only to fulfill his formal obligation, which his name in the film credits compelled him to do. He had made a decision he was committed to, so he lit up again. He glanced at his watch. I have to go, he said to himself.

After a few quick puffs, he threw away the cigarette butt and stamped it out. He never liked having to speak in public. Especially today. And today, he wanted to say something completely different from what he had carefully prepared. He sighed and set off, forcing a smile among his colleagues and acquaintances.

091 Prague, May 12, 1971

At the moderator's invitation, a number of filmmakers took to the stage in front of the screen. The microphone was passed from hand to hand. Karel Kachyňa was the first to speak, and Hofman was very pleased that he did not mention him as the screenwriter.

Then he handed him the microphone. Hofman thought for a moment, then began to speak: "First of all, I would like to thank Karel Kachyňa for taking on this film project and for choosing such excellent actors. He has done a wonderful job of bringing the script and the message of Alan Marshall's book to life. Thank you."

Then he was handed three carnations by a girl and quickly passed the microphone to Vladimír Dlouhý, the lead actor. He didn't listen any further, just waited until he could leave. He was startled by the applause from the hall and, as if in a dream, followed Karel Kachyňa down the stairs. They sat down in their designated seats in the front row, leaving an empty seat between them. Without consulting each other, they both placed their carnations on the empty seat. The curtain opened. The film began.

The title appeared on the screen: "Screenplay by Ota Hofman." Karel Kachyňa, who was sitting next to him, saw the title reflected in his glasses, which he almost never took off. At that moment, he was looking at Hofman. Hofman looked around as if someone might know who the real author of the screenplay was. He noticed Kachyňa's gaze.

He nodded, and another caption appeared on Kachyňa's glasses: "Directed by Karel Kachyňa." Hofman stood up and headed out of the theater. He went to the foyer to smoke. Director Vorlíček saw Hofman leaving, also stood up, and pushed his way through three occupied seats in the second row to the exit.

He headed toward Hofman. "I alveady saw it at the appvoval scveening, veally very nice, Oto. It's the best scveenplay you've wvitten so far.

Hofman looked away sadly. He'd had enough: "Are you sure? Then I'm not very happy."

Vorlíček, who had a slight speech impediment, doubted him: "Ota, veally? It's veally good, I think it's your best scveenplay so fav. I'm a little jealous of Kachyňa for finding such a talented wviter after Pvocháska turned out to be such a son of a bitch. Do you happen to have another tveasure like that in youv dvawer?"

Hofman took a drag on his cigarette, scratched his temples, and looked at Vorlíček: "There's a lot of interesting material in our group, Václav. If you're interested in something, we can definitely work something out."

092 Prague, May 12, 1971

Even though it was late in the evening, Ota Hofman and his wife, Irena, were playing solitaire and drinking red wine.

Irena waited for Ota to start talking. She knew what he had been through today and that it had probably been bad for him. But she didn't want to ask. She remained silent.

"Well, I feel like a scoundrel and a crook," Ota began. "It was the worst premiere of my life. I felt like the biggest fraud there."

Irena put down her glass and dealt another card: "By signing someone else's work, you didn't do anything wrong."

"But I've never, do you hear me, never had such a response to my work as I have now. Everyone is congratulating me on what a great script it is. They say it's the best thing I've ever written. I have to pretend that I'm pleased, thank them for something that isn't my work. Why didn't anyone ever say this about any of my work before? I'm starting to seriously doubt myself. What if I can't write at all?"

Irena tried to calm Ota down: "Ota, we both know you did the right thing. You couldn't have acted differently. And besides, you can write. You know the Germans are punctual, but they accepted your scripts on the first try. Who gets that kind of luck? And *Pan Tau* was a great idea; there will be more."

Ota Hofman took a card from the deck. He took a drag on his cigarette and drank some wine.

"I'll never sign someone else's work again," he decided.

Irena nodded and also took a card from the deck.

093 Prague, May 13, 1971

Hofman entered the dramaturgy group's office in Jindřišská late in the morning in a foul mood, looking gloomy. Bohunka Šourková had her face buried in Rudé právo.

As always in the morning, Hofman greeted everyone: "Good morning, Bohunka, coffee, please."

Bohunka, hidden behind the large format of the Rudé Právo newspaper, replied: "Good morning, Ota. So you've got the blessing from above. I'm reading some amazing reviews of yesterday's premiere by the great Kliment. Wonderful, wonderful. They say it's your best script." She paused for a moment and added, "I really don't envy you at all. You know what, I'll read it to you."

And she began to read aloud: "The power of the film begins with the excellent screenplay by Ota Hofman and Karel Kachyňa, based on a story by Australian writer Alan Marshall, whose book of the same name was published in 1962 by Mladá fronta in Czech translation."

She paused for a moment before finding her place again and continuing, letting Ota drink the truly bitter cup to the dregs. "This is definitely Ota Hofman's best screenplay to date. The entire work is deeply human. It testifies to the talent of its creators, screenwriter Ota Hofman, director Karel Kachyňa, and cinematographer Josef Illík. Especially them..."

The phone rang on the secretary's desk. Bohunka interrupted her reading and picked up the receiver:" Hello, children's film dramaturgy." She listened for a moment. "One moment, please." She covered the receiver and called out, "Oto, you have a phone call, it's Wagnerová."

Hofman shook his head dismissively.

Bohunka said into the phone, "I'm sorry, he's not here, please call back later."

Hofman couldn't take it anymore and ran out of the office: "Bohunka, I'm done here for today, and I won't be back." He gathered his things and left.

The tram ride to the tiny cemetery in Košíře didn't take long. It was a beautiful sunny morning, and as he walked among the graves, an old lady cleaning one of the older gravestones greeted him. "God bless you".

He greeted her in return and headed for a small, fresh gravestone a little further away. He recognized the figure standing next to it from a distance.

"Hello, Karel."

The inscription on the gravestone was brand new, not yet weathered by time: Jan Procházka, February 14, 1929 – February 20, 1971.

"Hello, Oto."

Neither of them wanted to start talking. They stood there in silence. Words were unnecessary.

But then Karel Kachyňa spoke. "I don't know why, but I thought you'd come." He reached into his breast pocket and pulled out a hip flask. Then he reached into his jacket pocket and pulled out a small glass.

He asked, "Would you like some?"

Ota nodded. Kachyňa poured and handed the glass to Ota.

He took another glass from his other pocket and poured himself a drink: "Here's to you, Honza."

They clinked glasses. They drank.

An old woman standing near watched everything, shook her head, and thought to herself: That's the way things are these days. These people have no respect even for the dead.

094 West Germany, Cologne, May 13, 1971

The hallway of the WDR television headquarters in Cologne, through which Gert was walking with his boss Müller, was long and bright. At the end, there was an elevator, which they were both heading for. Müller had a toothache and was going to the dentist that afternoon, so he wasn't in the best of moods: "Gert, if it's nonsense..."

But Gert assured him: "It's really very good."

Müller persisted: "I admit that *Pan Tau* is a name I like, but I don't like the idea of sending money to the other side of the Iron Curtain. Doesn't that leave you cold? We're supporting communism."

Gert shook his head, stopped at the elevator, and pressed the button to call it: "You can't look at it that way. Those people are poor. My dad fought at Stalingrad, and I grew up in such poverty you can't imagine. Have you forgotten what it was like here after the war? I think we both know how shitty it is when you're on the losing side."

Gert opened the elevator door, and they stepped inside. The doors closed behind them.

Müller pressed the button for the first floor: "Do you think the communists will lose in the end?"

The elevator started moving. Gert didn't hesitate: "Sometimes, of course, they have to."

The elevator stopped, and Gert opened the doors. A sign flashing PROJEKTIONSAAL was visible on the elevator door next to them.

Müller took Gert by the shoulders, and they entered the screening room.

The projection began. Jiří Malásek's catchy theme song *Pan Tau* started playing, and a bowler hat flew onto the center of the screen.

095 West Germany, Cologne, May 13, 1971

Müller, in a noticeably better mood, left the projection room with Gert. He immediately exclaimed cheerfully, "Gert, it's great. We'll sell it." Then he grimaced as a sore tooth made itself felt.

Gert was clearly pleased: "Sure. The Eastern Bloc is off limits to us; the Czechoslovakians sell it there themselves and then have to send it to Moscow, but the Western Bloc is ours. They have an embargo there. We'll offer it to the Austrians, the French, the Spanish, and see what happens."

Müller thought for a moment: "And who actually wrote it?"

Gert replied: "Ota Hofman."

"Is he German?"

Gert shook his head. "No, he's Czech. We met in Venice a few years ago, he won the main prize there with the film *Clown Ferdinand and the Rocket*."

"Oh, is that him? He's got good ideas. Does he speak German?"

"Of course." Müller suggested, "When can he come and see me?"

Gert hesitated, "It's not possible right now. He's got problems there, but I'll try to push it."

Müller nodded innocently, "Excellent."

096 Prague, May 14, 1971

Dr. Purš's office in Prague's Barrandov district was lavishly furnished, but rather tastelessly. A meeting of the Czechoslovak Film Company's management was taking place around a heavy oval table: "So, what else is on the agenda for today?"

Toman spoke up: "Here you are, comrades, the list of film festivals for this year," he said, handing out photocopied sheets of paper. "We need to agree who will go where and who we will send."

Purš took the list in his hand: "So what do we have here? Venice. Our western partner WDR sent three episodes of the new series *Pan Tau* to the children's section. We're not filling the adult section. "He looked up from the paper and cleared his throat:" I was there last year; the sewers stank so bad you couldn't stand it." He read on: "Tehran, you can't be serious! No one will get me there." His eyes scanned the entire list. "I don't see Cannes. Why isn't it on the list, Comrade Toman?"

Toman replied: "Cannes didn't accept our film for the competition, Comrade Purš."

Purš looked at him: "And what did you send them?"

"The best we've got. *I'm jumping over puddles again*. Well, they didn't accept it. They don't even want to talk to us. They say we've sidelined our best film directors, so they don't want our inferior films."

Purš looked back at the paper: "Well, we won't force ourselves on them. Moscow, I see you sent *The Key*. That's your work, if I'm not mistaken, Comrade Pixa. What's it about? I haven't had the pleasure of seeing it."

Pixa accepted the challenge: "It's about a communist hero who, even in times of greatest distress and fear, cannot betray the party."

Purš paused for a moment: "That's clear. I'll write note, to Moscow, Comrade Pixa. And who directed it?"

Pixa replied with a sour face: "Vladimír Čech."

Purš quickly decided: "Then you'll both go, as a delegation."

"He'll be delighted," Pixa remarked a little maliciously. "I'll let him know."

Toman joined the conversation again: "But they approached us from Tehran this year, and we're trying to improve relations between our friendly countries, so we sent *I'm jumping over puddles again*. But I'm willing to sacrifice myself.

Kachyňa can't go; he's still in big trouble with *The Ear*, and Hofman is unreliable. They might try to escape. But they're both good at their jobs, so we kept them. At least I won't look like an idiot there."

Purš nodded: "All right, then. I'll write to Tehran, Comrade Toman. And we'll send Comrade Brousil to Venice, he'll sort things out, and we won't look like idiots too."

097 Prague, May 17, 1971

The offices of the Barrandov children's film department were bustling. Toman burst through the door and grabbed Bohunka Šourková. "Is he there?" Without waiting for an answer, Toman burst into Hofman's office.

Ota Hofman was sitting at his typewriter, typing away.

Toman began: "Hi, Oto. Got a minute?"

"Sure," replied Hofman.

"I spoke to Jindřich Polák and your West German."

Hofman perked up: "Yeah, Müntefering."

"I can't pronounce that. Never mind. Listen, you asked me to go to Cologne, but they won't let you go. Only director Polák and Otto Šimánek will be going to the presentation of *Pan Tau*. I'm sorry. The German left this letter for you at the reception desk."

"He was here?" Hofman whispered.

"He was, but he can't just come up here, of course, you understand."

Toman handed Hofman the letter.

"I'm doing you a favor. I hope you understand. We're in the same boat," Toman added.

Hofman took the letter and opened it.

HI OTA. WRITE A LIST OF THINGS YOU WANT TO BUY IN GERMANY AND GIVE IT TO JINDRA OR ŠIMÁNEK. GERT.

098 West Germany, Cologne, May 24, 1971

Gert parked his Mercedes right in front of the restaurant in Cologne. He got out of the car carrying three huge, stuffed shopping bags. He walked over to the table where Otto Šimánek was waiting for him with a smile. Šimánek made a Pan Tau gesture and stood up from the table: "You are the real Pan Tau."

Gert, out of breath, smiled: "I feel like one. My secretary spent two whole days looking for this, but I think everything on the list is here. Where's Jindra?"

"He's still out shopping, he'll be here later." replied Šimánek.

"I've got everything you wanted, including for Ota, who they wouldn't let come with you. There are medicines, perfumes, jeans, men's shirts, and something from a sex shop. I don't know who wanted that," Gert assured him.

Šimánek blushed a little: "That's for me and my wife."

Gert was amused: "Sure."

Šimánek perked up with joy at the sight of Gert's wallet. "What are we going to eat?"

Gert had no reason to disappoint him: "We'll have something special." And he ordered a local specialty.

"I will take the same." Confirmed order Šimánek. He didn't understand what he had ordered, but he didn't want to ask.

A large portion of beautifully presented and expertly served food with various types of meat appeared on the table a moment later.

Delighted Šimánek looked at the plate and asked, "So this is the cancer, the capitalism that the Soviets are protecting us from?"

Gert smiled but said nothing.

Šimánek tasted it, closed his eyes with delight, and after a moment remarked, "But it tastes great."

099 Prague, May 30, 1971

At the main station in Prague, a train was waiting at platform 2 to depart for Gottwaldov. Václav Vorlíček was already sitting in the compartment, glancing at his watch from time to time. There were only a few minutes left before the train departed.

The compartment door opened, and a man with a suitcase squeezed in. It was screenwriter Miloš Macourek. Like every year, the two were on their way to the International Film Festival for Children and Youth. And like every year, they were traveling to Gottwaldov by train.

"Shit, I almost missed it. Hold the damn door," Macourek muttered.

Vorlíček reached out and held the door: "You've got five minutes."

Macourek took his suitcase and threw it up on the shelf: "What? Are you kidding me? I'm telling you, don't piss me off, Vašek."

"Sit down and calm down," Vorlíček reassured his colleague.

Macourek finally sat down and looked at Vorlíček: "Don't tell me to calm down. Don't you dare. You know that only pisses me off."

"It's okay, Miloš. We have a long way to go to Gottwaldov. By the way, I spoke to Ota Hofman yestevday."

Macourek perked up: "So?"

"He's coming with us and we'll sort it out with him. They found some good matevial fov us in his gvoup. It's a book by a woman who wovks in a phavmacy."

"Shit, another quack, or maybe even a witch."

Vorlíček chuckled amusedly: "You've not fav fvom the truth. It's called The Givl on the Bvoomstick. It's about a young witch. And do you know wheve she's flying to?"

But Macourek was in high spirits: "To Moscow... or to hell. Where do you think she's going to fly? How should I know where she's going to fly? Vašek, you're really annoying me with your questions!"

"No, she's a witch and she's going to fly to the wovld of people."

Macourek sneered: "That's going to win, man. I'd rather stay in a cottage on chicken legs."

100 Moravia, Gottwaldov, June 1, 1971

The Hotel Moskva in Gottwaldov was well located on a hillside, right next to the main festival cinema, which could seat over a thousand spectators. The International Film Festival was based here, and festival guests also gathered here.

Ota Hofman was drinking his coffee with Gert Müntefering in a small bar next to the hotel reception. A smiling waitress walked by and asked, "Would you like an ice cream sundae?"

Hofman thought about it. The waitress waited for his decision.

"You know, I think I'll have one."

A child with his mother approached their table. He was about seven years old. He looked at Hofman: "Hello, Mr. Writer. I saw you at the cinema this morning."

Hofman was amused. "Where did you see me?"

The boy was bold: "In the cinema, of course. You were presenting your film."

"Really? Are you sure you haven't confused me with someone else?"

"No, I haven't, Mr. Writer. I recognized you by your jacket. Then they showed the film. It was called *Pan Tau*."

His mother was embarrassed: "He's a screenwriter."

"Hello, Mr. writer and screenwriter."

Hofman was enjoying himself: "I'm also a dramaturg."

The boy repeated like a machine: "Hello, Mr. writer, screenwriter..."

"I was joking. I'm Ota."

The boy obediently continued: "Hello, Ota."

His mother slapped him on the head and added, "Be polite, okay?"

Hofman looked at her and felt sorry for the boy: "You shouldn't have done that. Maybe one day he'll come up with the theory of relativity like Professor Einstein. Do you know how many brain cells a slap like that kills? And how did you like *Pan Tau*?"

The boy replied, "I liked him. He was big and small and helped children. And he wore a hat."

"A bowler hat," corrected Hofman.

"That too," remarked the boy.

Ota Hofman smiled.

The mother took the boy by the hand: "Let's go. Don't bother the gentleman."

Amused, Hofman replied, "On the contrary, that was one of the best reviews I've heard of *Pan. Tau*. You have a great future ahead of you because you weren't afraid to come and tell me."

The waitress came over: "Here's your ice cream cup."

Hofman replied quickly, "That's for the critic, isn't it?"

His mother hesitated: "No."

"Yes, you are. I insist," Hofman looked at the mother, then saw the boy's shining eyes.

Hofman nodded to the boy, who sat down with the ice cream and began to eat. His mother stood shyly over him.

Gert didn't understand the conversation in Czech, but he seemed to be enjoying himself anyway: "What did he say?" he asked Hofman.

"That he liked the screening of *Pan Tau*."

Gert smiled: "I arrived yesterday morning and saw in the program that *Pan Tau* is playing today at seven in the morning. Do you understand? At seven in the morning. That's completely crazy. "

"And you see, it was full," replied Hofman, watching the boy stuff himself with ice cream.

Gert complained:" That really got to me. And then there's the way all your bigwigs look at me like I'm part of the scenery. No one even said hello to me."

"I don't know what to say to you, Gert. It's rude."

Two men entered the hotel in friendly conversation. Karel Zeman spotted Ota Hofman at the bar, said something to his colleague, and both approached the table where the little critic was finishing his fee.

"Mr. Hofman, allow me to introduce you to the composer Mr. Zdeněk Liška."

Hofman stood up and smiled at Zeman: "We already know Mr. Liška. We met in Karlovy Vary."

Zeman sighed: "Oh, I see. My apologies."

Gert watched them but had no way of joining the conversation.

Hofman then addressed Zeman: "Allow me to introduce Mr. Gert Müntefering from WDR production. Gert, this is Mr. Karel Zeman," Hofman switched to German.

Gert beamed: "Hello, it's very nice to meet you. I really liked your last film, *On the Comet*, and then... ah, *The Deadly Invention*, The Fabulous World of Jules Verne, right? I know it, very nice."

Hofman continued with the introductions: "Gert, this is the composer Liška. He composed the music for *On the Comet* and *The Deadly Invention*, and then for more than a hundred other films, right, Mr. Liška?"

"Do you speak German, Mr. Liška?" Gert asked.

"No, unfortunately," Liška replied.

"We were very pleased to meet you. Now, please excuse us. By the way, Mr. Hofman, would you like to stop by my place this afternoon for a chat? I live in a villa just above the studios."

Hofman was delighted and accepted the invitation: "I'd love to."

Liška added: "Around three, perhaps."

"Fine."

Zeman watched the conversation and said only to Hofman and Gert: "We'll see you at the reception this evening. See you later, gentlemen."

101 Moravia, Gottwaldov, June 1, 1971

Hofman sat in the study of Zdeněk Liška's villa, which had been designed for him by Slovenian architect Josip Plečnik, who was also the chief architect of Prague Castle. Although it was pouring rain outside, he didn't have far to go from his hotel, as the villa was within sight of the film studios.

Over his host's shoulder, he admired the large organ that the composer had built there. Hofman considered the invitation a welcome addition to the festival program. "You'll have your work cut out for you with our group, Mr. Liška. Last time we were in Karlovy Vary, we talked about an idea I had for a film. It's been approved. Two have been approved. I would be very happy if your music could be used."

"And who has the honor of directing, if I may ask, Mr. Hofman?"

"Karel Kachyňa will direct both, and Josef Illík will be the cameraman for *The Train to heaven* The second film is simply called *Love,* and Josef Pávek will be the cameraman."

Liška stood up for a moment, poured cognac, and brought the glasses to the table: "That's great news, they're all experts."

Then he thought for a moment: "You say simply... Love." He stood up again, walked over to the organ, and began to play. He sang a folk song: "Love, God, love, where do people find you, you don't grow in the mountains, they don't sow you in the fields..."

Hofman nodded in agreement with a smile: "That's it. We have our central theme. You know what? As soon as I get back to the office, I'll send you the script and the contract. Karel will be thrilled that I got you."

Liška returned to the table: "It's a pleasure working with you, Mr. Hofman."

Then they clinked glasses.

"The cameraman Kučera was in my office recently, and he mentioned you," Hofman continued.

Liška took a sip: "Yeah, I know. He takes nice pictures."

Hofman continued: "And he said that since he knows you're composing the film, he's shooting long takes so they can be used as title sequences for your music."

"Yeah. I have an agreement with a few guys from the camera crew, including Illík. But you must have some crutch too. Children's films aren't exactly three hours long, and I hear that sometimes you can't even get the required 70 minutes together to show it in theaters as a feature film."

Hofman smiled: "Sometimes the guys come to me and say they're short. So, I tell them to put in some fireworks. It looks good and fills a few minutes."

Liška nodded in agreement: "And you can put music under it."

Hofman felt comfortable with Liška; they understood each other. "Exactly."

Liška asked, "Would you like another shot of cognac with me?"

Hofman hesitated, but gave in: "I will, but it'll be my last. I have to get going."

Liška looked at Hofman: "Would you mind if I didn't go with you today? I've had enough for one day. They'll be drinking that clear alcohol again. And I hate that stuff. "

Hofman smiled understandingly:" Of course. Let me ask you one more question. You're a classical composer, so why do you mainly compose for film? Doesn't it bother you that your music won't be played in concert halls?"

Liška smiled too: "Who says it won't? Which of today's composers writes music that will be heard by millions of listeners in a year? How many times would I have to sell out the State Opera?"

102 Moravia, Gottwaldov, June 1, 1971

As every year, the festival reception took place in the studios in Gottwaldov. Ota Hofman joined the filmmakers as soon as he saw Macourek and Vorlíček.

Macourek had just put down his glass: "Good evening."

Hofman glanced at him and shook his hand.

Vorlíček greeted him: "Hi, Ota."

Hofman also shook his right hand. "Hi, Vašek. When did you arrive?"

Macourek was clearly in a good mood: "This afternoon. We were terribly delayed. Vašek came up with an idea for a *The Girl on a Broomstick*. We almost got into a fight over it, but I think we've got it."

Hofman continued smoothly: "I know. I read the book. So guys, if it makes sense, we'll go with it."

Director Pinkava approached them: "Hi, Ota." He and Hofman had known each other for years.

"Hi."

Pinkava took Hofman by the arm: "Can I talk to you for a moment?"

Vorlíček nudged Macourek: "I don't mind, but I can't speak for Miloš."

Macourek started up again: "What are you doing to me?"

But Hofman and Pinkava had already moved aside: "Hey, how do you see it this year? Will we get more awards here in Gottwaldov, or will you guys from Prague?"

"Does it matter?"

"Maybe to you. You live in Prague, but here it means something."

Hofman objected: "But I'm not a native Praguer. These things don't apply to me."

"Then write something for us."

"No way. You have your own authors here. That wouldn't be good."

Pinkava insisted: "Exactly the opposite. You know how they'll grow up if an author from Prague writes something for them?"

"I'll think about it," replied Hofman, excusing himself because he saw Zeman.

At that moment, the new director of the Gottwaldov studios, Jaroslav Šťastný, walked by, singing something in Russian.

Zeman was pleased to strike up a conversation: "Good evening, Ota."

Hofman replied humbly: "Good evening, Master."

Zeman looked Hofman in the eye: "You have to write it. We need those dinosaurs like a pig needs a scratch. And by the way, tomorrow you will receive an award with *Pan Tau*. The children chose your *Pan Tau* as the best thing they saw here. Congratulations."

103 Moravia, Gottwaldov, June 3, 1971

Macourek and Vorlíček met in a room at the Moskva Hotel in Gottwaldov to write. They took turns creating. One typed on a portable typewriter while the other drank a bottle of Pilsner beer. Macourek finished a page. Vorlíček read it. Then he sat down at the typewriter and wrote a page. When he took it out of the typewriter, Macourek read it.

Macourek grumbled, "What is this, Vašek? What is this?"

"It's an idea. Funny, isn't it?"

Macourek's temper flared again: "Hofman said he'd take it if it was good, not if it was crap."

Macourek took the bundle of papers and tried to tear them apart.

Vorlíček tried in vain to calm him down: "Miloš, don't be silly."

Macourek yelled, "You're crazy!" He stood up and kicked the chipboard cabinet so hard that his foot went right through it. He was still in a rage: "What the fuck is this shit! Fuck, that hurts like hell, do something, you moron!"

"I don't know who's cvazy. Is my leg in the cabinet?"

Macourek continued to yell on one leg: "Dude, don't act like a tough guy and get my leg out of there right now!"

Vorlíček was already amused: "Get it out youvself."

Macourek hopped on one leg: "How am I supposed to do that? I can't!"

Vorlíček ran to the kitchen. He pulled a plastic cutlery holder out of the table. A typical prefabricated item. He chose a knife, knelt down, and began to carve Macourek's leg out of the cabinet. Macourek held on to him with his hand and cursed like a sailor, but he couldn't be understood. It was a jumble of hissing, cursing, and sobbing. But in a moment, the leg was out.

Macourek, now a little calmer, remarked, "You're so lucky!"

Vorlíček didn't understand: "That I didn't catch you?"

Macourek added, "No, that you're working with me."

104 Prague, July 21, 1971

Back home but still full of impressions from Gottwaldov, Ota Hofman read the finished script for **The Girl on Broomstick** in his office at the Barrandov film studio in Jindřišská Street and laughed as he did so. He pressed the button and said, "Bohunka, please call Macourek."

After a moment, the connection was established: "Miloš, it's excellent. I've read it all, and we'll definitely make it. Really great. Hey, what are you doing this afternoon? Do you have time...? Our colleague from Cologne is here, Gert... On the Rhine, not the Elbe."

Macourek replied cheerfully, "That works for me. By the way, Ota, I heard you're looking for an apartment for your daughter. You probably don't know this, but I happen to be the chairman of the Writers and Filmmakers Housing Cooperative, and we're just building new apartments in Podolí, down the river. If you're interested, we can talk about it."

Hofman was taken aback by the remark for a moment, but then it dawned on him: "Yeah, it's rumbling there. We'll talk about it. See you at three in Jalta, and thanks."

Bohunka Šourková peeked into the office: "Sorry to bother you, Ota, Karel Kachyňa is here and says you need to see Toman."

Hofman hung up and saw Karel Kachyňa in the doorway.

Hofman asked Bohunka, "Is he back from Tehran already?"

Bohunka Šourková looked at him and shrugged, "I guess so, if you're going to see him. Immediately," she pointed out.

105 Prague, July 21, 1971

Hofman and Kachyňa had no idea what was going on, so they exchanged only a few words on the way there.

"Ota, do you know what's going on?"

"I don't know anything, Karel."

Both of them were racking their brains trying to figure out why Toman wanted to see them both so suddenly and urgently.

Toman's secretary was already welcoming them: "As soon as you arrive, you are to go straight in."

Toman was clearly still in his traveling clothes, but he was full of euphoria: "I wanted to tell you, comrades, as the first ones. We won big time in Tehran. Imagine we got diplomas for best film and best screenplay. I'll have copies made for you." Still elated, he continued: "That Shah Reza, he's a real guy. Look, I have a photo of us together. See, that's him, Reza, the Shah, and his beautiful wife, and here, here, that's me. If you could have seen the reception, there was a pile of luxury food and drink there...."

Toman got up from the table and opened the door of a cabinet full of various statuettes, cups, and festival awards. " And they gave me this for best film." He pulled out a large golden duck. "Isn't it beautiful? I don't even deserve it."

He showed the award to Hofman and Kachyňa, but didn't even let them hold it, quickly putting it back in the cabinet and closing the door.

Toman added with shining eyes: "Are you as happy as I am, comrades?"

Hofman and Kachyňa looked at each other. "Anything else, Comrade Toman?"

"No, that's all. You know, comrades, shared joy is double joy. You can go."

As they were leaving, Hofman asked Kachyňa at the door: "Come to my office for a moment, I have some news from Gottwaldov."

"Are you relieved, too, Ota? I was afraid of what would happen. Maybe they would stop our films, Train or Love."

"Yeah, I was scared too, but now it will be nothing but good news."

They understood each other and decided not to comment on Toman's performance.

106 Prague, July 21, 1971

Gert and Ota were sitting in the garden of the Jalta Hotel on Wenceslas Square, beer on the table.

Gert was also staying at the Jalta and was not in the best of moods: "Ota, I'll tell you, I felt like a fool when I arrived in Cologne thinking we'd won in Gottwaldov with **Pan Tau**, and they didn't even bother to give me the prize. I didn't even bring home a stupid diploma."

Hofman took a sip: "I'm glad they gave it to us at all. They don't give me any prizes either. I don't know where they all end up."

"So they're like socks. You put them in the washing machine and don't understand how you can only get one out," joked Gert.

"Sure. Gert, but now let's talk about Macourek, who's coming. Look, he's a peculiar guy, but he's an excellent author.

"Oh, I'm used to that."

"Not to this. You'll see."

A figure approached them on Wenceslas Square. It was Macourek. He looked quite nervous. Gert stood up and used a few words of broken Czech that he had already learned: "Good afternoon, Mr. Macourek. I don't speak Czech very well."

"I don't speak German very well either, Mr. Müntefering."

Gert didn't understand, so he turned to Hofman: "Never mind. Ota will translate for us."

Macourek looked gratefully at Hofman.

"Mr. Macourek, I really liked the script."

Hofman translated.

Macourek modestly lowered his eyes like a lover on a first date.

"It will need to be rewritten a bit. I estimate about half of the dialogue," Gert added with a completely stony expression.

Hofman translated.

Macourek's face turned red, and suddenly, he started spewing a torrent of profanities. After a moment, Gert and Hofman burst into hearty laughter.

"That's unique. I've never seen that before, Ota."

"Me neither, Gert."

Gert leaned toward Hofman: "I'm going to do that to him all the time."

"And I'm definitely not going to translate that," they both laughed.

Macourek didn't understand why they were laughing: "So what's going to happen?"

Hofman, once again acting as interpreter, translated.

"Don't worry, it'll be Sexana," said Gert. He enjoyed this little joke over and over again. Whenever the conversation turned to *The Girl on the Broomstick*, he never called the main witch hero by her name, Saxana. From the very first moment, she was, is, and always will be Sexana to him.

"And we'll buy her for our TV," he added dryly.

107 Prague, October 12, 1971

Toman sat down for coffee in his office. His secretary came in: "Comrade Director, Comrades Valtera and Hladký are here."

Toman looked at her and waved his hand as if to summon them: "Excellent, send them in."

Two comrades in their forties entered the room.

Valtera greeted him obsequiously: "Honor to your work, comrade."

Toman nodded to him to sit down: "Honor, take your seats."

They sat down.

Toman rested his elbows on the table and clasped his hands: "So you got the idea, and you understand the assignment?"

"Yes, comrade."

"We put all the characters you wanted in there," replied Hladký.

Toman wanted to make sure: "Procházka, Pavlíček, Vaculík, and all those other scumbags?"

Valtera sat almost at attention: "Yes, comrade."

Toman smiled: "Well, boys, let's hear it."

Valtera pulled out a stack of papers and began to narrate: "It's called *The Golden Osmar*, we kept the title you came up with, comrade."

Toman nodded: "Excellent."

Valtera added: "The main character is called Špacír."

Toman looked triumphant: "Sure, that's Procházka."

Already cheerful, Valtera continued: "Exactly. Špacír leaves school to write about socialist realism. He writes an optimistic script about bricklayers who love their work. But he runs into trouble with the dramaturgy. Roubíček laughs at him."

"Roubíček as Pavlíček. That's excellent. He'll go crazy when he sees that. A minister, no less. Well, don't let that disturb you, comrades," commented Toman.

Hladký felt it necessary to join the conversation: "Roubíček and his advisor will laugh at him. You won't get anywhere with that today. Do art! Do you know the new wave? Špacír is troubled by it, so he'll start going to Prague cinemas to see films like *The Fireman's Ball, Coach to Viena, The nun's night,* and we'll show them there, in the film, so that people can see them."

Toman's eyes lit up: "That's interesting, and then?"

Valtera took over: "Špacír realizes that in order to succeed, the bricklayers have to be slackers, they won't work, they'll go out for beer, and since they'll need money for that, they'll start stealing."

Toman nodded in agreement: "That's good. That has depth. Idleness leads astray."

306

"We've written it down for you here. Read it," Hladký handed the bundle of papers across the table.

Toman left them lying there, looking extremely satisfied: "Thank you, gentlemen. Where there's a will, there's a way."

108 Prague, October 19, 1971

The painting Absinthe Drinker by Viktor Oliva in the back of the Slavia café located opposite the National Theater in Prague, was a frequent witness to Ota Hofman's meetings, where he did not want or need any other attentive ears or eyes. In his offices, Mareček carefully monitored everything that was going on. Hofman was not sure whether StB operatives were sitting somewhere nearby with headphones on and tape recorders carefully recording every word spoken in the office.

Karel Kachyňa stretched himself out around the tables at the front of the café and headed without hesitation for the bench where Hofman was already sitting under the famous painting.

"Hello, Karel," Ota Hofman greeted the newcomer.

"Hi, Ota. What awful weather," said Kachyňa, taking off his soaked raincoat and leather cap. He sat down and removed his thick-rimmed glasses to wipe them dry with a handkerchief.

Ota Hofman waited for him to finish his ritual. "The usual coffee, or something else?"

The waiter noticed the new arrival and approached the table to take their order.

"I'll have the coffee and some water, please."

Ota Hofman waited for the waiter to leave: "I was at Toman's office. They've stopped us from continuing with the preparations for the film *Love.*

They don't like the main character, a writer who isn't allowed to write or publish anymore. "You know, Oto, I was a little worried that it wouldn't get through. The paranoia is terrible right now. They examine every word in every story, every script, and woe betide me if I don't follow the approved script to the letter on set. You know I've told you that before."

"Yeah, we've talked about it, but we can't keep watching ourselves all the time, wondering what will be allowed and what won't, and putting a muzzle on our work, as you say, permanent paranoid self-censorship. We'd never get anywhere. We're not just here to shoot, we're here to create!"

They both waited for the waiter to place the coffee and a glass of water on the table. When he left, Kachyňa started talking again as he stirred his coffee: "You know, Ota, they control me and everything I do. They forced me to give up working with Honza Procházka, *The Ear* and *The Nun's Nights* are now locked away in a vault, and they won't let me make adult films at all. The fact that I can work with you is actually a miracle. But let's not cry about it, knowing you, I'm sure you've already come up with something. Otherwise, you wouldn't have called me, even though I have plenty of time now, and I really don't like being out of work."

"Yeah, take a look at this, I rewrote it a bit," Hofman handed Kachyňa a folder of papers. "I rewrote the writer who can't publish into a hockey goalie who can't practice his profession anymore, as well, and I think it could work. I left in *Love* no politics, no allusions, just a calm sea. You'll have to add more imagery than we intended to make it at least a decent movie."

"A hockey goalie, you say. Fine, I'll be happy to read it."

But today was a day, Hofman thought to himself on his way to the tram stop on Jindřišská Street. It was evening, not exactly a pleasant dark autumn day; it had just stopped raining, but Hofman decided to take a walk anyway to clear his head. He headed familiarly from Národní třída across Wenceslas Square to the Jindřišská Tower. He looked at the building where Barrandov had its offices. The lights were still on in the windows. "They could at least turn them off, damn it." And he headed inside to do so himself.

109 Prague, October 19, 1971

Hofman entered the lit office on Jindřišská Street. Mareček was trying to unlock his desk drawer. Hofman turned red: "What are you doing at my desk, comrade?"

Mareček really didn't expect this. He stood frozen, staring awkwardly at Hofman. Hofman suddenly grabbed his stomach. He managed to gasp, "Get out, now!"

He unlocked the desk drawer and gathered all the files from the drawer into a bag. He only managed to notice the title page, which was on top of all the files. "Jan Procházka *Boys Will Be Boys* Literary script". Sweat poured down his face as he staggered out. Mareček had long since fled.

110 Prague, October 19, 1971

Irena Hofmanová had her ironing board set up and was just finishing one of her husband's shirts when the phone rang.

She picked up the receiver and immediately cried out anxiously, "When did it happen?"

She listened again. Her son Otto heard the cry and ran out of his room.

"How is he, where is he, where did they take him?"

Irena paused and listened to the voice.

"I'm on my way," she blurted out after a moment.

"What's going on, Mom?"

Irena, looking worried, began to explain: "Dad had a stomach ulcer at work. He's in the surgical ward at Vinohrady Hospital. Stay home in case they call again. I'm going to see him."

111 Prague, October 19, 1971

It was well after midnight when the key rattled in the lock. Irena Hofmanová was returning home. Her son was waiting for her and immediately asked, "So, how is Dad?"

Irena slipped into her slippers: "He's had the operation and is in intensive care. They said he was in a bad way. The ulcer burst inward instead of outward. That could have led to blood poisoning and who knows what else." Otto asked anxiously, "Will he be okay?"

Irena smiled at him, "He should be now. They have him under control. It's late, you should go to bed. I'll go see him in the morning and hopefully they'll let me in."

"But Mom, ulcers are caused by stress, I heard."

"You heard right, Otto. You know, Dad's been under a lot of pressure lately. He's had a lot of worries at work, and the current situation hasn't helped his health either. I'm sure he'll tell you everything, but please leave him alone now, and even though you're seventeen, it's still better not to ask him too many questions. He had to keep a lot of things to himself." Otto wouldn't let it go: "That sounds like something out of a spy movie."

Irena smiled:" You know, Otto, it's not about a movie, so don't ask any more questions. He'll tell you everything one day. When the time is right and the moment is right."

"Okay, I won't ask anymore."

112 Prague, October 22, 1971

Toman was in his office, checking the financial results of the Barrandov Film Studio again.

The phone rang on his desk. His secretary asked, "Comrade Purš is on the line, should I connect you?"

Toman agreed, and Purš came on the line: "Yes, it's me, honor to you, Comrade Purš."

"Honor to you. I looked at the financial statements, and it's pretty awful," Dr. Purš began.

"We're doing what we can, Comrade Purš."

"Do more. We need foreign currency. The republic needs foreign currency. Do you understand? Foreign currency and then more foreign currency. The only thing that brings us foreign currency is children's productions. I saw in the tables that children's productions account for as much as 80% of Barrandov's foreign currency income. Christmas is coming, and what are we going to buy bananas for the people? There won't be any bananas, people will be restless, there will be problems, and we definitely don't want problems. I also heard that your employee, chief dramaturge Comrade Hofman, is currently hospitalized."

Toman was well informed about Hofman's hospitalization: "Yes, Comrade Purš, he has health problems."

Purš yelled angrily into the phone: "I heard that too, damn it, why!"

Toman was shaken and breathed deeply into the phone. Purš was not usually foul-mouthed.

"You screwed up, comrade. You totally screwed up." Purš continued, and not in a calm voice.

Toman defended himself: "You wanted me to keep an eye on him!"

This made Purš even angrier: "Keep an eye on him, yes, but not kill him, you fucking faggot! Hofman is the only one we have; I could have a dozen directors like you. So, act like it. He has my blessing now. He wanted to go to Germany, so let him go to Germany, let him go whenever he wants, damn it. Start acting like my director! Everything is at stake! Do you know how much pressure I'm under from the Central Committee? "

Toman's adrenaline also began to rise: "Yes, Comrade Purš."

After hanging up the phone, Toman had beads of sweat on his forehead. That was a rush, he thought to himself. The financial results were sent out yesterday afternoon.

113 Prague, October 22, 1971

The secretary peeked into Toman's office. "I didn't want to disturb you, Comrade, but Comrade Mareček is here and wanted to speak to you."

"Send him in," ordered Toman.

Mareček entered and saw that Toman was red in the face, but he didn't know why: "Good day, Comrade Toman."

Toman glared at him. Then he began to speak, but very quietly: "Mareček, Mareček. What am I supposed to do with you?" His voice slowly grew louder: "What an idiot!"

Mareček shrugged his shoulders in confusion: "I don't understand you."

Toman was already yelling: "He says he doesn't understand! I must be dreaming! You screwed up, Mareček. Totally screwed up. Do you know the eleventh commandment, you idiot?"

"No, I don't," Mareček whispered.

"I won't let you catch me, you moron," Toman yelled.

Mareček began to defend himself: "But you wanted me to watch Hofman carefully, you said you wanted to know his every move."

Toman sighed and, as he calmed down, watched Mareček: "You watched him, you idiot, but you didn't kill him. I only have one Hofman, but I could have a dozen such Marečeks!"

He paused for a moment. Then he continued: "What's wrong with you, Mareček?"

Toman looked at the papers in front of him.

"Comrade Mareček, do you know anyone in Ostrava?" he asked in a calm voice.

"No, Comrade Director."

"That's good. Buy a train ticket and report tomorrow to Major Karásek, commander of the Ninth Administration of State Security. He is looking forward to seeing you. You will be assigned new tasks. Leave!" Toman commanded.

Mareček's eyes widened, and he gasped for breath.

He wanted to object, but Toman didn't give him a chance and shouted," I said leave!"

Toman remained seated in his office, trying to calm down.

The phone rang again. The secretary said dryly into the receiver: "Comrade Director, Comrade Hofman is on the line."

Toman put on the nicest voice he could muster: "Put him through..." Click, click.

"How are you doing? I heard about your health scare. Are you all right?"

114 Prague, October 22, 1971

Hofman was still weak from the operation, standing by the phone in the ward of the Vinohrady Hospital. "I was told to call as soon as possible. But if you ask me, Comrade Director, considering the circumstances, I'm doing quite well. I would like to..."

Toman interrupted him: "I have Comrade Mareček's resignation letter on my desk. He regrets to inform me that his artistic abilities do not meet the requirements of his current position in the dramaturgy group for children and young people, and he is requesting a transfer. You agree with that, don't you?"

Hofman was taken aback by the announcement: "Of course, I agree."

"And your request for a business trip to Cologne has also been approved. All future business trips will be a mere formality, so you have the green light. Let me know when you're fit for work. Anything else, Comrade Hofman?"

Hofman had nothing to add. "No, that's probably all. Goodbye, Comrade Director."

"You know what, call me Ludvík."

"I can't bring myself to say that," Hofman protested.

"Then call me Ludva."

Hofman paused: "Is that supposed to be a joke?"

Toman repeated: "You can call me Ludva."

Toman hung up. He was smiling.

After a moment, Hofman burst out laughing so hard he had to hold his stomach.

115 Prague, October 25, 1971

"Rrrrrrrrrrrrrrrrrrrrrrrrrrrrrrrrr."

Eva Košlerová, an attractive woman in her late thirties, editor and dramaturge at Czechoslovak Radio, was home alone and had just come out of the bathroom, where she had enjoyed a refreshing shower. Cinda, her spaniel, was barking furiously at the door.

Oh well, it's probably the fire department, she thought to herself, and wrapped a towel around her freshly washed hair.

The doorbell continued to ring: "Crrrrrrrrrrrrrrrrrrrrrr. Woof, woof, woof." The noise echoed throughout the apartment.

"I'm coming," she called, slipping into her bathrobe. "Is there a fire?" she called again and went to open the door.

When she opened the door, the doorbell finally stopped ringing.

Standing at the door was František Pavlíček's wife with a scowl on her face.

"I knew you were home," she said very loudly, so that the whole building could hear her.

She tried to shout over the dog's barking. "Woof, woof, woof."

"Quiet, Cinda," Košlerová tried to silence the dog and grabbed Cinda by the collar.

"I was really wondering where Franta had disappeared to this time, but this would never have occurred to me," Pavlíčková began, leaning her hand against the door frame.

Eva Košlerová was still unable to utter a word in response.

She tried to calm the dog down.

"I could show you photos of the children my husband so recklessly abandoned for a slut, but you know them well. I thought we were friends, that we understood each other. And you just stole my husband! And what's worse, you steal a father from his children!"

Košlerová stood there frozen, unable to find the right words, not knowing how to respond to the loud outburst.

"He's finished, completely washed up, they kicked him out of the theater and before that out of Barrandov, he's done for," Pavlíčková threw in her rival's face, and suddenly it dawned on her.

"So... you got a script at Barrandov, what a coincidence! What did you actually write, you pathetic slut? A radio editor, my ass! Now suddenly, the muse has kissed you and you've written a fairy tale about *Prince Bajaja*. Did Barrandov reject you before? Nooooo!" Pavlíčková answered her own rhetorical question.

"They didn't, so at least admit it. You're silent, aren't you? But I won't leave it at that, I'll see to it, and they'll get rid of you too, you bitch," she cried, turned around, and ran down the stairs.

Eva Košlerová closed the door.

116 Central Bohemia, Pečky, November 11, 1971

At the train station in Pečky, František Pavlíček was holding a broom in his hand, and five Gypsy men were standing next to him, smoking cigarettes and discussing something. They were looking Pavlíček up and down.

One of them remarked, "What's he doing here?"

Another replied, "I don't know, probably a cop."

Pavlíček overheard the conversation but remained silent, staring at the broom he had just been given as a new member of the work crew.

The foreman interrupted the group's musings: "Come on, guys, let's go. Or do you want to send them invitations in the mail, you fuckers?"

Pavlíček trailed behind the Gypsies with his broom in his hand. Suddenly, a figure appeared in front of him, a familiar female figure, the last person he wanted to see right now. Standing in front of Pavlíček was his wife, with whom he was in the process of divorcing.

Pavlíčková looked him up and down, glanced at the broom, then at the group of Gypsies. She sneered and said, "You got fired from the theater, huh? You fucking bastard!"

"How do you know?" Pavlíček defended himself.

Pavlíčková was already in full swing: "They called me. You're going from one mess to another, aren't you?"

Pavlíček looked at the amused Gypsies. They couldn't help but hear the angry woman.

"I signed the divorce papers, and so did you."

The Gypsies watched the confrontation with great interest and were undoubtedly enjoying it.

Pavlíčková was on a roll again today: "You're wrong, you bastard, it won't be that easy. You're not allowed to do that, and you're breaking the rules again."

This angered Pavlíček: "Excuse me?"

Pavlíčková was unstoppable: "You do things you shouldn't, don't you? You go to bed with other women. What's more, my former friend, when you have a wife and children at home!"

The master stepped by the amused Gypsies and listened to the argument between them. Pavlíček only noticed him now.

"Hey, stop it. Who's interested in you?" Pavlíček tried to silence her.

But Pavlíčková continued to yell: "Don't worry, they'll be curious. I sent a letter to Barrandov saying that you wrote *Prince Bajaja*. You think that just because you're banned and someone covers for you, you'll get away with it? And her, too, right? And then you'll use the money to start your new shitty life, right? You really haven't figured out why you're holding a broom instead of a pen, have you? Well, you've miscalculated, young man. You shouldn't have chosen my friend, she told me everything, you bastard!"

Pavlíčková turned around and walked away with her head held high.

The foreman was the first to recover: "Hey, you National Theater. Get a move on."

117 Prague, January 9, 1972

Hofman was sitting in Bohunka's office at the secretariat in Jindřišská, enjoying his coffee and cigarette. Toman burst through the door and commanded, "Come next door."

Both entered the chief dramaturge's office, and Hofman closed the door behind him.

Toman sat down in Hofman's chair. "Hello, Ota. I've received a denouncement," he began.

Hofman froze.

Toman continued smoothly: "I spoke to Kachlík, but I wanted to check with you first."

Hofman became nervous. "Check what?"

Toman looked at Hofman for a long time: "František Pavlíček's wife wrote to us saying that *Prince Bajaja* was written by her ex-husband, not Eva Košlerová."

Hofman didn't let on and replied decisively to Toman: "That's out of the question."

Toman probed further: "That's what director Kachlík, who is filming it now, said too. We got rid of Pavlíček for good, didn't we?"

"You can look in the film file. All the documents are there."

Toman nodded in agreement: "Of course, I've already looked. But you'd tell me, wouldn't you? I won't find out somewhere that you're playing some kind of game with me?"

"You can count on it. I'd tell you hundred percent, Ludvík. Definitely," Hofman declared resolutely.

Toman rose from the chair of the group's chief dramaturge: "All right, then. Never mind, I'll leave you to it. Just get on with your work."

He left the office, and Hofman breathed a loud sigh of relief. Suddenly, Toman returned. Hofman felt uneasy.

Toman remained standing, leaning against the door frame: "One more thing. I'm such an idiot. I forgot to tell you something. You won't believe it, but I have your permission to travel to West Germany. You're going to Cologne."

"That's impossible!"

Toman added slyly: "It is. And I also have a request that Wagnerová from the press will go with you. I envy you. She's a real catch."

Hofman didn't understand: "Wagnerová? The journalist?"

"What's wrong with her, Oto?"

Hofman was at a loss: "Of course I like her."

Toman waved his hand in a broad gesture: "What's the matter now?"

"Nothing, Ludvík. I was making sure that there is just journalism involved. Otherwise, I'm not interested in anything else."

Toman added, "You should probably be more interested in why she's going there. She'll be interpreting for you and representing us. They want her to write an article about the restoration of the Cologne Cathedral. And that suits me down to the ground, because I'll be tying her to me a little, if you know what I mean."

"But I speak German well," Hofman pointed out.

Toman snapped, "I know you know a little German, but your test results are marked with an exclamation mark, in case you've forgotten. She's a pro at this, you're a pro at being a Barrandov dramaturg."

"And besides German, is that girl a pro at anything else?" Hofman couldn't resist a snide remark.

Toman shot Hofman a hateful look.

Hofman ignored it and fired back at him: "Singles or doubles?"

Toman got angry: "What?"

"Well, I just don't know what to tell my wife if you order two single rooms or one double room," Hofman explained.

Toman waved his hand. He understood that Hofman was making fun of him. "I wish I had your problems. If the party books you a bunk bed, you lie down on it. You can also sleep on hay."

118 Prague, January 9, 1972

At his desk in his office, Hofman was mulling over his conversation with Toman. He stood up and walked past Bohunka. "Bohunka, I have to take care of something. I'll be back in an hour."

Bohunka nodded in agreement and picked up the newspaper. She would have some free time now and wanted to enjoy it.

Hofman went outside, reached into his pocket, took out a pack of cigarettes, lit one, and continued on through the park toward the Jindřišská Tower. He walked past it to Senovážné Square and headed for a phone booth.

He stepped inside, took out the number he had written on a piece of paper, and dialed.

"Hello, could I speak to Mr. Pavlíček, please?" he asked when a voice answered.

"He's not here right now, but I can call him."

"Okay, how long should I wait?"

"Try back in ten minutes."

Hofman hung up and threw his cigarette butt on the ground. He went outside and waited. He glanced at his watch.

Ten minutes later, he dialed the number on the piece of paper again.

"This is Pavlíček, who's calling?" came the voice on the other end.

"Hi Franta, I'm calling you at work on the number you gave me. I'm calling from a phone booth."

"Is that you, Oto?"

"Toman was here. He was reported that *Prince Bajaja* wasn't written by Košlerová, but by you."

Pavlíček was silent and listened.

"Kachlík covered for you, and he'll take the fall. I understand that he tried to refute it, and maybe he took it from him. He doesn't trust me, and I don't know if he really bought it. Do you know who could have reported you?"

"I know," replied Pavlíček.

"Then can you try to calm the informer down somehow. There are more people involved, and they could pay for it," warned Hofman.

"I don't know if I can do that," lamented Pavlíček. "Well, thanks for the information, I'll be more careful. And while we're on the subject..."

"What else, Franta?" Hofman wanted to end the conversation.

"I've been thinking about Cinderella. She always seemed so dull to me. I thought I'd mix the Cinderella fairy tale with the fairy tale about the three evil sisters, where there are also magic nuts. What do you think?"

There was a moment of silence before Hofman refocused his thoughts: "That sounds like a great idea, Franta."

"You know, Oto, I didn't know that when you're completely screwed up, that's when you come up with your best ideas. Now I finally understand."

"Take care, Franta."

Hofman hung up and headed back to his office. On his desk lay the reviews he was not looking forward to reading at all.

119 Prague, January 10, 1972

Hofman took the elevator to the top floor of the Short Film Studio. He had no idea why Kamil Pixa had called him and why he wanted to talk to him so urgently.

"Good morning, Comrade Hofman. Comrade Pixa will see you right away," he heard as soon as he opened the door to the director's office.

Soon the door flew open and loud laughter rang out: "Hi, Oťásek."

Hofman replied with some hesitation: "Good morning."

Pixa gestured invitingly and motioned him to come in.

"Would you like some coffee?" asked the secretary, Eva.

Pixa replied, "Oťásek prefers cognac, and I'll pour it myself. I'm not here for anyone else."

He took Hofman by the shoulders and led him into the office. He turned back to the secretary and licked his lips.

Pixa looked at Hofman for a moment: "I invited you here, Oťásek, so we could finally talk in peace. We have mutual acquaintances, we work in the same field, and yet we hardly know each other."

"We don't know each other, but I'd say you know more about me than many of my relatives and friends."

Hofman knew very well who he was talking to, and there was no point in playing blind man's bluff.

Pixa laughed: "You're right. Were you at Procházka's funeral?"

"I think you know very well, that I was," Hofman retorted.

Pixa didn't hide anything; there was no point: "And you're right again. I heard you're giving Karel Kachyňa another chance."

Hofman confirmed the information, but he knew that the less he said, the better: "Yes, he's preparing to shoot a film based on my screenplay, Train to Heaven."

"Is this your first collaboration?" Pixa asked.

Hofman got angry: "Is this supposed to be an interrogation? You know he already filmed I'm Jumping Over Puddles Again based on my screenplay."

Pixa didn't answer: "I'll pour us another drink."

Hofman shifted nervously and instinctively touched the knot of his tie.

"No, no interrogation." Pixa brought two glasses. "I was just testing you a little. And you can be sure that an interrogation would look a little different, don't you think? I asked for the script for that film and read it. It's good. Very good. "Pixa took the bottle of Hennessy cognac he had received from Gert. "I like memories of the war. Have you already chosen where it will be filmed?"

"Kachyňa would like to shoot it on a remote railway line in Slovakia. But we're a little worried that it's too far from civilization," Hofman replied.

Pixa handed Hofman a shot glass: "That'll be a good choice. The further away from Prague, the better. We've been instructed to focus a little on Kachyňa, and that goes against my grain, if you know what I mean."

Hofman nodded: "I appreciate that. Thank you for telling me."

Pixa clinked glasses with Hofman.

Pixa became serious, took another drink, and began: "Now on to the next thing. I read your requests and looked at the projects that would combine animation with live action. Honestly, it doesn't look bad. I'd be happy to support Karel Zeman's project and write a request to Toman for Krátký film to collaborate with Barrandov. I don't see a problem with that."

Hofman thought that was probably why he had called him:" Excellent, I'm glad to hear it."

"But don't get your hopes up. Toman will sweep it off the table. He can't stand me. But my conscience is clear."

Hofman shrugged.

"I heard you're leaving for Cologne tomorrow to meet with the West Germans," Pixa changed the subject.

"Yes, we'll be negotiating possibilities for cooperation on other projects," Hofman confirmed.

Pixa added, "The Republic needs foreign currency, and you're objectively good at negotiating, so don't screw it up for us. A broken money machine isn't good for anyone. Especially not for you. Are you going with Wagnerová?"

Hofman nodded and thought to himself. How does he know? But then he tried to answer himself.

120 Prague, January 13, 1972

Of course, this wasn't the first time Hofman had been preparing for a trip. He was always a little nervous, and his thoughts seemed to be elsewhere.

"So, do you have everything?" asked Irena in the bedroom of their apartment in Prague's Spořilov district. They looked together at the open suitcase.

"I think so, and even if I haven't, I'm going to civilization, so I can buy whatever I forgot there."

"Do you have a razor?" Irena wouldn't let him off the hook.

"How much time do we have?" Hofman asked.

"You're leaving in an hour and a half," Irena replied.

Hofman zipped up the suitcase and carried it to the hall. "So, we can have another game."

They went into the living room together, but Irena returned to the kitchen to make coffee. Hofman didn't forget to light up again. Half an hour later, they got up and took the elevator down.

The car was parked nearby. Irena unlocked it, Hofman put the suitcase in the trunk, and they got in.

"Are you sure you have everything?" asked Irena, who was driving, mainly reassuring herself.

He shrugged. The road was clear, and soon Irena pulled into the parking lane in front of Prague's main train station. She didn't get out.

"Be careful..." she said goodbye.

Hofman got out and took his luggage out of the trunk. He approached the open window and kissed Irena. "Bye."

"Bye."

He walked into the station building. Irena knew she couldn't stay there, so she headed home.

The train departure board announced that the train to Nuremberg was leaving from platform 2. Hofman headed there with his suitcase in hand.

As soon as she saw him, Klára Wagnerová waved at him from the train window. He boarded the carriage and made his way down the aisle to the compartment.

"Hello," said Klára, "I was getting worried, it's about to leave."

"Hello," replied Hofman, putting his suitcase on the rack.

"We're changing trains in Nuremberg, you know that, right?"

"Of course, Mr. Hofman, would you like to sit by the window?"

Both seats opposite them were already taken by an elderly couple.

"Thank you, but that's not necessary, I'm fine here," replied Hofman. A few minutes later, the train started moving.

121 Prague, January 13, 1972

Irena parked her car and headed home. She took off her shoes in the hall and went into the living room, picked up the empty coffee cups, and carried them to the kitchen. She noticed something on the dining table.

Isn't that Ota's briefcase? she thought. She put the cups in the sink, returned to the briefcase, opened it, and found his passport, an exit permit, cash in marks, and traveler's checks. She froze, but only for a moment. She glanced at her watch and knew immediately that the train had long since departed. She grabbed her purse with her documents, Ota's briefcase, and quickly put on her shoes. She didn't wait for the elevator and rushed down the stairs.

She jumped into the car. If only I hadn't asked him if he had everything! She cursed silently.

Oh well, the next stop was Karlovy Vary, Ota had mentioned that when he was playing cards. It'll be a showdown, she thought. She started the car and drove off into the darkness.

122 Train to Karlovy Vary, January 13, 1972

The train had picked up speed, and their conversation had slowed down a bit. The man and woman sitting across from me unpack a large amount of food. It seemed enough to feed a regiment. They eagerly began eating schnitzel and pickled cucumbers. The door opened, and the conductor entered. "Tickets, please."

He glanced at the pile of food and remarked, "The dining car is two cars back."

Klára handed over her ticket. Hofman stood up and began searching through his coat. When he couldn't find anything, he took down his suitcase, placed it on his seat, and opened the lid. "Just a moment, please," he apologized to the conductor.

Suddenly, he felt a wave of heat wash over him. His bag with his documents wasn't there. What now, damn it? He thought. This is a disaster!

"I think I left my documents at home," he said to Klára.

"Do you have a ticket or not?" asked the impatient conductor.

"At home, but that's not going to convince you, is it?" Hofman turned to him.

"No, it won't. If you don't have a ticket, you'll have to get off at the next stop."

"Where's the next stop?"

"Karlovy Vary." But Hofman already knew that.

The conductor left.

"What are we going to do?" asked Klára.

Meanwhile, the other passengers had cleared away all their food and were looking questioningly at the stowaway.

"I really don't know," replied Hofman, lost in thought. He felt like a complete idiot in front of Klára.

123 The Journey to Karlovy Vary, January 13, 1972

Irena Hofmanová revved the engine as much as she could. She considered herself a good and careful driver. But now all caution went out the window. She knew the road to Karlovy Vary well. She often drove there with Ota. But now she paid no attention to the potholes in the road or the town signs. She drove as fast as she could. Fortunately, it was late in the evening, around eleven o'clock. She glanced at the fuel gauge. Well, it should be enough to get to Karlovy Vary. It has to be. And she stepped on the gas again.

124 Train to Karlovy Vary, January 13, 1972

The train rode through the darkness and didn't stop at any of the stations it passed. Hofman and Klára were silent. Klára finally broke the silence.

"Of course, there's no point in my going there without you. I'll get off with you in Karlovy Vary."

Hofman looked at her. "I'm sorry. I feel embarrassed."

"What can you do? We'll find another date," she smiled at him.

Meanwhile, the train sped along the tracks through the countryside.

125 The journey to Karlovy Vary, January 13, 1972

Irena turned on her high beams to see better. Fortunately, there was little traffic at night. All the fines are on you, Oto, she thought. She read the sign Karlovy Vary – 34 kilometers. I have to speed up, she told herself and stepped on the gas. She vaguely remembered where the train station was in Karlovy Vary and how best to get there. I'm lucky, no police have stopped me yet, she continued to think. With her eyes fixed on the road and driving at a speed that could have cost her driving license, she raced towards Karlovy Vary.

She passed the sign for Karlovy Vary and drove down the winding road into the valley. Now where? Now where, damn it?

Someone was walking on the sidewalk. She stopped the car with a screech of brakes.

"Excuse me, how do I get to the train station?"

"Go straight ahead, turn left after about three hundred meters. Then straight ahead again and then right, and you'll arrive at the station," said the man, who happened to be wearing a station uniform.

Now, stay calm and don't get lost. She followed the instructions. In a moment, she was standing in front of the station and ran out of the car with Ot's bag. She left the car unlocked.

She saw a station attendant. "Excuse me, which platform is the train from Prague to Nuremberg arriving at? Or has it already left?"

She was terribly tense and waited for an answer. Maybe the effort was completely pointless...

"Platform three, ma'am. It should be here any minute."

Irena felt a weight lift off her chest, thinking that they must have heard them all the way in Prague. She ran to find the third platform. In the distance, she could already see the train arriving.

She wasn't alone on the platform. In the dim light, she thought to open Ota's bag.

She quickly found the train ticket and looked at the car number. Second car.

The train slowed down and came to a halt. She ran to the second car.

The doors opened, and there stood Ota in his coat with a suitcase in his hand, followed by Wagnerová.

Irena saw Ota and called out, "Ota!"

He stared at her in disbelief. "What on earth are you doing here?"

"All the fines will be on you, and if they take my driver's license, then all my groceries too," she shouted at him and handed him the bag. "Have a safe trip. You were lucky, Ota, five minutes later and..."

Wagnerová turned to return to the compartment. Hofman took the bag with his documents. "Thanks, Irena, you're a treasure."

Irena stood on the platform and waited for the train to leave. Then she waved to Ota.

126 West Germany, Cologne, January 15, 1972

A nice, cozy Italian family restaurant in Cologne was stylishly decorated. Gert often went there and enjoyed it. The walls were decorated with pictures of Italian landmarks— the Colosseum, St. Peter's Basilica in the Vatican, and the dé Trevi Fountain.

Gert sat down and looked at Hofman and Klára Wagneová: "I think we got a lot done today. I have to admit, Ota, your idea for the second series of *Pan Tau* is so great. You're right, we can't keep doing the same thing."

"As soon as I get home, I'll start writing. I'm glad you liked the story. I racked my brain trying to figure out what to do next. I believe that each time we need to approach the character of *Pan Tau* a little differently so that we cannot repeat ourselves and shoot all our powder too soon," said Hofman.

"The main thing is that you convinced Müller, he's good for me financially. And *Pan Tau* and Robinson, the doppelganger, uncle Alfons, it's so full of ideas! I do like it, Ota. Really, I do. And then there's the fact that you're here, that you can come anytime. Nothing but great news!"

"I'm glad too, Gert," Hofman replied happily.

But Gert became serious, and Hofman noticed the change in his face.

"Is something wrong, Gert?" he asked.

"Before we order, I should probably tell you something. I must report on the course of tonight's dinner to my superior."

Wagnerová joined in with downcast eyes: "Me too."

Gert and Klára looked at each other and laughed sourly. Hofman hissed in pain and clutched his stomach. "I don't usually have a problem with jokes, but I haven't been feeling well for a while and this atmosphere isn't helping my mood."

Gert seemed at a loss: "I understand. I wanted to..."

But Hofman interrupted him: "Excuse me, before you start, Gert. Ms. Wagnerová, who is your supervisor? I may have my own ideas, of course..." He paused. "I hope you're not recording this?"

Klára replied, still with her eyes downcast: "Mr. Hofman, we can talk here without fear. But I wouldn't talk much in your hotel room. I think there was something installed there."

Gert added, "Yeah, there was. There was a weird ear in the vase on the table, but the waiter 'accidentally' broke it a few minutes ago. They'll have a quiet night now."

Hofman grabbed his stomach again. He still thought it was a joke: "I'm sorry, I usually think your jokes are really funny. But now I insist on an answer, colleague."

Gert grimaced, looked at Klára, and answered for her: "Her boss is Kamil Pixa."

Hofman jumped up in his chair and squeaked weakly: "What? You didn't tell me that!" He took a sip of wine. "If it's Pixa, then we're going to have a nice dinner, and I'm supposed to go back to a hotel that's bugged from top to bottom? Are you serious? That guy even eavesdrops on his own family! He must do it for sport!"

Gert leaned toward Otto and said, "My dear friend from Prague, I'd love to hear your stories about the man in the bowler hat, Cinderella, or Sexana. But we must face reality, whether we like it or not."

"I know..." Hofman murmured.

Gert interrupted him: "You don't know. What I'm about to tell you will be unpleasant, but her orders are to inform Pixa if you want to emigrate."

"What?"

Klára nodded, and this time she took a sip of wine.

Gert leaned in closer to Hofman and said quietly, "If she doesn't answer his question, he might launch one of his infamous interrogations. If you're unaware of what Comrade Pixa can do, I can bring a colleague from Paris tomorrow. "He's also staying at your hotel and will be happy to tell you how they learn in Moscow to break and even kill a man without the cause of death being discovered."

"I really don't want to know that," muttered a frightened Hofman.

Gert continued: "You can't close your eyes to this."

Klára remarked: "Mr. Müntefering is right, that is the main purpose of my trip with you."

They both looked at her.

"To spy on me, in case I try to escape?"

"You're valuable to them, Ota, you bring Barrandov foreign currency. Your films win festivals, where they can then go themselves and collect the prizes for you. They like that. Believe me, Ota, you give them reasons for their occasional trips to capitalist foreign countries," Gert told Ota bluntly, revealing what he thought of his superiors.

Klára looked at Hofman and added, "No one's going to stick nails under your fingernails, but if you saw my dad's eyes when Pixa let me see him! I never want to see him so broken again."

"Ota, maybe I should tell you something else."

"Maybe you should, Gert."

"Well, Pixa had Klára's father arrested for alleged theft of socialist property, which I don't think she told you, did she, Klára?"

Hofman blurted out: "What?"

"And now my father is, how should I put it, Pixa's hostage to ensure my exemplary cooperation and loyalty. I had no choice. So, what should I put in my report to Pixa, Mr. Hofman? Do you want to emigrate or not?"

127 Prague, January 24, 1972

Klára Wagnerová went to Pixa's office dressed in stylish 1970s clothing. She was afraid, understandably reluctant, but she had to go; she had been given orders. The secretary looked her over, then smiled sourly and said dryly, "The director is expecting you."

Klára entered. Kamil Pixa was sitting in a chair with a high back, his back turned to her.

He ordered, "Lock the door behind you."

Klára turned, closed the door, and turned the key.

"Sit down," ordered her.

She sat down. Pixa turned around in his chair. He was dressed in women's clothes, and his lips were painted red. Klára stared at him, but said nothing.

"What do you say? Do you like me?" he asked.

Dismayed girl remained silent because she knew that if she said anything wrong to this psychopath, her father would end up in Ruzyně for God knows how long.

Pixa yelled at her, "Answer me!"

Klára looked at him, frozen, in a state of absolute shock. Nothing could have prepared her for this.

"Do you want help? Are you sure?" Pixa stood up. He walked over to her and showed her the stumps of his severed fingers.

She was overcome by a gag reflex.

"Put it in your mouth," Pixa ordered, holding out his stump.

Klára's eyes widened in horror. She closed her eyes and heard only the words: "I was in prison under the Nazis. I was beaten up by the Communists. The French secret service cut off my finger. Do you think I'm the kind of person who cares, what a pretty young whore like you thinks of me?"

Klára Wagnerová was on the verge of tears.

She didn't look at him. She heard him say," I'm sick of assholes who think they know how to handle me. I don't give a shit about them. Do you think I care about you? Or that I care about your father? I don't care about you at all. The only thing I care about is the game. I love it. It excites me. The feeling that I can snap my fingers and it can all be over. That really turns me on."

Klára didn't move.

Pixa returned to his chair, looked at the table with the documents, and glanced at her: "But why did I call you here?"

Wagnerová dared to open her eyes and muttered, "Well, I sent the report."

"Yeah, you sent it. Two pages about nothing. Well, that's not going to work, girl. Are you kidding me? Hofman forgot his documents at home on the train to Cologne. So what? Who cares about such nonsense? Did you at least sleep with him?"

"No, we didn't sleep together," Klára snapped.

"And I'm supposed to believe you? You already screwed that German guy. So why not Hofman?"

"We didn't sleep together," Klára repeated.

"And you want me to believe that he has no intention of emigrating, that he didn't even mention it when he has a friend like Müntefering there?"

"Girl, girl. You're really worrying me," Pixa remarked and thought for a moment.

"I want to know everything about that German. Who he is, who his parents were. What he did during the occupation. Whether his father beat me with a rifle butt when I was in a German concentration camp. Who he meets, who he talks about."

Wagnerová began to feel angry: "But you've already found that out, haven't you?"

"Don't be rude," Pixa admonished her, "trust but verify, that's true for the communists, but not for us. Check and double-check, that's our motto. I want every piece of information about him for this puzzle."

Pixa stood up and walked over to her, leaning in until she could feel his breath: "Do you know how to play checkers?"

"Yeah, my dad and I used to play." She stared into his face.

Pixa whispered, "Then refresh your knowledge. Right now, you're the little piece on the chessboard, and there are lots of other little pieces around you that have to be eaten before you become queen. And you definitely don't want to be eaten, you want to become queen, otherwise..." He paused. "Otherwise, your dad will wipe us out. Got it, young lady? ... So, what about that German bastard? I know you gave it to him. What did he say?"

Klára did not answer.

Pixa turned away: "Let's talk like girls. Like good friends."

He sat down on Wagnerová's lap and stroked her cheek. Klára closed her eyes. He kissed her.

Pixa whispered softly, "Open your eyes, beauty."

Klára opened her eyes.

Then whispered again, "We're friends, after all. Friends have to tell each other everything. Tell me."

Klára thought of her father and felt she had to say something: "They were there at the hotel in Cologne. The ones who caught you in Paris. The French officer didn't want to lose it. He said you killed his friend."

Pixa was intrigued: "But I didn't kill him. He just died. He couldn't take it. It wasn't my fault."

She added, "But now they have orders that nothing must happen to you."

"That's very good. Really very good." Pixa paused, then laughed.

He leaned toward Klára and kissed her. Then he whispered, "It's a good start, but it's not enough. I want more. Much more."

Shocked girl nodded.

Pixa waved his claw in front of her eyes: "And don't forget this! Never. Now get the fuck out of here!"

128 Moravia, Gottwaldov, February 2, 1972

Ota Hofman was slightly tired after several hours of driving on broken and winding roads from Prague to Gottwaldov.

He parked his car in front of the film studios and stretched a little to gather strength for the scheduled meeting.

He knew the way to the office of studio manager Pitr well, so he had another cigarette in front of the studio.

Inside, the studio staff and director Pavel Hobl were already waiting for him.

The studio director saw Hofman enter and greeted him: "Welcome, Ota. The muse with the bowler hat has come to kiss us."

Hofman smiled at them: "Hi, guys. So, I'm bringing it to you personally. I haven't written the musical yet."

Hobl was taken aback, so he asked, "What's the difference between a normal film and a musical?"

Hofman gave him a quick answer: "You have songs, and you just throw in some connecting dialogue, it's a piece of cake."

The director's answer made him laugh: "That's easy for you to say when you know how to do it. If you saw what I sometimes read here."

Hofman sat down: "And if you saw what I read in our group! But we won't have to talk about that today."

"But there's one thing. You wrote in the casting proposal that you want director Menzel to play Professor Ludolf.

Hofman nodded in agreement: "You know how he is right now. And he's perfect for the part."

Hobl supported Hofman: "He seemed absolutely ideal to me, so I told him so."

But the director still had his doubts: "I wouldn't get involved without approval from above, but my superiors are far away in Prague. And as you know, we're headed by Krátký film and Comrade Pixa."

"I know that, and between you and me, girls, I'm headed by Toman," replied Hofman ironicaly.

"Then you surely know that we spoke with Pixa on the phone."

"You know, nothing stays long as a secret at Barrandov," admitted Hofman.

"And Pixa laughed and said that we could hire Menzel because it would, and I quote, really piss off Toman."

"Yeah, I heard that too, that's why I'm here now, isn't it?" confirmed Hofman. "To discuss the details with you. If I didn't have the green light, I wouldn't have come," he added and lit up again.

Hobl lit up too: "I heard you were a hit with *Pan Tau* in West Germany, too."

The director snapped at him, "Why are you asking him that? Do you want to run away?"

129 Prague, September 7, 1972

Comrade Purš looked around the large table and the large director's chair in the office of the Czechoslovak State Film Company, with comrades Pixa and Toman sitting opposite him. Purš looked first at one, then at the other: "Comrades, I had to fire the head of Barrandov, Comrade Fábera. At first, he seemed like a promising cadre, but then it turned out that he wasn't serious about our ideas. He was only interested in money."

"No loss, I never liked that guy," Pixa commented on words of Dr. Purš.

Toman also added: "Everyone knows that, Comrade Purš."

Purš stopped them with a gesture: "Comrades, you are both responsible for film production in our already successfully normalized cinema. I hope you realize the seriousness of your task."

Toman readily agreed: "Of course, comrade. As the head of Barrandov, I have already proven that I understand the new direction of our film. Using my authority as chief dramaturge, I got rid of two particularly problematic screenwriters, František Pavlíček and Jan Procházka, for instance. Pavlíček is already out of the picture, and Procházka is now a closed chapter."

Purš looked at Toman: "Don't worry about Procházka now, that was more Comrade Pixa's doing. Ludvík, you'll get it in writing soon, but you'll be replacing Fábera."

"You've got to be kidding me, Toman and the forest virgin are going to be running Barrandov!" Pixa blurted out.

Purš pretended not to hear the remark: "Comrade Pixa, may I introduce you to the new head of the studio in the Barrandov hills. Congratulations, comrade. I trust you will not disappoint us."

Pixa managed to smirk.

But Purš continued: "And I have something for you too, Comrade Pixa. In addition to Short Film, you will also be in charge of the film studios in Gottwaldov."

"Even Karel Zeman?" asked Pixa.

"Even Karel Zeman."

Pixa looked triumphantly at Toman. "Thank you, Comrade Purš."

Purš looked sternly at Pixa: "But keep a close eye on them, Comrade Pixa. I'm a little uneasy about the people you're taking on. There are a lot of troublemakers among them, some aren't even in the party, and some never have been."

Toman cleared his throat, stifling a laugh.

Purš continued speaking directly to Pixa: "For example, we need to deal with the musical Thirty Virgins and Pythagoras from Gottwaldov. It was filmed by Pavel Hobl based on a story by Ota Hofman. Incidentally, Jiří Menzel also appears in the film, and he definitely didn't pass the party's vetting process. So, we watched it with our comrades, and there are quite a few people in it who aren't with us, as well as those who emigrated. It's beyond the question that we would show a film full of traitors. So, you'll arrange for it to be re-edited."

Pixa replied, "You can count on me, comrade. How much time do I have?"

"Hey, don't rush. Take your time. Make it your task for the next five years, until they send new directives from Moscow."

Toman, even though he knew that Pixa had bypassed him with Menzel, turned around: "But if you cut Menzel, you'll be left with about ten minutes of disjointed goulash, and what's that guy going to do? We've got dozens of letters at Barrandov saying we can't just sideline an Oscar-winning director. Even Hitchcock wrote about him to Barrandov."

Decisive Purš stood his ground: "That young whippersnapper should realize that he can only come back among us if he admits he was wrong. Let him fucking remember what Comrade Kliment said about socialist realism and let him fuck stick to it. Who does he think he is, having his own opinion? He's just a suckling pig. I'm twice his age and I don't have any opinions of my own! "

But Pixa wasn't willing to give up so easily: "How about putting him in a children's film? With Hofman. Hofman keeps quiet, we did kick him out of the party..."

Toman grumbled," I don't want him."

Pixa insisted and continued to annoy Toman: "Menzel could do *Three Nuts for Cinderella*, after all."

Toman shook his head again in disagreement. "Hofman brought it to me as a story for production, and I gave the green light to write the script. We suggested it again to Věra Plívová Šimková, but she's struggling with it. She's a good director, no doubt about it, but Cinderella going to dance parties to modern music and riding a scooter took even me by surprise, and I'm progressive man, comrades, you know that, don't you?"

Pixa couldn't resist the irony: "We all know that."

Purš finally decided: "Then offer it to Menzel. As soon as he starts complaining, we'll put someone reliable in his place."

130 Prague, September 13, 1972

The wine bar was full today. In a cloud of cigarette smoke, Ota Hofman and director Jiří Menzel arranged a meeting. They had glasses of wine in front of them, and Hofman had his indispensable cigarette between his fingers.

Menzel was already on his second glass and reminisced: "How long has it been since I played a cop in your movie?"

"Mr. Director, you remember Detective Martin films?"

"Of course, Mr. Hofman. Working with Milan Vošmik was a pleasure, a real pleasure. Didn't Juraj Herz also happen to play in it?"

"Of course he did, but in a different episode. I often think of Vošmik. He was a friend and we got along well. It was a terrible blow to me when he died suddenly at Christmas three years ago. We had several projects lined up together, which were then completed by others. But back to your question, Mr. Director, it's been about six years, I think," Hofman mused, "the lead actor Martin, Mr. Vízner, emigrated, so now the Martin films are lying somewhere in a warehouse gathering dust."

"Like my film *Larks on a String* and a whole bunch of others. But that's not why you called me, is it, Mr. Hofman?

"You're right. The opportunity has arisen for you to make the film again."

Menzel was very interested in this information: "Really? What is it about?"

Hofman stubbed out his cigarette in the ashtray: "*Three Nuts for Cinderella*. I know you'd rather shoot adaptation of Hrabal or Vančura books, but with our children's film group, you'd have freedom and a big budget. It's a co-production with DEFA."

Menzel replied: "With DEFA, you say? No way. I acted in a fairy tale there last year. And you want to entrust them with a fairy tale written by Božena Němcová? They can't do anything, the sets, the costumes, everything looks like cardboard."

131 Prague. September 15, 1972

The meeting with Ota Hofman in the Barrandov studio's film bar was booked a week ago by the director of Pixa Short Film through his secretary. She informed Hofman that the director wanted to finish the film musical *Thirty Virgins and Pythagoras,* which the director Hobl had already finished. When Hofman arrived, he saw Pixa sitting at the bar, a glass of cognac already in his hand.

As soon as Pixa noticed Hofman's arrival, he motioned for him to sit next to him: "Honor, Ota."

"Honor."

"How do you stomp rabbits? You wrote it, didn't you? *Rabbits in the Tall Grass*."

"I did."

"Good," Pixa remarked, and continued, "But how you wanted a child to die at the end, and a pioneer at that, you didn't mean it then, did you?"

"I thought so, but I guess that's not why you called me here."

"Of course not. I have your musical here."

"*Thirty virgins and Pythagoras*. But there were more of us working on that. Where did it ever end? It's been lying somewhere finished around for a long time."

"Don't even remind me. I'm also partly to blame for pushing Menzel in, but whatever. We've got to cut the cord. So I was wondering if you'd think about it."

"Why cut it? It's a musical, we can't throw anything away."

"We have to fire the whole role of that cow Chramostová. She's a nightmare. She's doing apartment theater, hanging out with those scumbags from the dissent, and that old Milota of hers, he's the one they're after in the Kremlin. He filmed Soviet tanks in the 1968 on a Barrandov camera and socialist material! The whole West saw it! He can be glad it's not the fifties, we'd sweep him away, the bastard."

"If you cut out Vlasta Chramostová," Hofman was horrified, "you'll get, I'd guess, twenty minutes out of the film. Then it won't make any sense at all. The plot won't follow; that's an absolutely crazy idea. Vlasta started out with me; she played the mother in *Johnny's Journey*. We had a standing ovation at the Lido. And that's not that long ago."

"Then there's nothing you can do about it?" insisted Pixa.

"How? I really can't. That's how many shooting days? I don't know, those girls look different now than they did then. They're all teenagers, and you can see them almost every month. It would look terrible, and the touch-ups would cost at least a million."

"Well, we have to welcome it, because otherwise they'd give us all a steal of socialist property, and we'd go to jail. Menzel doesn't mind so much anymore, because he's already filming what we've offered him, proving that he's finally grasped our idea. We'll show it afterwards."

"After what?" Hofman asked.

"Well, after his new socialist epic."

"But that doesn't solve the problem of this film's dramaturgy. It's going to be terrible. The critics will eat us alive," argued Hofman again.

"That may not solve your drama, but politically it will be fine and everything else is pretty much free to me, do we understand each other?"

132 West Germany, Cologne, September 18, 1972

In the conspiratorial apartment of the Federal Office for the Protection of the Constitution (BfV), the West German counter-intelligence agency, on Kardinal-Höffner-Platz in Cologne, Gert read a newspaper while waiting. On the table was an open bottle of expensive French cognac. He had been waiting for over half an hour, but he didn't mind. Finally, someone rang the doorbell. Gert went to answer it. Pixa was standing there.

Pixa started in fluent German: "Hello. I mean, getting here is a maneuver."

Gert ushered him in, "Hello."

Pixa walked over to the window. "Take a look out the window."

Gert approached him.

Pixa held out his hand and pointed with his finger: "That car over there, that's ours, State Security." Then he changed the direction of his index finger, "That car over there, that's yours."

Then he walked over to the other window of the corner apartment and summoned Gert with his finger. He held out his hand again. "There, that's Sergei from the KGB."

Gert turned and sat back in his seat, "You're enjoying this, aren't you?"

"Of course. I've been doing it all my life," Pixa confirmed.

Gert offered, "Would you like a drink?"

Pixa turned and looked at the expensive cognac on the small table.

He appreciated the bottle, "Hennessy?"

Gert nodded, "Yes."

"Now that's quality," Pixa nodded.

"I have a whole box for you."

"Great," Pixa remarked.

Gert raised his glass. Pixa took his own in his hand, and it was impossible not to notice that the links of finger of his left hand were missing.

Pixa noticed Gert's look, so he informed him, "I forgot you didn't know. You've only been working for them for a short time. I was cut off by your colleagues in Paris last year at the festival. Not the filmmakers, but the undercover ones you signed up for. But I don't blame them."

Gert was cautious: "Do you want to talk about it?"

Pixa looked at Gert appreciatively, "You're learning well. Of course, I don't want to talk about it. The walls have ears, don't they? Let's talk business, that's what I'm interested in.

How much goes to Czechoslovakia and how much goes to me? And don't spare me."

Gert smiled, "I'll do my best to keep you happy, but I expect the same from you."

Pixa shook his head, "Business is business. So, what are you interested in?"

"As you indicated, we can't shoot with Juraj Herz," Gert stated.

"Nothing has changed about that." Pixa leaned back in his chair and put his leg over his leg. "Herz is zigzagging like a rabbit. He's getting away with it for now, but if he doesn't join us, he's done for."

Gert didn't protest, "I see. We chose Saxana - *The Girl on the Broomstic* from Ota Hofman's offer." Gert forgave himself the joke about Sexana this time.

"Really? You like that?"

"Yes, and I think there is potential in director Vorlíček and screenwriter Macourek that needs to be developed."

Pixa took another sip from her glass, "I have good news for you. These ones can."

133 Prague, September 20, 1972

"This is Toman," came from the receiver.

Pixa just phoned Toman from his office at Barrandov. "Look, comrade, Vorlíček passed the West Germans. They bought *The Girl on the Broomstick*."

"Well, I'm looking at that. That's actually the first author we've helped, and he's going to make us more money. I thought they'd only take the bourgeois *Pan Tau* from us."

"Purš is very happy, he's thinking about what Vorlíček could do next," Pixa said.

Toman immediately thought that he could take advantage of this and take down Menzel, who was really drinking his blood: 'Hofman wants to be Cinderella. He's already done enough of that. I was thinking of letting Vorlíček do it and letting Menzel do something else, something educational."

"I'd pass on that if I were you. You're a first-class bitch; I'll give you that. For me, Chytilová, for instance, can do whatever she wants. But as you know, comrade Purš wants to give Menzel Cinderella, but he won't be here for a few days; he's gone on a business trip to Moscow, so Barrandov is yours now, you have free rein. Honour, comrade." And Pixa hung up.

134 Prague, September 20, 1972

Vorliček was frying eggs at home when his phone rang.

He announced into the intercom, "Vovliček."

"This is Toman. Honor the work, comrade director."

"Honouv," replied Vorlicek.

"I thought you could do Cinderella and make it with DEFA. You know speak German, don't you?"

"I can, but, comvade Toman, Jivka Menzel is supposed to be making it," Vorlíček objected.

"If Menzel was making it, he would be making it, and I wouldn't be calling you with this offer. Are you interested?"

"Cevtainly," he agreed.

Toman briefly added, "Then break a leg."

Vorlíček hung up and noticed that the eggs were now completely black. He threw them in the basket and opened the window.

135 Prague, September 25, 1972

The meeting of the dramaturgical team in the offices in Jindřišská Street took place regularly every week on Wednesdays from three pm. Ota Hofman, the head dramaturg, began speaking: "Ladies and gentlemen, I am working on the script for *Three Nuts for Cinderella* by the external author Zelenková." It will now be necessary to intensify the preparation. Director Vorlíček has already started to make his notes and comments. I have been in contact with my DEFA counterpart, Mr. Klaus Richter de Vroe, head of children's films, and dramaturge Mrs. Hannelore Neupert-Unterberg. The script was very well received by the German side. It was recommended to keep Cinderella active until the end of the story and to strengthen the slipper motif. A date for a working meeting with representatives of DEFA Studio will be arranged as soon as possible. For the time being, they have put forward a request to start filming in Germany at the beginning of December and to finish work on their territory by the end of January next year. It is already clear that it will be a challenging project, especially in terms of logistics and frequent border crossings."

Hofman continued, "We will have our own airline link to Berlin. The German side has started scouting, and now they are talking about the possibility of filming in a real castle in addition to the studios in Babelsberg, to keep with the tradition of the Czechoslovak fairy tale. They chose the baroque castle Moritzburg near Dresden. We offered the water castle Švihov. The budget is a bit higher, but both parties will cover the standard part for their regular production, so there will be money for Cinderella. Does anyone have anything to say?" said Hofman.

They all shook their heads.

Hofman added, "The only thing I'm puzzling over is that I don't like the scene with the ball and the hunt. I've looked up the background in the literature, and I think Mrs. Zelenková will have to rewrite it. It must be winter season. It doesn't make a lot of sense to me, and also, frankly, the timing doesn't work out for us to shoot in the summer. We've got to get it done in wintertime. I'm sure Mr. Theodor Pištěk can get the costumes ready. I've seen his original design, and it's beautiful."

136 Prague, September 25, 1972

Pavlíček's apartment had been tidied up, and the boxes were gone. Hofman stopped by briefly, so he stayed in the hallway and didn't go any further: "Franta, you have to rewrite it. It must be wintertime. How long will it take you?"

Pavlíček paused: "Come on, you're the author, you know how it is."

"That's exactly why I know. A week?"

Pavlíček: "Or two?"

Hofman interrupted him: "Ten days and a case of Gruzignac."

"I have to leave for a few days, but I'll stop by when I get back."

Pavlíček looked at Hofman as he was leaving: "All right, then."

Hofman turned back: "I've been told that your friend, Šimáčková quit her job in Vinohrady to stick with you."

Pavlíček just swallowed in amazement: "Helena?"

"Yes. Apparently, she told them in such a way that they won't be able to frame it."

137 Central Bohemia, Pečky, September 26, 1972

A pensive Pavlíček went to see the foreman in the warehouse hall of the Central Bohemian railway station in Pečky.

Pavlíček waited a moment before the foreman acknowledged him: "Boss, I need some help."

The foreman snapped, "What is it?"

Pavlíček didn't want to provoke him, so he asked quietly, "I only need to work half the week."

The foreman looked him up and down: "And who's going to do the other half?"

"Boss, that's the advantage of a centrally planned economy, I don't care. I'm a worker. Who's more important than me?"

The foreman was amused: "There's something about you, Franta. You can tell you've been to school. You're going to write subversive texts against the party, aren't you?"

"Fairy tales for children."

The foreman laughed loudly: "That's just as bad. Children will recognize evil anyway. But your pay will go down a lot, I hope you've thought of that."

"I'm counting on it, but I don't know if I'll get it. The main thing is to have a stamp in my ID card saying that I'm working, otherwise they'll lock me up."

The master considered the conversation over and returned to his work: "But that goes for everyone."

138 Prague, September 28, 1972

Helena Šimáčková was walking down Londýnská Street in Vinohrady. She was carrying a shopping bag. František Pavlíček, who had been waiting for her, saw her. He ran up behind her and called out. Šimáčková turned around.

Pavlíček, out of breath, greeted her: "Hi, Helena. I heard you quit your job."

Šimáčková nodded. "I couldn't stand it anymore, František. It was impossible to work in that atmosphere."

"I really admire your determination. I could use a dramaturge," Pavlíček remarked.

Šimáčková looked at him: "So, where did they take you? Did you go back to Barrandov?"

Pavlíček smiled: "No, nothing like that. I work in a warehouse in Pečky, but I have a good boss..."

Šimáčková's eyes widened in disbelief: "What?"

Pavlíček persisted: "It's not so bad, as long as they don't deliver any goods..."

"And what does a warehouse worker need a dramaturge for?"

"I'm writing a fairy tale," he explained.

"For your drawer?"

"I hope not. I'm writing **Three Nuts for Cinderella**, but it will be signed under a different name, of course."

Šimáčková smiled: "František, I'd love to. You know I'll take a look at it."

"You know, it's very urgent," he said, handing her a folder of papers.

"You were waiting for me, weren't you? Don't say you weren't. Admit it."

"I'm not saying I wasn't," replied Pavlíček.

139 Central Bohemia, Mukařov, October 1, 1972

Theodor Pištěk was holed up in his studio, painting a picture of a car. The studio wasn't far from Prague, so director Vorlíček didn't have far to go.

He knocked on the door. Dóda, as everyone at Barrandov called him, put down his brush. He had no idea who had come to see him. So, he cautiously invited the visitor in: "Come in."

Vorlíček entered, knowing full well what would make Dóda happy, and greeted him: "Zdvávstvuj, tavávyšč palkovnik Pištěk."

Pištěk turned from his easel and immediately recognized his visitor: "Zdrávstvuj, taváryšč Vorlíček," he replied in kind.

As always, they both laughed. Theodor Pištěk wiped his hands on his apron before shaking Vorlíček's hand.

Of course, he knew that the fairy tale Three Nuts for Cinderella was in the works. Nothing ever stayed secret for long at Barrandov.

That's why he knew that the director had come to ask for his daughter's hand in marriage.

"We've got the budget approved from Bavvandov and DEFA, and I despevately need the costumes. Cindevella is going into pvoduction," Vorlíček informed him.

Pištěk asked, "Would you like some coffee? Who's doing the finances?"

Vorlíček didn't refuse: "I'll have some. Fovtunately, Hofman is the main cveative team."

"So what's the problem?" Pištěk asked.

"There's still the creative team for the commissions."

"Ah, Metro Goldwyn Kadlec?"

Vorlíček laughed: "Yes." It was a common joke at Barrandov film Studio.

Nobody named production team headed by Jan Kadlec anything other than Metro Goldwyn Kadlec.

"But you'll keep an eye on him, Václav, won't you?" Dóda poured coffee into the cups and added hot water.

"You can count on me. Bavvandov is giving four million, and DEFA is giving a million maveks."

"What's the exchange rate?"

"I don't know," admitted Vorlíček, "you know it changes depending on the weather in Kveml. But it's roughly the same amount. There are a few more days, but not many. According to the contract, sixty for us and forty for them."

"And how much time do I have?" Pištěk invited Vorlíček to sit down at the small table.

"A month and a half."

Pištěk muttered, "That's not too bad. I can work miracles on demand. Do you have the script and the cast?"

"Yes. The scvipt has just been vewvitten for winter, but the plot has been finalized since Autumn."

Vorlíček handed Pištěk photos of the cast and a folder with the script.

Pištěk took a sip of coffee and looked Vorlíček in the eye: "You have two budgets, I'll want double the fee."

"You'll get it."

Pištěk looked at the photos of the actors. He showed one to Vorlíček: "Libíček. His pants are always unbuttoned. I hate that. Unbuttoned buttons. He can't even button them up. The guy supposedly eats sixteen goulash with dumplings in one sitting! Damn it."

"He has to be in it, he's a big shot," admitted Vorlíček.

"For that kind of money, Vašek, I'll sew him some Renaissance underpants when his Dederon fabric loosens up and his huge belly pops out."

"If you sew him some Renaissance underwear, I know you'll win an Oscar one day," Vorlíček teased Pištěk.

They both burst out laughing.

140 Prague, Střelecký Ostrov, October 4, 1972

Pavlíček sat with Šimáčková on a bench on Střelecký Ostrov. They looked at the Vltava River. It was already quite cold, but the sun was still shining a little.

Pavlíček, staring at the surface of the river, said, "The most beautiful office in the town."

Šimáčková laughed. "You're right. But aren't we a little cold here?" She reached into her bag and handed him some papers. "It's beautiful, Franta. There's action, humor, and it's poetic. I have a suggestion."

Pavlíček read: "His face is smeared with soot, but he's not a chimney sweep. He has a feathered hat, a bow, and a camisole, but he's not a hunter. She has a dress with a train, embroidered with silver, but she's not a princess, that's for sure."

"Heleno, that's wonderful," sighed Pavlíček.

141 Prague, October 6, 1972

Hofman gave it a try and stopped by Franta Pavlíček's place on his way home from work.

"Did you manage to rewrite it?" Hofman asked him as soon as Pavlíček opened the door.

Pavlíček invited him into his apartment: "Don't you want to come in?"

"No, I'm in a hurry, Franta, I'm just checking if you're done."

"Yeah, I rewrote it for winter, like you wanted. But it wasn't easy. Instead of a tree frog, there's now an owl named Rozárka. Three nuts don't fall from a tree but fall out of a squirrel's nest. Cinderella doesn't meet the prince and his cronies by the stream, where she would take their clothes, but in a snowy forest while hunting a deer, and she takes the prince's untamed horse."

Hofman didn't hide anything and spoke directly: "Franta, I know how hard you worked on this, but you know how things work at this stage of the script. It's signed by Mrs. Zelenková, and she'll be working with the director from now on."

"Which one?"

"Václav Vorlíček."

Pavlíček frowned: "I don't know him. Has he worked with us before?"

"No, not when we were working together, but he's just worked on the children's film Saxana," explained Hofman.

"Unfortunately, I haven't seen it."

"Defy will also have a say in it, but we both know that no one can take the foundation away from you. I can tell you that it's a beautiful fairy tale and a fantastic script."

Pavlíček smiled:" Thank you... And the Gruzignac?"

"I have it in the trunk of my car. I hope you can help me with it; I can't carry heavy things yet."

They both laughed.

142 West Germany, Cologne, Interrogation room of the Federal Office for the Protection of the Constitution (BfV), October 8, 1972

Gert Müntefering sat in a chair in a completely empty room. He had been brought here like a criminal. He knew he was in the interrogation room of the German secret service, the BfV.

But he had no idea why. And why on a Sunday, he had no idea.

The voice of the investigator standing over him was completely neutral: "Mr. Müntefering, last year you were on twenty business trips to socialist Czechoslovakia."

Gert was not afraid and replied decisively: "Yes, I can confirm that."

He heard the investigator's voice again: "Westdeutscher Rundfunk television projects are produced according to your analyses, mainly in studios in Prague's Barrandov district."

Gert confirmed without hesitation: "Yes, I stand by that. Of course, my colleagues originally planned to shoot more abroad. As you know, Czechoslovakia has no sea, which is quite limiting for many fairy tales. In the case of the *Pan Tau* series, the plan was to film in Paris, New York, and Tokyo. In the end, it was my idea to stay at home. They have a beautiful country with a rich history and many beautiful castles and chateaux. And, of course, it's much safer."

The investigator asked another question: "How would you describe the StB agents?"

Gert sat and tried to answer calmly and firmly: "They contact me every time I arrive. Most of them are filmmakers. Most often, one sound engineer with a strange name, Vorisek, who is difficult for me to pronounce and remember, tries to get information out of me. But I haven't been able to find out if he's really a sound engineer."

"What have you heard about the fairy tale project *Three Nuts for Cinderella*?"

"It's a project involving several creative groups in Barrandov. It's being produced by a creative group on commission, but it's more for show, to get foreign currency. All foreign currency is strictly controlled in Czechoslovakia. It's monitored by a separate working group," said Gert.

"Were you asked to join the production?"

"Why?" Gert didn't understand the question.

"Please answer."

"We discussed this with Mr. Hofman, the dramaturge at the Barrandov film studio."

"We know who Mr. Hofman is."

"Then yes, I was approached informally by Mr. Hofman."

"I strongly advise you not to get involved in the production itself. It could cause you a lot of trouble," said the investigator again.

Gert didn't understand why, so he said, "I don't understand."

"We have received independent information that you are cooperating with the East German intelligence service," said the investigator's voice.

Gert froze: "What? With the Stasi?"

The neutral voice continued: "Yes, East German secret police. This information comes from our agents. We are also concerned that you are meeting with Mr. Pixa."

"Pixa is my production counterpart. Without his cooperation, and I assume without his partial protection, it would be extremely problematic. What's more, he has put his man on me."

"All right, take it easy, Mr. Müntefering. If I were you, I would try to settle this and send them a clear signal that they cannot treat you this way."

Gert nodded emphatically.

"And rest assured, we will also send them a signal they will not soon forget."

143 Prague, October 16, 1972

The dramaturgy group was in the middle of its regular meeting. Everyone was seated around the table: secretary Bohunka Šourková, Marcela Pittermannová, and Ota Hofman. The meeting was coming to an end. Hofman was summarizing today's discussion: "Well, the tasks have been assigned, and we'll meet again in two weeks."

Someone knocked on the door. Quite loudly.

"Come in," Hofman invited the visitor.

Gert appeared in the doorway. His face was red. He began in Czech with an accent: "Good day."

The doorman ran up behind him, protesting: "You can't come in here, foreigners aren't allowed. You must leave immediately!"

"It's all right, Mr. Večeřa, he'll be leaving right away, I'll see to it."

Mr. Večeřa wanted to add something, but Hofman pushed him out of the door and closed it.

"But that's not possible, Comrade Hofman, I have my orders," protested Mr. Večeřa from behind the closed door. Hofman completely ignored his clamor.

Hofman offered his right hand. ,"Hello, Gert, I didn't know you were here."

"I'm not going to report every time I need to come here," Gert snapped at him.

Hofman looked around the room. "Come have a beer, we're almost done. Looks like we both need one."

Gert nodded.

144 Prague, October 16, 1972

They were already sitting at the table, with glasses of beer with rich foam in front of them.

But Gert was figuratively speaking foaming at the mouth: "I'm coming straight from Wenceslas Square. I had a meeting there with that Vorišek."

"With whom?"

Gert confirmed the name: "Well, with Vorišek."

"I don't know him," Hofman replied.

Gert took a sip and then continued: "He's my personal StB agent. You have, or had, your own crook, Mareček, and I have Vorišek. Every time I arrive, this idiot happens to bump into me, as if by accident. He smiles and asks questions. Oto, I'm used to pressure, but I can't put up with this. That idiot wrote a report saying I'm a Stasi agent. "

"What?" blurted Hofman.

"For me, but also for you, it means that the sword of Damocles is hanging over me now. I don't know if they'll let me continue our cooperation, and I've been tasked with sorting things out. Ordnung muss sein, lieber Ota."

"Gert, please, what did you tell him?"

"I told him clearly that I don't work for any East Germans, and if he doesn't stop lying about me, I'll take him down. Then I told him that I would make sure he never saw the

West again, and given that he had managed to send his adult son to Munich, I warned him that my colleagues knew all about him."

"And what did he say?" Hofman hung on his every word.

"He shit himself with fear."

"How long are you staying, Gert?"

"I'm leaving already. I just came to take care of this, and besides, I've been advised not to stay here too long."

"Is there anything else going on that I don't know about?"

Gert shrugged. "You never know," he muttered. Gert raised his hand and called for the bill.

Hofman looked at his watch. "One more thing, Gert, what about Cinderella? Are you going for it?" Hofman asked.

"Ota, weren't you listening to me?"

"Yes, I was."

"Then you must have misunderstood. Cinderella is completely out of the question for me right now. I have to protect my ass and stay away from DEFA. But I'll give you some advice. Call Müller or write to him. Drive to Cologne and it'll work out."

"Okay, Gert, I'll call him. Now, excuse me, I have to get back to the office. I need to finish writing a nasty review of a really stupid script."

145 Prague, October 18, 1972

A key rattled in the lock of the Wagners apartment. Klára Wagnerová entered. She was well-groomed again, and her clothes suited her. Her mother sat at the dining room table like a body without a soul. Klára greeted her mother as she always did: "Hi, Mom."

This time, her mother did not answer, lost in her own thoughts.

"Is something wrong?" Klára asked.

Her mother looked at her: "How can you ask that? Of course, something is wrong. It's been going on for a long time. When will this end, for God's sake? It's impossible to live like this."

"What happened, Mom?" Klára sat down at the table.

"They called from prison. Dad is in the infirmary. That's all they told me."

"Is he okay?"

"They said you'll tell me."

"Me? I don't know anything."

"They said you'll explain everything to me, even why Dad is in prison."

"No, Mom. We're not going to talk about things like that. I have nothing to say." Klára didn't have the strength to tell her mother the truth.

"I brought you into this world. Do you think I'm completely stupid, that I don't know what's going on? I don't understand why you're traveling to capitalist countries while your father is in custody?"

"Mom. Not now. I can't talk about it. I'm... I'm so ashamed."

"What are you ashamed of? That you're like me? Sometimes you have to grit your teeth when you need to protect your loved ones."

Klára couldn't take it anymore and burst into tears.

Her mother stared blankly ahead: "They'll only let you in. Visiting hours are from three to five. You'll still make it."

Klára wiped her tears and looked at her mother.

Her mother smiled sadly: "Now go."

146 Prague, October 18, 1972

The infirmary at Ruzyně Prison detection was certainly not comfortable. It was a bare room with a barred window and a bed bolted to the floor. Before Klára Wagnerová entered, she had to show her ID to the guards again. He frisked her, even her breasts. What a pig, she thought to herself. He also searched for the purse with her ID and keys that she had with her. The whole procedure was extremely unpleasant and humiliating. Only after it was over, permit the guard let her see her father. Nevertheless, at last, he called the prison doctor to make sure he was allowed to let her in.

Wagner was lying in bed, feverish and hooked up to an IV stand.

"Dad, how are you? What happened?"

"Hi, Klára. You have no idea how happy I am to see you. They took out my gallbladder."

"Does it hurt?" Wagner smiled sadly: "It's better now. But it was better before. How are you?"

"I'm in the press department at Barrandov now, and in a week, I'm going back to Cologne with Mr. Hofman."

Wagner looked around. Then he motioned to his daughter to come closer. She leaned toward him, and he whispered in her ear: "Please don't come back. Mom and I will manage somehow."

Klára burst into tears.

147 West Germany, Cologne, October 20, 1972

Gert Müntefering went to the WDR offices to see director Müller, carrying a folder of papers under his arm.

Müller greeted him: "I called you, Gert, because you haven't talked to me about Czechoslovakia in a long time. Is something going on? Have you stopped working with them or what? "

"No, it's not like that. We're developing new projects, but you're right, I'd rather not go there too much at the moment. "

Do you have anything new? "

Gert perked up:" It's called *The Little Mole*. It's by the animator Miler."

"German?" asked Müller.

Gert laughed: "Ha, ha. It's pronounced the same as you, but it's spelled differently."

"So, what's it about?"

"When I was in Prague, they contacted me themselves. Zdeněk Miler showed me his drawings. Then we talked about which animals Disney hadn't done yet, and I thought of a mole."

Gert showed Müller a picture of the mole.

"Nice... and what about *Pan Tau*?"

Gert replied, "We're working on new episodes, the ones Hofman showed you."

"Is something wrong, Gert? You seem to have lost your enthusiasm."

"No. But..." Gert didn't want to talk about it.

"I heard something that they badmouthed you..."

"And they gave it to me good," Gert confirmed.

"I'm sorry."

"Don't be, it just annoys me."

"I'm asking because Ota Hofman called me and said he'd be coming on October 30th," Müller told Gert.

"And you're asking me what for?" Gert asked.

"I'm asking why he wants to come. What do you know about it?" Müller insisted. "Whether I should confirm the date. That's what I'm asking you."

"Then it's because of the new Cinderella project. He gave me the script to read; they're working on it with DEFA, and that's why I told him in Prague to call you directly. I'm not too fond of East Germans right now, and I also have to protect my ass, so to speak."

"And what's this Cinderella project like?"

"It's good, but to make it really good, they need our money," Gert said.

"Do you think I should agree to it?" Müller asked another question.

"Keep an eye on sales, you won't lose money in the West. I just don't know if it will pass politically. You know, we and DEFA are in the same boat. Pretty strange, don't you think, in this day and age? "Gert remarked.

"I'm also wondering if you'll be meeting with him, or if I should just meet with him here? "

"Of course I'll be happy to meet with him," Gert agreed.

148 Prague, October 27, 1972

It had been raining all day, and taxi driver Šmejda was reading the newspaper in his new Simca car. He was proud of the new car, which his wife had received as a wedding gift and which he was enjoying to the fullest. He realized quite early on that his father-in-law didn't like him very much, but it was he who was enjoying the benefits of his current position.

He was third in line at the taxi stand on Old Town Square at the exit from Pařížská Street, with the statue of Jan Hus in view through the front window. He was startled out of his reading by a knock on the side window. He was surprised, as two colleagues were waiting for customers in front of him. Nevertheless, he put down his newspaper. He saw two men in wet coats, so he rolled down the window and asked, "Where to, gentlemen?"

One of them took a cigarette out of his mouth, threw it away, leaned toward him, and announced, "Into the ass and back, dude. You're coming with us." And he shoved his State Security badge under Šmejda's nose.

149 Prague, October 27, 1972

The three of them couldn't fit into the tiny elevator of the Short Film office, so they climbed up to the fifth floor on foot, with Šmejda in the middle. They led him to the director's office, where they all sat down on chairs for guests. Pixa came out of his office and motioned for Šmejda to come in. Pixa returned silently to his desk and motioned for Šmejda to sit down. Šmejda waited and said nothing.

"I read your reports. Nothing. Nothing interesting. Absolutely nothing," Pixa said from behind his desk. "Boring. In all the time you've been working for me, nothing. Instead, as part of your job, you have two kids and you're married." Then he took a deep breath and shouted, "Now explain this to me!" He threw several photographs on the table in front of him. The photographs showed Šmejda in the U Koziček pub, rampaging while drunk. Šmejda glanced briefly at the photographs. Pixa had a tape recorder on the table, pressed the start button, and continued shouting, "Now listen to this, you bastard."

The tape recorder played the voice of a completely drunk Šmejda, babbling: "I don't give a shit about him. Pixa is the biggest bastard under the sun. Now I'll stop snitching forever. I'll tell everyone what that bastard is like. I swear on my children's health that..." Pixa turned off the tape recorder.

Pixa glared at Šmejda. "I made your life a bed of roses. You live like a pig in clover. You're about to move into a three-bedroom apartment in Spořilov, now that Hofman has cleared the field and is moving to Podolí himself. You got a new car from the West as a wedding gift. And don't tell me that your visits to luxury Tuzex shops are paid for by your pathetic taxi driver's wages! According to your reports, you hardly ever see Hofman, and he doesn't give a damn about you."

Pixa waited for a moment a glared furiously at clearly shocked Šmejda. "And what do I get for that? News about nothing, and what else, well, fucking ingratitude!"

"We were celebrating the birth of my second daughter. I have my head completely empty. I do not remember anything" Šmejda finally understood what was going on and tried to make amends.

But Pixa continued to rage until he was gasping for breath: "Then I'll open that window in your head wide right here and now, you bastard. I've decided you're going to disappear, and whether you like it or not, I really don't give a shit." Pixa stood up, leaned over Šmejda, and yelled, "Right here and now, you're a pain in my ass. A security risk, and I can't afford that!"

"I can't, I have a wife and children," Šmejda protested.

Pixa sat down again and stopped yelling: "Yeah, as a side effect of the task I entrusted to you. If you really want your wife to be a widow and your children to be orphans, fine, I can arrange that too," he snapped at Šmejda.

He reached into his desk drawer and pulled out an envelope. He threw it in front of Šmejda.

"Here's your new passport and travel permit, as well as your new credentials. By the way, from now on, your name is Beckenbauer, so get used to it, you scum. Hofman is going on a business trip to Cologne. Not the one near Čáslav, but the one on the Rhine, and you'll be following him. I've arranged for Klára Wagnerová to go with him again, and she'll keep an eye on him. But I don't trust her very much, so you keep an eye on her too. Kraus will be in charge there, and he'll keep an eye on you. Now get out of here. The two men standing outside will help you find your way to the border and make sure you disappear immediately."

Pixa paused and then added: "And if you think about coming back, you can be sure you won't come out of jail alive. Got it, you bastard?"

150 Prague, October 29, 1972

Hofman remembered well the place Klára Wagnerová had given him over the phone. He used to live in Vinohrady on Londýnská Street. Jiřího z Poděbrad Square was part of his neighborhood during his student years. Without hesitation, he drove his Saab to her apartment. Klára saw him through the window and, carrying a large suitcase and a bag over her shoulder, dragged herself down the stairs to the car where Hofman was waiting for her.

When he saw her, he opened the door and went to help her load the suitcase. They got into the car and Hofman set off towards Pilsen. A long journey awaited them. Wagnerová reached into her jacket pocket and took out a Montblanc pen. She examined it ceremoniously.

151 Prague, October 29, 1972

They had been driving for quite some time, and neither of them had spoken. Hofman grew tired of the silence and asked, "Are we going to sit here in silence the whole way to Cologne?"

"I'm not really in the mood to talk," replied Klára.

Hofman glanced at her briefly and asked, "Did something happen?"

"They haven't released my dad from prison yet, and now he's had gallbladder surgery. I just feel like crying," Klára told him.

Hofman didn't want to let it go: "What was the last report?"

"Pixa thinks we're sleeping together."

"That's all I needed," Hofman remarked. "Are we? I don't know anything about that."

152 West Bohemia, Rozvadov, border crossing, October 29, 1972

A uniformed customs officer stopped Hofman and Wagnerová in front of the barrier with a paddle. Hofman rolled down the window.

"Border guard," said the man in the green uniform, "your documents, please."

Hofman handed him his passport with an exit permit. Klára leaned over, stretched out her hand, and did the same.

"Are you traveling for work or pleasure?" he asked.

"For work," replied Hofman.

The customs officer leafed through the passports with the exit permits. Suddenly, he stopped.

"And you?" he snapped at Klára.

"I'm with him. We have a business meeting at Westdeutscher Rundfunk."

A second man in a similar uniform approached the car and asked, "Do you have anything to declare? Are you carrying any weapons, drugs, or antiques?"

"Of course not," replied Hofman.

The second man looked at the documents again. "Get out," he ordered, "let's check."

"Do you have any reason for that?" protested Hofman.

The customs officer ordered, "Comrade driver, open the trunk."

Hofman went to open the trunk, and the customs officer addressed Klára: "Comrade, I'll take a look in your handbag."

Klára's heart was in her mouth. She looked around nervously. She grabbed Hofman's sleeve and handed him a pen. He took it and looked at it.

Then he instinctively put it in his breast pocket. She handed the customs officer her handbag. He took it and walked away to a table. He rummaged through it for a moment. Finding nothing, he left the handbag on the table. Then he began searching the trunk of the car.

"Please put that suitcase over there on the table," he asked Klára.

Klára grabbed her suitcase, and Hofman, like a gentleman, helped her carry it to the table.

The customs officer asked, "Can you open that suitcase for me?" He began taking pieces of clothing out and placing them on the table.

When the suitcase was empty, he took it in his hands and shook it. "You can pack your things back in," he said dryly.

Girl set to work. The clothes that had been carefully folded now lay in a heap. She began to fold the skirts, blouses, and dresses again and put them in the suitcase. When she was finished, Hofman helped her put the luggage back in the trunk of the car.

"Everything's fine. You said you were going to state television?" asked the customs officer.

"Yes."

The customs officer turned to Hofman: "You haven't filled out the customs declaration. Fill out this form." He handed Hofman an A3 size form in duplicate.

"I don't have anything to write with," Hofman remarked.

"Comrade Hofman, you don't have anything to write with? You're a writer and screenwriter," said the customs officer in surprise, holding Klára Wagnerová's pre-filled customs declaration in his hand.

"Do you know who I am?" asked Hofman in amazement.

"Yes, and I would find it very strange if you didn't have a pen with you." The customs officer looked Hofman in the eyes.

"Mr. Hofman, you have it in your jacket breast pocket," remarked innocently Klára.

Hofman smiled kindly and reached into his pocket for his expensive Montblanc pen. He looked at it again and took off the cap. The customs officer looked at Hofman. Wagnerová lowered her eyes.

"Nice pen," remarked the customs officer. Hofman shrugged and, as soon as he had finished writing, put the pen back in his pocket. He handed the document to the customs officer.

On the mat that the customs officer had with him was a stamp on a chain. He stamped both customs declarations without reading them and handed them to Hofman along with their passports and a copy of the exit permit.

"Have a good trip," he said as they got into the car. He nodded toward the building, and the barrier lifted.

153 West Germany, Motorway service station near Frankfurt, October 29, 1972

The car with Hofman and Klára Wagnerová had long since entered the motorway, and their physical needs dictated that they stop at a motorway restaurant just before Frankfurt am Main.

Hofman drove up to the gas pump first. He filled up, then drove over to the restaurant to take a break; he felt like having a coffee.

Over a good cup of coffee, Hofman remembered something, reached into his pocket, and handed Klára a pen.

"Your pen, you probably don't want to lose it."

Klára smiled. She took the pen and put it in her purse.

A black car pulled up in front of the restaurant, and two men got out. The one in the passenger seat entered Hofman's field of vision for a moment. He perked up, but the man immediately disappeared behind the car.

"Is something wrong?" asked Klára.

"No, probably not. But I thought I saw my son-in-law outside."

"Your son-in-law? What would he be doing here?" asked again Klára.

"Exactly, what would he be doing here? I must have been mistaken. But it's a long story," said Hofman, losing his train of thought.

"We have plenty of time," Wagnerová remarked.

"I always do my own laundry, Miss Wagnerová," Hofman replied curtly. "But may I ask you something?"

She nodded.

Hofman continued. "Are you worried about your father?"

"Yes, I don't know what will happen to him."

"I saw those things; I saw the suitcase. It's none of my business. It's a lot of stuff for three days."

Klára lowered her eyes and said nothing.

"So, I'm going to assume that you don't intend to return to Czechoslovakia," Hofman remarked.

Wagnerová looked him in the eyes for a long time, then shook her head and lowered her eyes again.

"You know, as a father, I've thought about it too. If Otto or Irena came to me and said they wanted to emigrate, I wouldn't try to talk them out of it."

"You wouldn't be afraid of what would happen to you? I think you know very well what the communists are capable of."

"Of course I would be afraid, but do you think that would help me in any way?"

411

She smiled slightly.

"You'll see, everything will turn out fine."

Two men sat down behind them, and one of them opened a large newspaper.

154 West Germany, Cologne, October 30, 1972

The family-run Italian restaurant in Cologne was Gert's favorite place to eat. Hofman and Wagner entered the familiar premises. Gert was already waiting for them, and when he saw them, he automatically stood up. He looked absent-minded, almost angry, but after a moment, he smiled, and Hofman smiled back. They approached each other and shook hands. Gert kissed Wagner's hand. She smiled but looked very distracted. Hofman lit a cigarette. Gert ordered shots of Hennessy.

"How was your trip?" Gert asked.

"Long," Klára replied.

"Come on, let's have a drink, and you'll feel better right away. I'm nervous too when I cross the border, but you're among friends here."

Hofman looked at her. She hastily knocked over her glass of water.

"I'm sorry."

"Everything okay?" Gert asked.

"It's just the trip, I've been sitting for so long, I'd like to stretch my legs. I'd like to go for a walk, if you don't mind."

"Not at all," Gert smiled.

"Are you okay, Mr. Hofman?" she asked.

"Of course."

Klára headed for the door. At that moment, a young, well-built man in jeans got up and followed her.

155 West Germany, Cologne, October 30, 1972

Klára walked down the sidewalk. She reached into her pocket for a pack of cigarettes. She lit one. She blew out the smoke and continued on her way. She glanced at the name of the street she was on. She took out a map of Cologne, where her destination was circled. She looked up the route. A car was parked a short distance away. It drove off slowly, following her. The man in blue jeans was also watching her. She crossed the street and turned a corner.

There was a large sign on the building she was approaching that read AUSLANDSAMT. The car sped up and braked just in front of Klára. A man jumped out of the car.

"Comrade Wagnerová, what's this I see? I hope you're not about to turn the handle," the man said to her.

The man in jeans from the restaurant watched the situation from a distance.

"Who are you?"

A gun was pointed at her side. "Get in."

"No. I'm on the territory of the Federal Republic of Germany."

The agent laughed: "We had a good laugh, now get in immediately. You're just a snitch, and I'm trained. I hope we understand each other."

Wagner looked around, the gun pressing into her side, so she obeyed and got into the car. The agent helped her and slammed the rear door shut behind her. He jumped in from the other side, still pointing the revolver at Wagner.

"Drive," he ordered the driver. The car pulled away.

The blue jeans took off running, but it was too late. All they could do was stare after the speeding car. However, they pulled out the radio hanging from their belts and pressed the button: "Central, this is PY42. Suspected kidnapping. White Mercedes. German license plate MA JT 2002. Detain them."

"Yes, understood," came the reply over the microphone.

A police patrol parked at a highway rest stop spotted the white Mercedes through binoculars, which they were using to monitor traffic. The patrol held a microphone connected by a cable to the interior of the car. They filed a report.

"What did you think, you idiot, that we'd just let you get away?" Agent barked.

"You have no business here. You're operating in a foreign country," Klára replied, nearly crying.

"Have you ever wondered why we're called the Secret Service? This is a secret operation, I don't have to answer anyone. I have orders, and if I hand you over at the border, I'll be paid very well. For me, it's just business."

"You don't believe that?" she asked.

"What? What don't I believe?"

"Communism."

"I have an apartment in Cologne, a decent salary, and I don't work myself to death. I think communism is fine. I don't have to live under it, so what's the big deal? If they catch me, I'll go to Brussels or London to work in foreign trade. I really don't give a shit."

Klára tried to soften the agent: "My dad is being held in a detention center, and I have no choice. I just want to live a normal life."

"Well, it seems to me that you've taken the short end of the rope, but like I said, I don't give a shit... Fuck."

At one point, the highway was blocked and diverted into the turning lane.

Behind the roadblock, they saw a police car. The other cars in front of them slowed down and obediently pulled over to the side of the road.

The driver stepped on the gas, swerved sharply into the left lane, and broke through the roadblock at full speed.

But the car ran over the spike strip. The tires deflated instantly. Sparks flew from the rims. The StB agent's car came to an involuntary skid at the side of the highway. Police officers with their guns drawn ran up to the white Mercedes from both sides. They opened the doors, forced both agents to get out and lie down on the road, and handcuffed them.

A car with black windows stopped at the roadblock. A man in blue jeans jumped out. He showed his badge to the shaken Klára and then led her to his car.

156 West Germany, Cologne, October 30, 1972

Hofman and Gert were drinking red wine. They were talking and having a good time. They were waiting for Klara Wagnerová and were both certain that she had gone shopping.

"I know we've been yelling at each other a lot lately, but we're still friends, Ota."

"Even friends yell at each other sometimes, but I'd hate for it to become a habit," Gert replied to Hofman. "And about Cinderella. The machine will soon be set in motion, and the money will definitely come."

"Have Filmexport write to me officially, and I'll see what I can do about it. As far as I'm concerned, it's a go. Ota, let's get down to business. I'm sure that when they let you back in, you called a family meeting to discuss whether you should leave or not?"

"Shall we at least have an appetizer?" suggested Hofman.

"Before our lady arrives. We did have a family meeting. We really appreciate your offers to help us in the beginning. We thought about it a lot. I have a wife, children, and elderly parents who are definitely not going anywhere. It's a problem for me to go on a month-long business trip to Karlovy Vary. I couldn't manage it without my wife."

"The offer still stands. You're welcome to stay with us, but can you promise you'll write here as if it were your home? Even I can't promise that. It's different here."

"It's just as you say, Gert. You know me very well. This job is a calling, but sometimes it really sucks."

"That's the first time I've ever heard you swear," Gert said in surprise.

Hofman took a sip of wine. "The boy doesn't speak German, neither does the girl, I can't write German either, and most importantly, I couldn't handle it here. Not being able to take a walk through Kampa in the evening when I feel like it would probably break me. Munich, Cologne, they're all beautiful cities, but I couldn't live there."

The restaurant door opened, and Klára walked in, man wearing blue jeans behind. Wagnerová approached the table.

Gert signaled to the waitress that they would have three shots. "Sit down, Klára. I don't see any bags. Ota and I thought you'd gone shopping."

Then he saw the still frightened expression on Klara's face and asked, "Is everything all right?"

"I really don't know. I'm still shaking."

"What happened? You've been gone for over two hours," Gert glanced at his watch. "Almost three hours."

"When I've recovered, I'll tell you everything, but right now I need a drink of water, or better yet, a shot of something stronger," Klára asked. "The bottom line is that I don't want to go back, I want to stay here in West Germany, and two guys threw me in a car and tried to kidnap me."

Gert and Hofman stared at her and said nothing.

The restaurant door opened, and a policewoman in uniform entered, carrying a folder of papers, which she handed to the young man in jeans who had brought Klára.

"Excuse me, gentlemen," said the man in jeans, approaching the table. He was holding a folder of papers. An asylum application. "They filled it out for you at the station based on your visa application. Now all you have to do is sign it."

Klára took out her Montblanc pen and signed her name.

"What shall we drink to?" asked Hofman.

"Welcome to the Federal Republic of Germany, Frau Wagner. By the way, that's a beautiful pen. Is it a Montblanc, by any chance? May I take a look?" Gert examined the pen for a moment and then returned it with an admiring smile.

They clinked glasses.

"Excuse me, am I missing something?" asked Hofman, puzzled.

"Well, sort of, Ota, look out the window. Do you see that beautiful shiny Mercedes over there?"

Ota focused on the spot Gert was pointing to: "You mean that white sports car, Gert?"

"You could have that for this pen, and you'd still have enough left over for coffee."

Ota looked at Klára angrily: "Are you telling me that I smuggled the latest Mercedes model across the border in my breast pocket?"

"Mr. Hofman?" asked the blue jeans.

"Yes, that's me."

"You see, I have to ask you something. When we questioned one of the kidnappers, he told us that he was your son-in-law."

"What? You can't be serious! Some kind of stupid joke?"

"We don't know what to make of it either. According to his passport, his name is Beckenbauer."

"I don't know any Beckenbauer. I don't know what else that guy made up."

"I'm sorry."

Blue Jeans stood next to the chair where Klára was sitting.

"Could I invite you to dinner? I guess you didn't have time to eat, and the gentlemen, as I understand, have already eaten."

"How could I refuse my savior?"

"You must be tired. If you'll allow me, I'll drive you back to the hotel."

422

She stood up: "I'm still shaking. That would be very kind of you."

The blue jeans and Klára got up to leave: "Goodbye, gentlemen. See you at the hotel," she said.

Gert and Ota looked at each other and burst out laughing.

157 Prague, November 1, 1972

"I'm home," said Ota Hofman as soon as he opened the door to his new apartment in Prague's Podolí district, opposite the famous yellow swimming pool.

"Hi, Ota," said Irena, kissing him hello. "Don't even bother getting changed, we have to go to Spořilov to see Irena."

"What's happened?" Ota hung his coat on the coat rack.

"Well, Milan has disappeared somewhere, he hasn't been home for a week, and the car is gone too. That's what's happened," blurted out Irena.

"Let's go then."

158 Prague, November 1, 1972

"Have you reported it to the cops?" asked Hofman.

"I already reported it. I went there the day after you left..." replied his daughter. "They took my statement. I call them every day. So far, they have nothing, they know nothing."

Irena sat in the dining room with her baby in her arms. "I don't know anything else, only that he didn't come home. He didn't take any of his things; only the car disappeared with him."

Grandmother Antonie from Jiřice near Kostelec nad Labem, Hofman's extremely kind and devoted mother-in-law, who had come to help her with the child, sat next to her.

"Make me some coffee, please," Ota asked his wife.

"Dad, I don't know what to do," Irena cried.

"So, he's missing? He didn't say anything and just disappeared? Do I understand correctly that the cops don't know anything about him or the car?"

"That's right," confirmed Grandma.

"What about his friends, acquaintances, relatives? Did you call them?"

"I called everyone I know. No one knows anything. They don't know, or maybe they're just pretending. I…"

"That's all we needed," her father consoled his daughter. "I'll tell you something. The journalist who went with me to

Cologne hasn't come back. She ran away. I'm probably going to have trouble at work now. I have no idea how much trouble. And now this is on top of everything else." Hofman thought for a moment. "Look, Irena, it's not the end of the world. We need to figure out how to organize everything. Grandma, can you stay here for a few more days?" he asked.

She nodded:" Of course, I'll stay."

"And you, Irena, go back to Security tomorrow, there's not much else you can do now. Yeah, you have to report the car to cops as stolen; it's registered to you anyway, maybe they'll find out something. I'll finish my coffee and then we'll go to Podolí," he said, looking at his wife.

She nodded.

"I'm really tired from the trip. It was long and boring."

"I'll drive," Irena decided.

159 Prague/Cologne, November 2, 1972

Late in the evening, Pixa was in his office reading Klára Wagnerová's file again. He picked up a photo of Klára. "Good job, girl, what would I do here without you? Just fly away, little dove."

He lit a cigarette, then used the lighter to burn her photo and threw it into the ashtray. It was exactly 10:08 p.m. when he wondered what she might be doing now.

*

The music was so loud that you couldn't hear yourself think. The DJ on stage was half-naked. In front of him was a lit-up console, and he was adjusting the speed of the record he was playing. A Creedence Clearwater Revival song was rocking the crowd of dancers on the dance floor of the Paradise disco club in the center of Cologne. Klára Wagnerová felt like she hadn't felt in a long time; she had an exhilarating feeling of freedom and was going wild on the dance floor. Her partner, a tall, slim man, never seemed to take off his blue work jeans. The only change in his attire was the loose shirt he was wearing today.

Suddenly, it dawned on Klára... That blackmailer, Pixa. She remembered him, his painted lips, and the hideous claws he had shown her.

The clock showed twenty-two minutes past ten. What was he doing now, maybe torturing someone else at home? But that wasn't home for me anymore. And what about Dad? Where was home now?

*

Pixa picked up the phone; his secretary had long since gone home, so he dialed the number himself: "Hey, Volod'a. Listen, I've got the Koh-i-noor accounts to check. Let Wagner go in the morning and tell him to get back to work like he's used to. The local party cell will take care of him. He's dead to me now; I don't care about him. I think he's had enough of his vacation. Let him start earning money for our cause again." Pixa laughed at his own joke.

*

Blue jeans searched for keys in his pocket. They ran up the stairs to the second floor together. He and the beautiful and charming girl from Czechoslovakia. She hugged him at the door and kissed him. It was magical and intoxicating.

He quickly unlocked the door, and they stumbled inside, embracing and kissing. As soon as he closed the door with his foot, she began to unbutton his shirt. He led her in his arms through the unfamiliar apartment to the bedroom.

She was already unbuttoning his blue jeans. The pendulum clock in the living room showed twenty-three minutes past eleven.

*

"Volod'a, please check Comrade Holinka from the prop room. Something doesn't seem right... Oh, and don't forget to file a criminal complaint against Wagnerová with the prosecutor's office... Well, as usual, for the crime of leaving the country. If that little minx comes back, put her in a jumpsuit. So, film star, beautiful lady, oh well, it was boring with you."

Pixa closed the folder on his desk and went to lie down on the couch.

*

Lovers in an apartment in Cologne embraced each other tenderly, and at that moment, nothing else mattered to them.

*

A lonely man in an empty office in Prague reached for the light switch by the couch, turned off the light, and tried to fall asleep. But he kept thinking about what game he would play tomorrow and with whom.

160 Prague, November 6, 1972

Hofman went to see Toman, who had summoned him to his office. They sat opposite each other at the table. Both were smoking freshly brewed coffee. Comrade Husák looked down at them benevolently from the wall above them.

"So how did the business trip go? Have you written your report yet?"

Hofman raised his eyebrows. "Are you kidding me? You put a hen in my car to follow me..."

Toman interrupted him with a wave of his hand: "That's Pix's business, I'm not involved in that."

"Oh, right, I forgot, you put that idiot Mareček in my office. You two can shake hands. You hate each other to the core. I'm the head scriptwriter for children's films, I deal with fairy tales and stories for children, I focus on stories about first loves, art, childhood, gingerbread houses, princesses," Hofman said angrily.

Toman remained calm: "I see you're getting as angry as a writer. Look, I'm not blaming you for anything, I know you're not involved, so calm down, okay? This is Pixa's mess. Let him deal with it now," he laughed.

To cover it up, Toman addressed Hofman: "So, Ota, I read your request for financial support for the children's film festival in Ostrov. Where is that, please?"

"Right next to Karlovy Vary. The festival is organized by enthusiasts, and they need help. I got back from there two weeks ago. There are lots of children and really enthusiastic organizers. The festival has a great atmosphere."

"Oto, we can't contribute to every film festival in the country, but you know what? Prepare a letter for me, I'll run it by Purš, and we'll send it to the Ministry of Culture. They're responsible for these things, so they should do something useful for people, right?"

"Well, I'll prepare the letter, and we'll see. I highly doubt the ministry will budge an inch."

"And how did it go with Cinderella? Are the West Germans getting involved?"

"Gert will try to push it through," confirmed Hofman.

"That's good. Especially after the unpleasantness the comrade from Stasi put him through."

"It wasn't comrade from Stasi, it was comrades from the StB," corrected Hofman.

"That's very good, because I already wrote a letter to DEFA asking if they would mind a capital investment from a West German partner in Popelka. We can't do this behind their backs," remarked Toman. "You have to realize that my job isn't just to read your fantasies; I also have to watch you. Watch you, above all, from yourself. Because that's how I protect myself. The party has given me the trust that you have lost. And if I don't watch you, whether I want to or not, I'll have to step on your neck. I can afford to make mistakes, but you can't. Because if you make another mistake like you did during the checks, remember that we don't forgive mistakes."

"We? Who's 'we'?"

"We. The watchdogs."

161 Prague, January 10, 1973

Nostic Palace in Malá Strana was built between 1660 and 1676 by Jan Hartvík of Nostic, the highest chancellor of the Kingdom of Bohemia. František Václav Nostic then commissioned a late Baroque renovation. Some of the preserved interior elements are remarkable, such as the Baroque star-patterned parquet flooring, Baroque door frames with original doors, tiled stoves, and stucco work. In addition to the gallery and library, the well-known palace rooms include the Chapel of the Assumption of the Virgin Mary and the minister's study. It is therefore no surprise that the palace has been designated a protected monument.

And it was here, to the current headquarters of the Ministry of Culture, that Ota Hofman headed for a meeting with Minister Milan Klusák. He entered the richly decorated minister's office.

One of the two secretaries behind the desk immediately asked when she saw him in the doorway: "Can I help you?"

"Good morning, my name is Ota Hofman and I have an appointment with the comrade minister on behalf of Barrandov Film Studios."

The secretary checked the list on her desk: "Yes, of course. Please excuse the minister, he is delayed. Please take a seat."

Ota Hofman took out a pack of cigarettes with a practiced gesture and was about to light one.

"You can't smoke here, we are in a protected cultural monument, comrade. Even the minister is not allowed to smoke in the building," the secretary admonished Hofman.

Hofman humbly put the pack back in his pocket.

"May I use the restroom in the meantime?" asked Hofman.

"Certainly, third door on the right," replied the secretary.

Hofman got up, went out, and headed for the restroom.

He opened the toilet door and saw a figure standing by the open window. He recognized him. He had seen that face somewhere before. Then it dawned on him: "Good morning, Comrade Minister."

The minister looked him over. Hofman continued: "My name is Hofman, and we have an appointment on behalf of Barrandov Film Studios."

"Ah, good morning, Comrade Hofman," greeted the minister, pulling out a lit cigarette hidden behind his body from the visitor. "I'm glad it's not anyone from the ministry; they might report me."

"Would you mind if I lit up too?" asked Hofman.

"Not me, why? This is pure terror, not being allowed to smoke in your own house, but what can I do?"

He stubbed out his cigarette, threw the butt into the bowl, and flushed it.

Hofman took out a pack and lit one.

"So, what's on your mind, Comrade Hofman?"

"It's about financial support for a film festival for children and young people in Ostrov. I go there every year, and I'm completely captivated by their enthusiasm. There are lots of children there, and everything is organized by volunteers for free. Your ministry should support events like this, especially with regard to the education of young people."

Hofman took out the box again. "Can I offer you one, Comrade Minister?"

"Ah, Stuyvesants, I haven't had those in a long time. Thank you." He took a cigarette out of the box. Hofman lit it with his lighter.

"I've passed the matter on to my deputy, so it would be better if you stopped by his office. I think activities like this should be supported. He has my instructions to accommodate you. And while I'm talking to you, I really liked your book *The Escape*, a very enjoyable read. I like short books."

"Well, you know, I'm not very good at writing long pieces. A three-page Balzac-style description would be torture for me. But thank you."

"What are you working on now?"

"Scripts. Most of my time is taken up with the next series of *Pan Tau*."

"I look forward to it. It's a shame you cast those undesirable actors in the first series."

"Who do you mean by undesirable actors, Comrade Minister?"

"That's not my decision, Comrade Hofman; it's decided by others. However, Comrade Landovský and Comrade Werich, for example... That's why the episodes with them definitely can't be broadcast now."

"I see, and the others can be broadcast?"

"Yes, they were found to be acceptable. So be very careful with the casting. Comrades are very sensitive about that these days."

"Thank you for the advice. Where can I find the deputy minister?"

"If you go down the hall, it's the fifth door on the left."

"Thank you, Comrade Minister, and now, if you'll excuse me." Hofman stepped up to the phone and relieved himself. He still had the cigarette in his mouth. But he knew what to do with it. He threw the butt into the bowl and flushed it down.

"Goodbye, Comrade Minister."

"It was a pleasure, Comrade Hofman. I'm glad we sorted it out so nicely. Goodbye."

Hofman went out, leaving the Minister of Culture, who was enjoying his Stuyvesant, to contemplate by the window.

162 Prague, January 10, 1973

Hofman knocked gently. "Come in," he heard.

He entered and stood frozen. "Well, Bureš! What are you doing here, Bureš?"

"Deputy Minister, Comrade Hofman." He was clearly pleased. "You know, life has taught me that it's better to make a living as a deputy than as a screenwriter or writer. Now I have security. But let's sit down. The secretary has gone to chat in the next office, so we'll be alone, and no one will disturb us."

"I'm amazed, Comrade Bureš."

"How are you, Comrade Hofman? It's been a long time since we last saw each other. You were the only one who understood my creative talent, and I will never forget that. Now, about your request, "he pulled a letter from the pile on the desk. " It has, of course, been approved. From now on, the Ostrov festival will receive a subsidy in the form of a mandatory item from the Ministry of Culture, that is, every year. All you have to do is send me a request and the amount of the subsidy you require."

"I'm speechless, Comrade Bureš. Thank you. I won't keep you any longer." Hofman offered his hand in farewell: "Goodbye."

Bureš stood up, reached into his pocket, took out the banknotes, counted out three hundred crowns, and offered them to Hofman. "Thank you, I'll give them back."

Hofman stared at the banknotes for a moment, fascinated, then took them.

"Well then, goodbye, Comrade Deputy."

They shook hands.

"Anytime, anything, Comrade, I mean, Mr. Hofman. Come by, give me a call, my door is always open. Goodbye."

163 Prague, January 10, 1973

Bohunka Šourková was checking her perfect makeup in the mirror behind her desk in the dramaturgy group's office when she heard the door open.

"Good morning, Bohunka, what a beautiful morning we're having."

Bohunka put down the mirror. "Hi, Oto, you seem to be in a good mood."

"You bet. Please dial the director of the cultural center in Ostrov."

"You must have scored big at the ministry yesterday, huh?"

"Bohunka, guess who I ran into ministry yesterday!" Hofman fired off a rhetorical question and raised his eyebrows.

"How should I know? Klusák?"

"Yeah, him too. We had a nice chat in the bathroom."

"What?"

"Yeah, it's the perfect place to meet with ministers. We agreed on everything there, and we didn't even need an office."

"And the other one? That wasn't all, I presume."

"Well, no, it wasn't. I ran into Bureš."

"That Bureš..."

"Yeah, that Bureš. He's Klusák's deputy now."

"You've got to be kidding me, Oto," Bohunka blurted out.

"Come on, Bohunka, I've never heard you use words like that."

Hofman reached into his pocket and pulled out three hundred crowns. He handed them to Bohunka.

"What's this?"

"Our bet, I lost."

"He gave it back to you. I'm really surprised."

Bohunka took the three hundred and put it in her wallet, which she took out of her purse. Then she looked at her phone book and started dialing a number.

164 East Germany, Moritzburg Castle, January 15, 1973

Director Vorlíček checked the prepared scene one last time. The entire film crew was frozen to the bone under the walls of Moritzburg Castle. Cameraman Illík checked the camera position once more. Vorlíček explained to Cinderella, Libuše Šafránková, once again how he envisioned her role.

"You'll vun up the staivs. You'll dvop the slippev. You'll hesitate, but you won't pick it up. The hovse will be in the shot with you. But you won't mount it until the next shot. Cleav? Let's do it."

The lighting technician checked the lighting one last time. The sound engineer with the microphone announced, "Ready."

Libuška Šafránková ran up the stairs. She nodded down.

A voice called, "Camera."

"Take 8961, first time. Clap." The clapperboard clicked in front of the camera.

Vorlíček gave the command: "Action."

165 East Germany, Moritzburg Castle, January 17, 1973

The surface of the lake surrounding Moritzburg Castle was dark, as was the entire January day. Everywhere else except for the lake, there seemed to be nothing but mud and mud. The temperature was just above freezing. There was no sign of snow anywhere. A member of the crew led a horse. Václav Vorlíček sat huddled in the director's chair.

A voice addressed the director: "Director, are we shooting today?"

"Not yet. I'm not veady yet."

"What's going on?" asked the voice.

"Evevything's pvetty much scvewed up, that's what's going on. There's supposed to be a lot of snow in the scvipt. Do you see any? Theve's none heve. Wheve's that guy from DEFA production?"

"He's over there in the heated tent."

Vorlíček got up and walked over. He pulled back the tarp and saw who he was looking for. "Comvade, wheve's the snow? Didn't you ovdev it in Moscow? Undev socialism, we can command snow and rain. Isn´t it"

"Comrade director. We're already working on it."

"What?"

"We've got snow. We're bringing it."

"All vight," Vorlíček calmed down. "I'll wait heve for a while."

After a moment, he heard the sound of cars approaching. The cars stopped, and the sounds indicated that they were unloading their cargo.

"What's all this noise?" asked Vorlíček, looking at the DEFA producer.

"We ordered snow from a nearby fish farm; we couldn't get it anywhere else," DEFA producer defended himself.

Vorlíček got up and ran outside. He saw a pile of strange slush. He covered his nose. A little further away, he saw one of the actors vomiting.

"How the hell am I supposed to shoot a wintev faivy tale without snow and in this slush?" cried Vorlíček in despair.

He was interrupted by a crew member: "Comrade Director, you have a phone call from Prague."

"Who is calling?"

"Ota Hofman."

"Gentlemen, I'm sovvy, but I have to take this."

Vorlíček headed to the castle to answer the phone.

Downstairs in the hall, he was handed the receiver.

Hofman asked with a smile, "Hi, Vašek, how's it going?"

"Tevvcible," Vorlíček informed him.

443

"Now you finally understand why screenwriters don't go to film shoots, right?"

Vorlíček began to laugh: "Look, this veally isn't possible. We'll finish filming today, as it is, and then we have to get back to Czechoslovakia. One move day with that smell from fish and I'll be dead too."

"What are you talking about, Vašek? What's that fishy smell?"

"Don't even mention it. There's not a snowflake in sight for miles avound, but they've bvought in a load of stinky fish from the neavby fish mavket. The stench is unbeavable."

"But there's no snow in Švihov," Hofman pointed out.

"Even if I had to bving polystyvene theve, it would be wovth it. But it's bound to snow."

"As if that weren't enough, I have more bad news, Václav. I spoke to our producer, and he said to tell you that you need different horses in Švihov than the ones we have here."

"What?" Vorlíček exclaimed.

"There's an epidemic of foot-and-mouth disease, and no horses are allowed across the border."

Vorlíček cursed: "Damn it, but the actovs ave used to them!"

"Václav, that's why I should have told you."

166 Prague, January 18, 1973

Hofman, dressed in his usual suit and tie, was typing furiously on his typewriter. Bohunka entered his office. "Toman called. He wants to see you as soon as possible, Ota."

Hofman nodded imperiously. He didn't let anything show. It seemed that over the last few years, he had finally smoothed out his rough edges.

"Sit down, Ota," Toman invited Hofman. "How's it going with Cinderella? Are they managing? Are they having any problems with our East German comrades? I've received a few letters..."

"Nothing out of the ordinary. As far as I can tell, anyway. I only ever visit the set once. But they're having problems with the snow. As luck would have it, it's not snowing, and their solutions are expensive and not always effective."

Toman listened to the information: "All right. I'll call the producer."

"I spoke to director Vorlíček, and he's already getting ready to move to Švihov, but I'm afraid that won't solve the snow problem. There's nothing there either."

"From a political point of view, it's good that he's coming back. When I found out how they were transporting the film material across the border, I was quite shocked. Imagine, Ota, they're so afraid of the Stasi that the young actor

Trávníček is carrying the discs full of film material through customs himself, so they don't get into the trunk of the company car."

"Trávníček?" Hofman was alarmed. "That barely legal kid who plays the prince?"

"Yeah," confirmed Toman.

"Are you completely crazy?"

"I don't know, probably. Their secrecy is making the comrades nervous, and me too. I'm tired of being a lightning rod. After my urgent request, DEFA director Albert Wilkening responded to my question about WDR's capital investment in the production of Cinderella. The ministry rejected it because of the lack of an agreement regulating cultural relations between East and West Germany."

"Damn it, damn it. I haven't even got to tell you yet. I saw footage of Cinderella's entrance that DEFA shot in December. It looks like cardboard, and they've reduced the extras compared to the script. We'll have to reshoot everything here. We discussed it the day before yesterday with Marcela Pittermannová and the DEFA production team in Dresden. Vorlíček was really not happy about it. If they don't want to put their own money into it, why are they blocking our WDR funding? Damn it. Damn it!" Hofman vented. "You know what, you've got a lot on your plate. But so do I. Anything else?" Hofman didn't want to prolong the meeting.

"How are things at home?" asked Toman.

Hofman looked at him in astonishment: "Excuse me?"

"What about at home? I'm asking because I heard your son-in-law ran off, and your adult daughter came back home with two girls?"

"How did you find that out?" Hofman stared at Toman.

"Ota, don't fuck with me, you know who you're talking to, you fucker. I've got my people at Pixa too!"

"I get it. You're both obsessed with spying. Hofman flushed with rage.

"We have to defend the interests of the working class. At any cost."

Hofman suddenly lost control: "I was thinking, Ludvík. Have you seen Animal Farm?"

"What am I supposed to have seen?"

"George Orwell."

Now it was Toman's turn to stare blankly. "Some capitalist crap again. No wonder you need supervision."

"It's nothing my wife and I can't handle." Hofman was slowly regaining his self-control.

"Well, whatever you say. But you're probably going to miss that car he took from you, aren't you?"

"I'll buy my daughter a new one in time," Hofman snapped. "But there's something I'd like to ask you, Ludvík," he continued.

"Yes, Oťásek?"

"I'd appreciate it if you didn't talk to anyone at work about my private life. It's nobody's business."

An angry Hofman got up and left without saying goodbye.

167 Prague, January 18, 1973

As Hofman left Toman's office, his mind was in turmoil. He passed the bathroom door and went in. With trembling hands, he took out a cigarette with a practiced movement. He lit it and took a long drag. He looked at himself in the mirror. Through his own reflection, he began to see images of his daughter Irena, and granddaughter playing in the garden. The smiling Šmejda suddenly looked directly at the camera and said something to him. He couldn't hear what.

Hofman punched the mirror with his fist. It shattered just like Šmejda's image.

168 Prague, January 18, 1973

Bohunka bandaged his wounded, bloodied hand in her office. He refused to go to the emergency room. A company car with a driver took him home. When Irena saw him with the bandage, she was startled.

"I have to tell you something, come sit down, but first make us some coffee."

"I should at least bandage your hand," Irena suggested anxiously. "It's bleeding. What happened? You're as mysterious as a castle in the Carpathians."

"I spoke to Toman today. And he let slip that our son-in-law has run off to West Germany with Irena's Simca."

"What? So he's not missing, as we thought?" Irena stared at him.

"No, he's not."

"Then why cops are lying to us?" she asked.

"I don't know, maybe they don't know either. You know, I think I saw him at a rest stop near Frankfurt, but I thought I was just imagining things."

Irena was now really angry: "That bastard didn't forget the car we gave Irena as a wedding present. He forgot the children, though, the bastard."

Hofman added, "It must be Pixa's doing. Pixa and Toman literally hate each other! Otherwise, Toman wouldn't have told me. I really don't know."

Irena continued to rage: "So one bastard puts a spy in your office and the other one in your family? Is that what you're telling me? For God's sake, what kind of world are we living in?"

Hofman asked: "Light my cigarette, please."

Irena did as he asked. She put the cigarette in his mouth.

"We can't tell Irena he was a snitch; it would completely destroy her. It's bad enough that he ran away from his family in a stolen car."

Irena remarked sadly, "Those children aren't to blame for their father, but hopefully they didn't inherit his thieving genes and..." Irena couldn't find the right words for a long time.

169 West Bohemia, Water Castle Švihov, February 10, 1973

"What are we going to do?" asked Vorlíček.

They were standing with cameraman Illík outside Švihov Castle. According to the shooting schedule, they were supposed to be preparing the scene of the royal procession passing by. In the script, full of handwritten notes, director Vorlíček had written that the landscape would be snowy. They were standing there alone because there was no point in bringing the whole crew to the set. At this time of year, there was always snow, but not this year. Not even a flake.

"Should we pack up and postpone?" the cameraman asked the director.

"Do you know how much that costs? And we don't have that kind of money, damn it!" the director vented.

"I'd like to try an idea," the cameraman bowed his head and looked at the planned shot from the knees.

"Get a truckload of Styrofoam from production," he said to Vorlíček.

"I already thought of that," Vorlíček remarked, "but we'd need at least ten or a hundred to make it look right. I only managed to get one, and it's got problems."

"When can it be here?"

"I don't know, would one be enough for you?" asked Vorlíček in amazement.

"I guess so."

"Let's go," Vorlíček commanded. "Come with me, I'll call production."

With the receiver in his hand, Vorlíček inquired, "So it can leave immediately and be here when, in how long?" He covered the speaker. "This afternoon, it'll be here at one," he informed Illík.

"Let's all eat quickly and get the crew ready. We're shooting at one," Illík told Vorlíček and the production cameraman.

"Really?"

"Yeah, really. I'll show you when the truck arrives."

"All right, everyone, stop messing around. I want everything ready at one o'clock," ordered the director.

"Take a look." Illík took a bag of polystyrene from the back of the truck and dumped it on the ground. "What are you standing around for?" he snapped at his colleagues.

"Go make a royal procession. Walk a hundred meters down this road, then turn around and come towards us."

Then he lowered the camera on the tripod and framed the road. He lay down on the wet ground, not caring that he was getting dirty, and changed the shot. "Look through the viewfinder," he told Vorlíček.

"Holy shit," Vorlíček exclaimed.

The crew members walked through the snowy landscape, but it was just an illusion.

"All right, everyone, get ready and let's go, go, move," Vorlíček commanded.

170 Prague, Vorlíček's apartment, February 12, 1973

Vorlíček had a glass on the table and a bottle of Vat 69 whisky next to it. He was reading the German magazine Spiegel, and Rudé právo newspaper was lying on the table. At the same time, he was watching television with one eye – they were showing the old film *Moon Over the River*.

Vorlíček was captivated by a scene in the film and thought to himself, That's filmmaking.

The phone rang. Vorlíček looked at the clock. It was already past eleven. He picked up the phone. "Comrade Director…"

"Pepa, damn it, man, you were supposed to call by ten. Weren't you paying attention in civics class? Am I supposed to look out the window?"

The sleepy film producer Kadlec, leaning over an open black notebook with the cast list, began calling the actors.

Vorlíček also sat by the phone, dialing number after number, completely forgetting about civics class. He gave everyone the same information: "Alert. Hurry up, it's snowing. It's snowing!"

Soon, the phone rang at his home: "Hello!"

"Šafránková is in Brno," he heard from the receiver.

"What is she doing in Brno when it's snowing? Oh, she lives there. That's her only excuse. Send a car for her. She has to be on set."

Everyone at the Šafránek house was asleep, which is why no one answered the phone for so long. Ring, ring, ring. The phone rang and rang. Finally, a sleepy father in his pajamas picked up the receiver, yawned, and muttered, "Is there a fire or something?"

"No, it's snowing. Wake up, Libuška Šafránková, the car is coming for her."

The entire film crew was already up, and feverish preparations were underway. "We have to be on set at five in the morning. It's snowing. It's already snowing!"

171 West Germany, Cologne, June 14, 1973

After arriving at work at the WDR building in Cologne, Gert made coffee. Yesterday's mail was waiting on his desk, which he hadn't had time to open yet.

He sorted through the envelopes, throwing some unopened ones into the trash can next to his desk. However, one envelope caught his eye. He opened it and took out a letter from Filmexport in Prague. In the invitation, written in German, Director Moravec invited him to Prague to see a rough cut of the film Three Nuts for Cinderella by director Vorlíček, which was to be screened on June 26 in the Filmexport screening room in Prague's Lucerna.

172 Prague, June 26, 1973

Three people sat side by side in the Filmexport screening room watching the rough cut of the film, without music: Gert Müntefering, Moravec, the director of Filmexport, and Vorlíček, the director of the film.

"That Šafránková is a very pretty girl," remarked Gert, clearly enjoying the screening.

"She really showed them, haha."

The screening ended.

Gert turned to Vorlíček: "This is a comedy, not a fairy tale."

"But that's how we make films in Czechoslovakia," replied Vorlíček.

Gert thought for a moment. Then he got up from his chair. "I like that Cinderella is an action girl... Westdeutscher Rundfunk will definitely buy the license. And who's doing the music? It needs some good music."

"Kavel Svoboda," replied Vorlíček.

"Good choice, but tell him I don't want any Gott in it."

"Kavel is supposed to sing the final song. We've already agreed on that."

Gert frowned: "No way. Maya the Bee was enough for us."

"Wait, Svoboda and Karel Gott are best friends, you can't do that to them."

"You know, Václav. Here in Czechoslovakia, you have a one-party government, and you promote your friends. We have a competition. And *Maya the Bee* is on our rival TV station. Even if I wanted to, which I don't, it's not worth it to me for the backlash."

"But you'll tell him youvself," Vorlíček challenged Gert.

"No, Karel Svoboda will tell him, why me? He's the head of music. Karel Gott is a professional; he'll handle it."

173 Prague, June 26, 1973

Ota Hofman and Gert sat in the bar of the Alcron Hotel in Prague with a glass of wine so many times that no one could ever count them. It was the same this time. Ota Hofman, once again with a cigarette, listened to Gert, who had just informed him: "So I bought it."

"Great! I'm happy for you, my friend. Everyone will be relieved. It cost a lot of money, but now we're basically in the black."

Gert laughed: "According to my business judgment, our TV will be too. A lot of countries will buy this."

"That's great. I hope it works out the way you think it will. You deserve it. Anyone else in your position would have given up on this madness long ago."

Ota took a drag on his cigarette and stubbed it out in the ashtray on the table.

Gert laughed and waved his hand.

"If I didn't enjoy it, I wouldn't do it. At least I'll have something to talk about in retirement. It's an adventure."

Hofman laughed too. "Tell me about it. I still remember the stitches in the hospital."

"But I'd like to ask you something."

"Anything, Gert."

"About when they kicked you out of the party after the checks, can I ask you why you actually joined the Communists? We've known each other for a few years now, and you're different from the other guys I see around here."

"You know, I did a lot of stupid things when I was young. For example, in high school, I stole the gym teacher's girlfriend, and that's unforgivable. My dad had to deal with it. I was seventeen. Churchill once said that anyone who isn't a leftist at twenty has no heart, and anyone who is a leftist at forty has no brain. I kind of got ahead of him. But after that damn August, I might add that I also sold my soul and lost my memory." "I don't understand, Oto, why didn't you come with us? You know I would have taken care of you. And you had a chance with Klára. By the way, she's doing fine."

"We've already discussed that, Gert."

"Don't be sad, my friend. I've thought about it too. You could come work for us on TV and start writing. But even here, you wouldn't be able to write what you want. And when I see how things are at your job, I'd be surprised if they let you do what you do there. I'm so happy I was able to buy Sexana, that I helped you with *Pan Tau*, and now we're sure to be a hit with Cinderella. You're flying the flag for Hollywood of the East. Without you and your enthusiasm, Barrandov would be just another subjugated regional Moscow studio."

461

"Maybe you're right," Hofman smiled and invited Gert to clink glasses. "Actually, we should be happy that we managed to see it through to the end."

"When you think about it, neither of us is sitting still, and the brakes on our cars still work."

Hofman laughed. "So what are you up to now? What are you going to do next?"

Hofman shifted in his seat. "I don't know, Gert."

"I'd really love it if you and Jindra Polák finally came to shoot here. I'm sure Pixa and Toman would let you. Shoot something family-oriented, about parents who don't have time for their children. That's your thing. And it's a big issue here in Germany right now."

"You're right. I have an idea. A combination of live action and animation. We shot something like that once, years ago, at Barrandov, and it could be developed further. It's about a little girl. Her name is Lucie and she's always up to mischief, which annoys her neighbors, who can't stand her. She's the ruler of the seven seas, she's a force of nature, and she brings stuffed animals and inanimate objects to life."

"She's the terror of the neighborhood, so Lucie, the terror of the street?"

Hofman looked at him. "She's the terror of the street, exactly."

"So, get to it."

174 Prague, October 4, 1973

The Hofmans were playing cards at home. Ota Hofman came to take a break from writing and sat down with Irena for a cup of coffee.

"How's it going today, Ota?" Irena asked.

"Well, it's going, but not really," Ota complained. "I think I've got a block or something. I'm stuck and don't know how to continue. I can't do it."

The phone rang. Ota got up to answer it. He heard Vorlíček's voice: "Hi, Ota, I need to meet with you."

"What's up, Vašek?"

"Don't play dumb. The festival in Ostvov stavts in five days. You talked Toman into it, and the pvemieve of Cindevella is on the progvam. We have to get veady. We have to wvite a pvess velease togethev, and I don't know what else we have to do, man."

"Are you nervous or something? Yeah, I know, your first time in a big cinema. The premiere with children. It's going to be awesome."

"So, Oto, can you make time fov me?"

"Of course I can. Come to my place tomorrow, I'll be in Jindřišská from the morning."

175 West Bohemia, Ostrov, House of Culture, 7 October 1973

"Welcome to Ostrov," said a smiling woman in her thirties wearing a red dress as she greeted Ota Hofman and Václav Vorlíček in the accreditation room of the House of Culture in Ostrov, "My name is Marie, Marie Cruel, and I will be your guardian angel for the duration of the festival."

Vorlíček quickly remarked: "Well, I hope it won't be too cruel."

Oh, another one of his jokes, Marie thought to herself, but she didn't lose her smile.

"Comrade Hofman, here you are..."

"Marie, we can certainly be on first-name terms, but I'm no comrade. I'm Ota."

Marie Cruel looked him in the eye and started again. "Oto, here's the festival program. We've booked you a room in Jáchymov, and don't forget to come to the discussion with my class tomorrow. The children are really looking forward to meeting their dad of Pan Tau."

"I haven't forgotten. I've written it down in the program."

"Oto, I can pick you up here at the cultural center. I'll show you the way. You might get lost. And here are the invitations to today's reception, which will be up here in the large hall. By the way, thank you very much, Oto. The National

Committee has already paid us the ministerial money, so this year we have enough left for the reception and the fireworks in the evening. You will be here in the evening, of course..."

"It's not my money, so don't thank me."

"Ota, we know, everyone knows, so please... We have to celebrate in the evening after the lantern parade and fireworks. You're invited, Oto, and you can't turn us down."

"Come on, Václav, we have to go to your discussion now," Hofman said, leading Vorlíček to the cultural center's café. He knew his way around here well.

176 West Bohemia, Ostrov, House of Culture, October 11, 1973

Vorlíček and Hofman handed out the carnations they had just received to random women passing by. They had just finished their obligatory speeches before the start of the preview screening – and, in fact, the world premiere – of the new Czechoslovak fairy tale *Three Nuts for Cinderella*. Vorlíček sat down in an empty seat in the front row, but Hofman left the hall, which was filled to capacity with children. He went out for a smoke.

After a moment, the doors to the hall opened.

"Václav, you're such a wimp. What are you afraid of? You should be sitting in the hall."

"Oto, I've got tevvible stage fvight." The sound of film music and raucous children's laughter could be heard from the hall.

Vorlíček confessed: "This is an oppovtunity that comes once in a lifetime, I'm afvaid I've messed it up."

"Messed it up, you didn't mess it up, you can hear it, can't you?" Another burst of thunderous laughter rang out.

"I saw you yestevday evening. Was she intevested in you?" Vorlíček changed the subject.

"Please, I'm a happily married man."

"That's not a physical defect, is it? I'm quite envious of you, Oto. evevy spavvow on the voof is alveady whispeving about it."

"Are you kidding?"

"No, I'm not," Vorlíček insisted.

177 Prague, October 20, 1973

After returning from Ostrov, Ota Hofman immediately met with František Pavlíček for a glass of wine.

"Franta, long time no see."

"I'm glad you called me."

"It didn't look like it at first, but Cindarella is a hit. It's already been sold to more than fifty countries."

"To the East?" asked Pavlíček.

"The East doesn't have that many countries. To the West, too, mainly thanks to Gert, of course."

"It's a dream come true, my friend." They clinked glasses.

"I forgot to tell you and now hold on to your hats. That bastard secret police guy they put in my band has been fired!"

"You're kidding," Pavlíček said in surprise.

"No, really. I can feel something's happening."

"That's so nice to hear, my friend. It makes me think of a comparison between life and theater. You can't deny, Oto, that there really is a certain similarity here without having to look too hard. In life, just like on stage, laughter and tears often alternate, comedy and drama. Here and there, we see stories of rise and fame, but there are also falls. Sometimes tragic, sometimes more grotesque..."

Hofman took a sip of wine but did not interrupt Pavlíček.

"It seems to me that right now, on the stage of our world and our lives, a play is being performed that is at times quite amusing, but at times bitterly embarrassing, and sometimes even a little gloomy. We see a large number of eccentric and remarkable costumes, yet this is not a historical costume drama."

Pavlíček paused and took a sip himself.

"Something has to change, Franta. It can't go on like this. Everyone can see that," Hofman remarked.

"But, Oto, despite the similarities, there are differences, and they are not insignificant. On stage, the play ends after two hours, the audience applauds, and the actors take off their costumes behind the scenes. Tomorrow, they will easily put on different costumes, perhaps for roles completely opposite to those they played today. Unfortunately, in real life, it's not that easy. We keep playing our only dramatic piece, and unlike theater, it lasts a lifetime, and the consequences of our actions on the world stage don't end with the curtain falling on one comedy today and another being performed tomorrow."

178 West German, Cologne, October 22, 1973

Gert was sitting at his desk in his office in Cologne. He heard a soft knock on the door. "Come in." He couldn't be distracted from his work. He was writing notes for next year's WDR children's program. He looked up. Wagnerová, with a large belly in front of her, opened the door with one hand and tried to push the pram inside with the other. Gert looked up, smiled, and ran to help her. When she finally managed to get the pram inside, he hugged her.

"I bought that pram in half an hour."

"So?"

"There's a waiting list for baby carriages in Czechoslovakia."

"Oh, and how long is the wait?"

"About half a year, and for this one, probably forever. You can't even buy it there."

179 Prague, Offices of the Czechoslovak State Film Company, November 6, 1973

Dr. Purš sat behind a large desk like a boss. Standing before him in a humiliating posture, he did not feel comfortable at all. And he knew very well why.

"I called you here, comrade, personally. I received the financial results for Barrandov, which we entrusted to you, and it's terrible." He waved the paper in his hand. He pointed to the underlined passages with his finger. "Here, here, and here. Attendance for political films is almost zero. If we didn't send schools to see these films, there would be no reason to show them. And no one wants them abroad. We paid the same amount of money for the film about Klement Gottwald's life story as we did for *Marketa Lazarova*, which ruined three creative groups. The director got enough money to buy two family houses, and the result? Shit. Complete shit, Comrade Toman."

Toman tried to defend himself: "We managed to sell a few titles to the Soviet Union."

"Don't talk to me about that," Purš snapped at him. "They didn't pay us anything. I had film director Vávra here, and he was complaining about how his comrades from Mosfilm told him that we should be honored that they were even taking our films, let alone paying for them."

471

"We need to work harder with our comrades, not only politically, but mainly economically," argued Toman.

"Yes, that should work. Are you already doing that?"

"Hofman has results. He may be politically misguided, but he knows how to choose material that sells. Cinderella has been sold to fifty countries. *Pan Tau* also smacks of bourgeois culture, but he brings in foreign currency for us. Let them do it here if the imperialists pay for it. It doesn't have to be broadcast here. What's more, Hofman understands what's necessary and knows how to get rid of authors who are undesirable and politically unreliable. Procházka and Pavlíček, for example, have long since left the group, and things are going well without them. I know I can rely on him."

"Procházka has been dead for two years, Comrade Toman."

Toman blushed: "I said it as an example."

Purš laughed. "I know what you meant. So, let's put it this way... It's an advantage that you managed to get Hofman on your side. He gets results. And what's going on with Pavlíček now? I heard he got cleaned up pretty good."

"I think he's working in the boiler room now," replied Toman, "going from one menial job to another. His work ethic is more suited to an intellectual from Vinohrady than a Marxist-style worker."

"Right. There he'll finally understand that resistance is futile. We'll wipe his intellectual superiority out of his head. But listen. Trapl's creative group spent eight hundred thousand on the synopsis alone, and what's the result?"

"It's mostly purely political work, but..."

Dr. Purš interrupted him with a wave of his hand: "Sure, they can't handle it artistically. I suggest a complete replacement. And don't think, comrade, that I don't know you have your own ideas there. Hofman's group is the only one that can stay. They have all their papers and accounts in order, and they earn foreign currency as well as crowns."

Toman was about to object: "But..."

"I have direct orders from Moscow, where comrades in leading positions change even faster than in five-year plans..." Purš stood up and put his hand on Toman's shoulder. "Comrade Toman, this won't do. Ludvík, damn it. You have to take decisive action. I want your recommendations on my desk tomorrow. And remember what happened to your predecessor. You don't want that. Talk some sense into Hofman, tell him that the film about the youth of Klement Gottwald is still not ready for production, as I ordered, and put a knife to his throat. I expect it to be the most-watched film of the year, so he'd better get to work on it. If I remember correctly, it was in his dramaturgical plan the year before last, last year, and this year. Maybe the screenwriter of the highly successful Cinderella, Comrade Zelenková, should take it on. And also explain to me why the heroes of these children's films are just anonymous figures, why aren't they little communists? I would really like someone like Fučík."

"I'll take it as a party assignment."

"Those are the words of a true Bolshevik. I like you, Ludvik."

180 Prague, November 19, 1973

Hofman walked thoughtfully down the hallway to his office. He had taken a vacation and spent last week with Irena in Karlovy Vary.

He met a man who was clearly a stranger. "Hello, are you looking for something?"

"Not really, I'm the new head dramaturge of the group, my name is Vojtěch Trapl, and who are you?"

"Hofman," replied Hofman, astonished.

"I haven't heard of you at Toman's, and we were all there."

Hofman's eyes widened.

"My God, my God." He didn't answer the man. He continued down the hallway past another open office. He stopped and peeked inside. He saw new people sitting there, people he didn't know. He looked at the window and saw another new comrade he didn't know. He was unpacking things from a box onto the desk. He noticed a frozen figure in the doorway.

"Good morning, Comrade Hofman."

"Good morning. Who are you?"

"I'm your new colleague," said the stranger.

"And where's the old one who was sitting here last Friday?"

"I really don't know," replied the man and continued unpacking.

Hofman entered Bohunka Šourková's office in the children's film department. "Thank God, I was afraid Toman had replaced you, too."

Bohunka sighed: "It's terrible, Ota. Not a stone left unturned."

END

The financial plans for both Barrandov and DEFA were flawless. Cinderella met expectations during the year and exceeded a million viewers in both countries. It became a permanent fixture on cinema screens. In Czechoslovakia, it was still being shown in cinemas in the second half of the 1980s and became evergreen on television. Every year, it attracts 85 million viewers in Germany during Christmas reruns. But it wasn't just German-speaking countries and Czechoslovakia that fell in love with Cinderella. Cinderella is also well known in Mexico, Switzerland, Russia, Poland, and especially Norway. As one Norwegian journalist once jokingly remarked, "If Cinderella weren't shown at Christmas, there would be a revolution."

In 1973, the first phase of normalization after the occupation by Warsaw Pact troops came to an end.

František Pavlíček spent his official professional life in blue-collar professions until the Velvet Revolution. He himself said, "Right after the premiere of Cinderella, people came up to me saying that I was the author of the script. It even got to my friends in the dissident movement. So I told him to keep it to himself. But I'll tell you one thing. The changes that director Vorlíček made didn't harm my story, and I'm glad that he's also named in the credits."

The public only learned about Jan Procházka's authorship of the screenplays from the 1960s and 1970s after the Velvet Revolution. To this day, Procházka's screenplays are not properly credited in official copies of the films or in film databases. Jan Procházka died on February 20, 1971. In democratic Czechoslovakia, his friend Karel Kachyňa filmed his other unrealized screenplays, *Nicholas Walks Through the Town* and *The* **Cow** won many film festivals, and if it had not been a television production, the Czech Republic would have sent it to the Oscars.

Ludvík Toman was fired from Barrandov in 1982. He then worked for Filmexport, a company that sold licenses for Czechoslovak films abroad, especially to the Eastern Bloc, and was directly linked to the secret State Security Service. Toman died during the Karlovy Vary International Film Festival in 1988, where, heavily intoxicated, he choked to death on his own vomit. Despite his extraordinary position, there are no official photographs of him, and no documents about his life have survived.

Jiří Purš was the director of Czechoslovak State Film from September 23, 1969, until his happy retirement in 1988. He was never afraid of confrontation and was always willing to stand in front of the camera and defend his opinions. It was discovered that he used his Dr. title without any authorization.

Kamil Pixa worked at Krátký film until 1985. He managed co-productions with West Germany until the end of the regime. Although Czech Television made an hour-long documentary about him and there are many credible testimonies about him, there are many gaps in his life. He died in 2008.

Ota Hofman was head dramaturge for children's films at Barrandov until 1983.

He wrote more than 45 screenplays for award-winning films, such as The Third Prince, Meeting in July, The Last Butterfly, and the highly successful series Pan Tau, The Visitors, Lucy -Terror of the Street, and The Octopuses from the Second Floor, which are still staples of television channels' annual Christmas programming. He did not live to see the Velvet Revolution of November 17, 1989, dying on May 17, 1989. The film about the youth of Klement Gottwald was never made by the children's film group at Barrandov.

List of Czechoslovak films mentioned in the story

Pan Tau TV series, 1971-1977

Director: Jindřich Polák

Screenplay: Ota Hofman, Jindřich Polák

Music: Jiří Malásek, Jiří Bažant, Vlastimil Hála

Pan Tau, a magical man with a bowler hat, helps children and can transform into a small puppet. The television series has 33 episodes and feature film.

Clown Ferdinand and the Rocket, 1962 (Klaun Ferdinand a raketa)

Director: Jindřich Polák

Screenplay: Ota Hofman, Jindřich Polák

Music: Evžen Illín

Clown Ferdinand embarks on a space adventure with his friends, saving a spacecraft from disaster.

Fireman's Ball, 1967 (Hoří má panenko)

Director: Miloš Forman

Screenplay: Miloš Forman, Jaroslav Papoušek, Ivan Passer

Music: Karel Mareš

At a firefighter's ball, organizers struggle with a stolen raffle and a disastrous beauty contest.

Rabbits in the Tall Grass, 1961 (Králíci ve vysoké trávě)

Director: Václav Gajer

Screenplay: Ota Hofman, Václav Gajer

Music: Evžen Illín

When his rabbits die, a young boy begins to question his faith and the hypocrisy around him.

Robinson Girl – 3 adaptations (Robinzonka)

Director: Milan Vošmik, TV 1954

Jaromír Pleskot, 1956

Karel Kachyňa, 1974

Screenplay: Ota Hofman

Music: Jan F. Fischer, 1956

   Zdeněk Liška, 1974

After her mother's death, a 13-year-old girl takes charge of her family, inspired by Robinson Crusoe.

I'm Jumping Over Puddles Again, 1970 (Už zase skáču přes kaluže)

Director: Karel Kachyňa

Screenplay: Jan Procházka

Despite being struck by polio, a boy continues to dream of becoming a skilled horseman.

Music: Zdeněk Liška

Orange moon, 1962 (Oranžový měsíc)

A father and son in Prague share a humble life, hoping to win the lottery and change their fortunes.

Director: Antonín Moskalyk

Screenplay: Ota Hofman

Music: Ladislav Simon

The Kissing-time ninety, 1965 (Délka polibku devadesát)

Director: Antonín Moskalyk

Screenplay: Ota Hofman, Irena Hofmannová

Music: Luboš Fišer

Eva and Jarda's life changes when they have quintuplets. They're given a modern villa and Jarda gets a new job, but soon they're overwhelmed by strangers and intrusive questions.

Ikarie XB1, 1963

Director: Jindřich Polák

Sreenplay: Pavel Juráček, Jindřich Polák, Stanisław Lem

Music: Zdeněk Liška

In the year 2163, the spaceship Ikarie XB1 sets out to find life beyond Earth. The crew faces human emotions, threats, and a surprising encounter with a 20th-century ship carrying nuclear weapons.

The Key, 1971 (Klíč)

Director: Vladimír Čech

screenplay: Vladimír Čech, Kristián Topič, Kamil Pixa

Music: Štěpán Lucký

The Gestapo captures a wounded Czech resistance leader, member of the Communist Party and finds only a key on him. They suspect it may unlock a secret, but the man refuses to talk and remains faithful to his ideals and the Communist Party.

Three Nuts for Cinderella, 1973 (Tři oříšky pro Popelku)

Director: Václav Vorlíček

Screenplay: František Pavlíček, Václav Vorlíček

Music: Karel Svoboda

In this Cinderella adaptation, the main characters have new qualities. Cinderella is lively and skilled, while the prince is headstrong and prefers hunting to court etiquette.

The Escape, 1967 (Útěk)

Director: Štěpán Skalský

Screenplay: Ota Hofman

Music: Zdeněk Liška

Two boys, Saša and Ruda, meet in a garden shed. Ruda is on the run, and Saša tries to force him to confess to a crime. But Ruda takes Saša as a hostage, and they embark on a journey that changes them both.

On the Comet, 1970 (Na kometě)

Director: Karel Zeman

Screenplay: Jan Procházka, Karel Zeman

Music: Luboš Fišer

A French colony is torn from the earth's surface by a comet and hurled into space. Petty disputes and rebellions ensue, but the director focuses on exaggerated comedy and caricatures.

The Deadly Invention, 1958 (Vynález zkázy)

Director: Karel Zeman

Screenplay: Karel Zeman, František Hrubín

Music: Zdeněk Liška

A brilliant inventor, Professor Roch, is forced to finish his world-destroying invention by the sinister Count Artigas. The professor's assistant, Hart, tries to free him and prevent destruction.

Káťa and Crocodile, 1965 (Káťa a krokodýl)

Director: Věra Plívová-Šimková

Screenplay: Ota Hofman

Music: Zdeněk Liška

A young animal lover takes home all the animals from the school's nature corner, causing chaos. Káťa helps by taking the animals in, but they escape, and the children must round them up again.

The Transformation of a Knife, 1969 (Proměny nože)

Director: Eva Sadková

Screenplay: Ota Hofman

Music: Karel Svoboda

Dana, a young waitress, longs for love and beautiful things. She has short-term relationships, but her life changes when a group of students stops at the diner, and one of them, Martin, takes a liking to her.

Markéta Lazarová, 1967

Director: František Vláčil

Screenplay: František Pavlíček, František Vláčil

Music: Zdeněk Liška

The film depicts the feud between two bandit families, the Kozlíks and the Lazars. Mikoláš Kozlík kidnaps Markéta Lazarová, and they fall in love, but their families' conflicts tear them apart.

This film is concidered as the most beutiful film in the history of Czechoslovak cinematografy.

Loundryboy, 1960 (Práče)

Director: Karel Kachyňa

Screenplay: J. A. Novotný, Karel Kachyňa

Music: Miloš Vacek

A young Czech boy, František Bureš, is liberated from a Nazi concentration camp and joins the Soviet Army. He wants to fight, but is assigned to a laundry unit, where he befriends the soldiers.

Granny, 1971 (Babička)

Director: Antonín Moskalyk

Screenplay: František Pavlíček

Music: Luboš Fišer

Božena Němcová's classic novel Grandmother is adapted into a two-part television epic. The story is a testament to memories, capturing folk customs and traditions of the time, and is a beautiful picture of great love.

The Ear, 1970 (Ucho)

Director: Karel Kachyňa

Screenplay: Jan Procházka

Music: Svatopluk Havelka

Banned in 1969, this film follows Ludvík, a high-ranking official, and his wife Anna. They're trapped in a world of fear and uncertainty, surrounded by "ears" - State Security listening devices that monitor their every move.

Long Live the Republic, 1965 (Ať žije republika)

Directed by Karel Kachyňa

Screenplay: Jan Procházka

Music: Jan Novák

In the midst of World War II, a young boy named Olin must save his family's mare. This poignant film blends memories, dreams, and vivid imagery to expose the darker aspects of human nature.

Marathon, 1968 (Maraton)

Director: Ivo Novák

Screenplay: Jan Procházka

Music: Zdeněk Liška

As the war ends, 19-year-old Ruda joins the revolution and finds refuge with Karla, a young maid. Together, they face danger and uncertainty, all while Ruda's brother Jarda leads a Soviet tank column towards Prague, searching for him.

Johnny's Journey, 1956 (Honzíkova cesta)

Director: Milan Vošmik

Screenplay: Ota Hofman

Hodba: Svatopluk Havelka

Five-year-old Honzík visits his grandparents in the countryside. He makes friends with local children, but has a problem with a naughty boy named Ferda. Honzík gets lost in the forest, but is found and returns home.

Beauty and the Beast, TV 1971 (Kráska a zvíře)

Director: Antonín Moskalyk

Screenplay: Ota Hofman

Music: Luboš Fišek

A poor merchant is rewarded with riches for picking a rose. His daughter Beauty goes to the castle to take his place, and the monster falls in love with her. Beauty eventually returns to the castle, and her love transforms the monster into a prince.

A Journey into the Primeval Times, 1956 (Cesta do pravěku)

Director: Karel Zeman

Screenplay: Karel Zeman, J. A. Novotný

Music: E.F. Burian

Four curious boys travel back in time to the prehistoric era, experiencing many adventures along the way.

The Outrageous Baron Munchausen, 1961 (Baron Prášil)

Director: Karel Zeman

Screenplay: Karel Zeman, Josef Kainar, Jiří Brdečka

Music: Zdeněk Liška

Astronaut Toník lands on the moon and meets Baron Prášil, who takes him on fantastical adventures.

Prince Bajaja, 1971 (Princ Bajaja)

Director: Antonín Kachlík

Screenplay: František Pavlíček, Eva Košlerová

Music: <u>Vladimír Sommer</u>

Prince Bajaja sets out to find his parents' killers, meets a magical horse, and falls in love with Princess Slavěna. He eventually rescues her from a dragon.

The Train to Heaven, 1972 (Vlak do stanice nebe)

Director: Karel Kachyňa

Screenplay: Ota Hofman, Karel Kachyňa

Music: Zdeněk Liška

A mother takes her daughter to a mountain village to escape the war. The girl is fascinated by the local railway and uses it to go to school.

The Girl on the Broomstick, 1971 (Dívka na koštěti)

Director: Václav Vorlíček

Screenplay: Miloš Macourek, Václav Vorlíček

Music: <u>Angelo Michajlov</u>

Saxana, a young witch, prefers life among humans to her supernatural privileges. She escapes from a fairy-tale realm and finds true human feelings among humans.

The Nun´s night 1969 (Noc nevěsty)

Director: Karel Kachyňa

Screenplay: Jan Procházka

Music: Jan Novák

A former nun returns to her hometown after her father's suicide and gets caught up in tragic events that culminate on Christmas Eve.

Boys Will Be Boys, 1975 (Páni kluci)

Director: Věra Plívová-Šimková

Screenplay: Jan Procházka

Hudba: Petr Hapka

Three friends, Tomáš, Jožka, and Hubert, live in a small town at the beginning of the century. They get into mischief and eventually flee to a local castle.

Larks on a String, 1969 (Skřivánci na niti)

Director: Jiří Menzel

Scrteenplay: Bohumil Hrabal, Jiří Menzel

Music: Jiří Šust

The film takes place in a steelworks in Kladno, where "political offenders" are sent to work. The story follows the lives of the workers and their struggles.

Thirty Virgins and Pythagoras, 1973 (Třicet panen a Pythagoras)

Director: Pavel Hobl

Screenplay: Zdeněk Svěrák, Pavel Hobl, Milan Šimek, Miloš Noll

Music: Angelo Michailov

A new math teacher, Ludolf, tries to make the subject enjoyable for his students. He discovers a new teaching method that uses modern songs, making math accessible to them.